SEO 2019

Actionable, Hands-on SEO, Including a Full Site Audit

By Dr. Andy Williams

W0009351

ezSEONews.com

Version 1.0

Updated: 14th January 2019

What people have said about my other SEO books

My first SEO book (from which this one evolved) was published in 2012. That's when the SEO upheaval started with Google moving the goal posts. I updated and re-released major versions of that book in 2013, 2014, 2015, 2016 & 2017. The copy you have in your hands now is the updated version for 2019 and contain some major additions.

The following comments are from customers over this timespan and may refer to any one of the major versions released since 2012.

"Read this book and anything else you can get your hands on by this guy."

"Dr. Andy Williams is, to my mind, the man to listen to when it comes to the subject of building a website in a clean ethical manner. His explanations of what Google, and the other search engines, consider as part of the ranking process cannot be bettered. If you wish to create a long-lived website that does not need to fear the latest Google update(s) then pay heed." **Jim**

"A MUST READ for SEO professionals who need to get themselves updated" **Bryan Grandy**

"Five Stars - game changer, eye opener" **Nahum Pierre**

"After 10 years online, building and promoting websites, I became quite adept at SEO (both on-page and off), but that was then and this is now! Having read this eBook from cover to cover, I think you would be hard pressed to find more informative, descriptive, and easy-to-understand material on the subject of present day SEO anywhere." ~ **Andy Aitch**

"This is the right way to build websites. There is a lot of rubbish written by many so-called experts, but this is not one of them. If you want to learn the best way to do SEO, then this is the leading book I have read, and I have read many." ~ **Dobsy "Dobsy" (UK)**

"Basically, I loved this book and highly recommend it. It is the best couple of bucks you will ever spend. It is easy to read, succinct, and brilliant. He offers a lot of great tips without all the fluff that some authors throw in to add page count. Thanks, Andy, for a good read that upped my SEO IQ." ~ **Nicole Bernd**

"Since Google's Penguin update was released in April 2012, SEO has been turned on its head. Creating themed content with Latent Semantic Indexing (LSI) in mind, instead of keyword focused content, is now the way forward.

Amazingly, this is exactly what Andy has been teaching for the past ten years. I only wished I had known him when I started out in internet marketing. His style of teaching is the best. He's a very genuine and generous person, so if you've been hit by Panda or Penguin, then this book is exactly what you need." ~ **Carole**

"Great book, super helpful, and makes SEO easy to understand, especially for an ecommerce novice! I would definitely recommend this to anyone trying to get a handle on best practices in SEO." ~ **cswaff**

"Andy was warning of a Panda type hit at least two years before the Panda was born. Although the Penguin update has changed things more than a bit, in this book, Dr. Andy clearly, and in simple terminology, explains the strategies and tactics needed to stay on the good side of Google." ~ **Tony Crofts**

"Great at teaching the difference in old SEO practices Vs. new techniques." ~ **Ms. WriterGirl**

"Andy is one of the few people that I listen to when it comes to SEO. Rather than "follow the usual crowd", that tends to share rehashed information with little value that's based on fact, Andy does his own testing to determine what is actually working for him, and then shares his own results." ~ **J. Stewart**

"This book was a very quick and easy read from start to finish. I found it to be an excellent work with some very mature insights into the nuances of how to get in good graces with Google. It took a few of my beliefs and approaches to Search Engine Optimization and turned them upside down." ~ **Jonathan W. Walker**

"This is groundbreaking Internet marketing information. Stuff you won't find elsewhere. Being a long-time pupil of Dr. Andy, I have put much of it to the test myself and I know it proves out. If you are in the Internet business, you need to read this book." ~ **Norman Morrison**

"After following Andy Williams for over 8 years now, I had a hunch his new SEO book would be a winner . . . and it is. It's simple, straight forward, and on target with respect to the latest updates, upgrades, and algorithmic mods by our friends at Google. Do what Andy teaches, especially with reference to great content creation, and you will be successful in your SEO efforts." ~ **Chris Cobb**

Contents

DISCLAIMER AND TERMS OF USE AGREEMENT

How to Use This Book

This book divides into two main sections.

The first section is a complete overview of modern, white hat SEO, that you can use for reference as you build your site. You'll learn the best way to optimize your website, both on-page and off. You'll also learn about the strategies that successful sites employ to build powerful, white-hat, natural backlinks.

The second section of this book is an SEO trouble-shooter, or SEO audit, that you can use on existing sites to check for any problems. Use it to check specific factors of your site or use it to perform a complete SEO audit.

A note about UK v US English

There are some differences between UK and US English. While I try to be consistent, some errors may slip into my writing because I spend a lot of time corresponding to people in both the UK and the US. The line can blur.

Examples of this include spelling of words like optimise (UK) v optimize (US).

The difference I get the most complaints about is with collective nouns. Collective nouns refer to a group of individuals, e.g. Google. In the US, collective nouns are singular, so **Google IS** a search engine. However, in the UK, collective nouns are usually plural, so **Google ARE** a search engine.

There are other differences too. I hope that if I have been inconsistent somewhere in this book, it does not detract from the value you get from it.

Typos in this book?

Errors (and inconsistencies previously mentioned) can get through proof-readers, so if you do find any typos or grammatical errors in this book, I'd be very grateful if you could let me know using this email address:

typos@ezseonews.com

A Note About Page Rank (PR)

Many people think that Page Rank is dead, but they are wrong. Even if that term is no longer used in SEO circles, the principles of Page Rank still exist, and probably always will. If you've never heard of Page Rank before, here's a short introduction.

Every page on the internet has something called Page Rank, more commonly known as PR or PageRank. PR is an algorithm used by Google Search that helps to rank websites in its search engine result pages (SERPs). It is measured on a logarithmic scale from 0-10. A new page will have a PR0. Actually, it won't be zero, but "Unranked", which is very close to zero. Note that Google may still index unranked pages.

When page 'A' links to page 'B', page 'B' gets an increase in its PR that is a proportion of the PR on page 'A'. If page 'A' has a PR of zero, then page 'B' gets very little additional PR. However, if page 'A' has a PR of '5', then page 'B' gets a huge boost in its PR status.

If a page has a lot of incoming links, it gathers PR from each of those pages, thus making it more "important". This is where we get the idea of a link being a "vote" for a page. The more incoming links a page has, the more PR it gets, and the more important it becomes. In other words, the page gains in status & reputation. The more important a page is, the easier it will rank in the Google SERPs.

For many years, PR was thought of as some kind of ranking Deity. PR was an all-powerful property of a page that could be sculpted and used to make other pages rank better. It was a measure of how important a page was to Google.

The search engine giant even provided a toolbar (no longer available) for webmasters so they could check the PR for pages on their websites.

For many webmasters, SEO became a game of chasing PR. Getting links pointing back to their site from other high PR pages was the only thing that mattered.

By giving webmasters the toolbar, Google gave them the power to rank at will. It allowed them to funnel PR to important pages. It gave them the ranking power they needed to dominate the SERPs.

For the last 4 - 5 years, Google has been trying to distance itself from PageRank. It has done this to convince webmasters that PR is no longer important for ranking. Google even stopped updating the PR on its toolbar so that no one could tell the true PR of a web page.

In October 2014, Google's John Mueller said

"We are probably not going to be updating it [PageRank] going forward, at least in the Toolbar PageRank".

Clearly, Google didn't want webmasters knowing the PR of their web pages as it gave them too much control.

With PR covered, let's define SEO.

What Is SEO?

SEO stands for **S**earch **E**ngine **O**ptimization. It's best defined as the steps a webmaster takes to increase the visibility of his/her web pages in the search engines organic search results.

Let's define a couple of terms at this point.

A **webmaster** is simply a person who is responsible for a website.

Organic search results are those listings in the **SERPs** (**S**earch **E**ngine **R**esults **P**ages) that are there on merit because of their relevance to the search term typed in. It's important to differentiate between organic and paid listings. With paid listings, webmasters pay the search engines to have their pages (in the form of ads) listed at the top of the SERPs. You can identify paid listings in Google because they have the "Ad" label next to them.

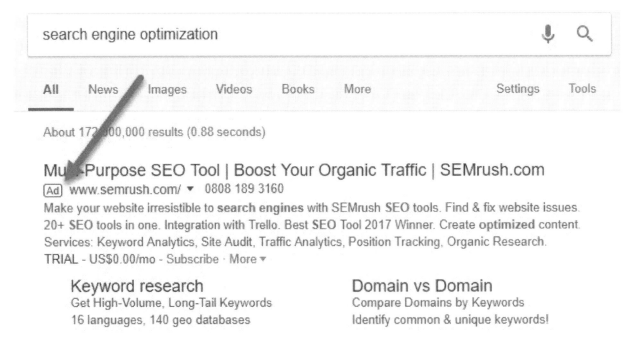

There can be several Ads at the top of the SERPs before any organic listings appear.

Before we go on any further, I should just mention that this book focuses on Google SEO. Google is the largest search engine on the planet. In fact, most search traffic from around the world comes directly from Google Search. Google has become synonymous with the term "search engine". It's an expression that has even found its way into the English dictionary as a verb. I expect you've heard someone describe how they "**googled**" something or other. Google is the most important place to rank well, and if you rank well on Google, chances are you will rank well on Yahoo and Bing too.

Why Is SEO Necessary?

The answer may be obvious, but let's start at the beginning.

When you build a website, how are people going to find it?

The sad truth is that you can have the best website on the planet, but if people cannot find it, it'll be a very lonely place. This brings us back to search engines.

Fact: Search engines are the number one way people find websites.

The good news is that it is easy to get your pages into the search engines.

The bad news is that it is difficult to get your pages to rank high enough to be visible in the search engines.

Data from May 2018, published by Smart Insights on their website, showed that the page which ranks on page one in position one of the SERPs typically gets around 30% of all clicks on that page.

The web page ranked in position two gets 14%.

The page in position three gets 10%. In positions 9 to 10, the clickthrough rate is as low as 2%.

From this information, you can see that it is important to not only rank in Google but to rank as high as possible. Even one or two places can mean big changes in potential search engine traffic.

I should point out that these figures are just averages. As you will see later in the book, click-through rates are related to how appealing your listing is on Google. Increase the appeal, you can increase the CTR. If you increase CTR, your rankings may also improve.

What Makes a Page Rank Well?

To rank high in the organic search results, your page needs to be one of the best matches for the search term typed into the search box. Your page needs to **match the "intent"** of the searcher. Your page also needs a certain level of trust and authority. How much is defined by the competition in your niche and even the niche itself. For example, after the "Medic update" in August 2018, it's now very difficult to rank in health and finance niches without a lot of trust and authority.

A little later in this chapter, we'll look at the top-ranking factors in a little more detail, but to fully understand how SEO is different today, we should consider the SEO of the past.

How We Used to Rank Pages

In the good old days (that's up to about 2010), ranking in Google was relatively easy.

At that time, Google's algorithm (the complex code that determines where a web page will rank) was heavily based on two things. The keywords found on the page and the links pointing to it.

These were the main ranking factors and webmasters knew it. Since both of those factors could be controlled and manipulated by the site owners, many webmasters began to organize and manipulate things so that they could rank well in the SERPs.

Here was the process for doing this:

1. Identify the keywords you want to rank for (the ones people type in at the search engines).
2. Create a page that was "optimized" for that keyword or phrase. The quality of the content was not important back then. You simply needed to include your chosen keyword in as many places within the HTML code as possible. This was aptly named keyword stuffing. The keyword would be placed in the title of the page, the opening header, in the body of the content (maybe five times or more per 100 words), and in the ALT tags (a text alternative for an image or object on a page). Keywords were also sometimes stuffed into the domain name itself. The more times you could get your term on the page, the better your results.
3. Build backlinks to the page. These were often built by the thousand using automated backlinking tools that dropped links into a variety of spammy, worthless pages around the net. These backlinking tools would use your chosen keyword in the link text.

Basically, that was the strategy, and it worked. You could rank for literally any term using that simple formula.

Webmasters were able to rank in the SERPs for anything they wanted, for whatever they wanted. Back in the very early days, if you got into the first top 10 positions on page one of Google, you would remain there for three months, until the next update came out.

Google had lost control.

As you can imagine, the SERPs started to fill up with junk. Pages were ranking because of the spammy techniques employed by webmasters, rather than on merit, and that made Google look bad.

As a search engine, Google's goal was to return the best, most relevant and high-quality results as possible. The reality was very different. In many cases the top 10 was filled with trashy content; spammy sites that offered little or no value to the web surfer.

Over time, Google refined its algorithm, making it more and more difficult for webmasters to game the system. In Google's ideal world, its prized algorithm would be based entirely on factors that webmasters could not control or manipulate.

As you will see later in the book, Google's Panda and Penguin updates (as well as several other major updates) were designed to take back control from the webmasters. By removing factors from the algorithm that webmasters could easily manipulate, or give these factors less importance, Google made it increasingly difficult for webmasters to game the system. Bear this in mind when we look at the top-ranking factors later in this chapter.

Personalized Search Results

In recent years, Google has been applying more and more personalization to the search results. So, what does that mean exactly? It means that what you see when you search for a phrase in Google, may not be the same as what someone in a different part of the country would see for the same search term. In fact, it might not even be the same set of results that your neighbor sees, or your mom sitting next to you on the couch while searching on her mobile phone.

It is important to realize this. Not everyone sees the same results for the exact same search query.

You see, when someone searches on Google, the search giant will apply filters to the results to show that searcher the most relevant results, based on their own personal circumstances and viewing history.

As a quick example, let's say you search Google for an antivirus program on your iMac. The chances are you'll probably see a bias towards Mac anti-virus tools and the discussions of Mac users as to whether antivirus is needed on a Mac computer. Do the same search on a PC and you'll get PC antivirus software discussions and reviews. Repeat the search on an Android phone or iPhone, and you'll get results tailored to those operating systems.

This is one simple example. Google looks at much more than just your operating system. Other factors it'll try to use include:

- Your location (whether that is your reported location, IP address, or GPS location as given out by mobile devices).
- Your search history, which looks at what have you been searching for in recent days or weeks.
- Your social networks, including your likes, your friends and your circles.
- Whether you are searching on a mobile device, desktop, or even SmartTV.
- Your preferred language.

Personalization of the search results is meant to make our lives easier, and in many ways, as a consumer, it does. However, as far as SEO is concerned, personalization can be a pain if we don't know what other people are seeing in their SERPs.

Top Ranking Factors in 2019

Earlier I suggested that in an ideal world, Google would build its algorithm around factors that were not easily controlled (and therefore manipulated) by webmasters.

In this section, we'll look at some of the factors we know are important. Think about each one in turn, and how much control a webmaster has over it.

Ranking Factors can be split into two groups, namely "on-page" and "off-page".

On-Page Factors

1. Quality Content

Google is looking for high-quality content that is relevant to the search query. It will look at the language used on a page, and for words and phrases that are related to the search query. I call these "theme words". Longer pages tend to do better, and the inclusion of photos and/or video works to your advantage too. Furthermore, pictures and videos also help to retain the visitor's interest. Google also looks at the design of pages, and what a visitor will see "above the fold" (before scrolling down) when they land on a page. Good user experience is essential. If a visitor landing on your page sees a bunch of adverts and very little else, you can imagine how Google would view that page.

2. Page Load Time

Nobody likes waiting around for a page to load. If your web pages are taking five or more seconds to load, your visitors may not wait and hit the back button. According to research, your average web user has an attention span of just a few seconds, less than a goldfish. So, it's important that your pages load quickly. Slow page load times are unlikely to be directly penalized by Google, it's more how a visitor reacts. If the searcher came from Google, a slow loading page will make that visitor unhappy and even click the back button to Google. Google sees both the "bounce" and "exit" rates as negatives for your page. An unhappy visitor from Google means an unhappy Google.

3. Internal Links from Other Pages on the Site

If you look at a website like Wikipedia, you'll see a lot of **internal links** on the pages. Internal links go from one page on a website to a different page on the same site. These should be distinguished from **external links**. External Links point to a different website. Internal links are there to help the visitor navigate around your website's pages. As someone reads a page on Wikipedia, they might come across a word or phrase they do not understand, or simply want to know more about. By "internally" linking keywords or phrases to other pages on Wikipedia, visitors get to navigate around the site more easily and find the information they are looking for quickly. Internal links also help

Google fully index your website.

4. Bounce Rates

We mentioned bounce rates earlier in the context of fast loading pages. A "bounce" is simply a visitor who clicks a link in the SERPs and then returns to Google. The quicker the return, the worse it is for your page as it tells Google the visitor was not satisfied.

Let's think how this might work.

Say a visitor on Google searches for "vitamin A deficiency" and visits the first page in the SERPs. Not finding what they want, they then click the browser's back button to return to Google. They may then click on another site further down the SERP to see if that can provide what they are looking for.

What does this tell Google about the first page?

The visitor did not find the information they wanted on that page.

Google knows this because they returned to the search results and repeated (or refined) their search. If lots of people around the world search for a certain phrase, and an unusually high percentage of them bounce back from the same web page that is ranked #1 in Google for the search term, what do you think Google will do?

Doesn't it make sense that it would demote that page in the SERPs - **for that search phrase** - since lots of people are not finding it relevant to their search query?

Bounce rates go hand-in-hand with searcher intent. If visitors find a page relevant, they'll stay on the page for longer. They may even browse other pages on that site, so don't bounce right back. This tells Google the visitor was happy with that recommendation, and Google is happy.

5. Time a Visitor Stays on Your Page / Site.

Google monitors the time visitors spend on web pages. One of the ways it does this is through its Google Analytics platform. Google Analytics is a freemium web analytics service for site owners. What it does is track and report on your website traffic. Because it's free, a lot of webmasters install it on their sites. This gives Google the ability to accurately track the site's visitors. It'll track lots of variables including things like time spent on the site, the route a visitor takes through your site, how many pages they visit, what operating system they use, the screen resolution, the device they are using, and so on. Even if a site does not have Analytics installed, it is possible that Google monitors visitor behavior through its popular Chrome web browser.

6. Trust and Authority

I'll cover this here even though it is controlled by off-page factors, simply because we think about the authority of a site as an on-site property.

This factor became huge in 2018. It was always important, but with the introduction of the "Medic Update" in August of that year, high trust & authority is now vital for ranking in health and finance niches (and other niches will follow). Essentially, if a site can hurt your health or your financial well-being with the information (or products) available, it will require a lot more trust before Google will rank its pages. It is my opinion that the way Google is monitoring these factors is down to what other authoritative sites (and people) are saying about you and your site. As we've seen, votes (links from other sites) pass on this authority. Now more than ever it is important to focus on high-quality links, relevant, and authoritative links, rather than high numbers of links. Quality over quantity is the key. While trust and authority is something your site will build up, but as I've said, it is largely controlled by off-page SEO and we'll come back to this later.

Those are the main on-page factors used by Google in its ranking algorithm.

Except for the last factor, most of the on-page factors are within the control of the webmaster. Even bounce rates and the time the visitor stays on your site is within your control, to a certain extent. If you provide quality content and the rich experience visitors demand these days, then you'll get lower bounce rates while keeping the visitor on your page/site for longer.

Off-Page Factors

1. Click-through Rates (CTR)

As webmasters, we do have a certain level of control over Click-through Rates.

Let's say a web page ranks in position #5 for a search term, and searchers seem to like that listing because 15% of them click on that link. Usually, a page listed in position #5 would get around 5% of the clicks. When Google sees more people than expected clicking that link, it may give the page a boost in the rankings. After all, it's apparently what the searchers are looking for and therefore deserves a higher slot on the first page.

On the other side of the coin, imagine a spammer. This is an "official" term used by Google to describe someone trying to manipulate rankings for one of their web pages. Let's suppose the spammer manages to bypass Google's algorithm with a "loophole", and ranks #1 for a search term. Remember, in position #1, a link typically gets 31% of the clicks. However, this #1 ranking page only gets 15% of clicks because searchers are not impressed with the link title or its description. On top of that, 99% of people who do visit that link bounce right back to Google within 30 seconds or less, because it's rubbish. Google now has clear user signals that the web page ranking #1 is not popular with searchers. Because of this, Google starts moving the page further down the rankings until it finally drops out of the top 10. It will continue to drop.

Today, bad content will rarely get to the top of Google, and if it does, it won't get to stay there for long.

2. *Social Signals*

Social signals like Tweets, Facebook shares, Pinterest pins, and so on, are clearly used as ranking factors in Google, though they are not major factors. Any boost that social signals might offer your site will be short-lived. This is because of the transient nature of "social buzz".

For example, let's say that a new piece of content goes viral and is shared around by thousands of people via social media channels. This is typically done within a relatively short space of time. Google will take notice of this because it realizes the content is something visitors want to see, so gives it a ranking boost. After the social interest peaks and the shares inevitably start to decline, so does the ranking boost in Google.

Social sharing is a great concept and should be encouraged on your site. Even so, don't expect the backlinks created from social channels to give you a big or long-lasting ranking boost, because they won't.

3. *Backlinks*

Re-read what I wrote about trust & authority a minute ago.

When "web page A" links to "web page B" on another site, page B gets a "backlink". Google sees this as page A (on site 1) voting for page B (on site 2). The general idea is that the more backlinks (or "votes") a page gets from other sites on the web, the more important or valuable it must be.

Today, and probably for the foreseeable future, backlinks remain one of the most important rankings factors in Google's algorithm. However, more is not always better. Let me explain.

A web page that has **dozens** of links from authority sites like CNN, BBC, NY Times, etc., is clearly an important web page. After all, quality, authority sites like the ones above would hardly link to trash.

On the other hand, a page that has **thousands** of backlinks, but only from spammy or low-quality websites, is most probably not very important at all. Backlinks are a powerful indicator of a page's value, but the quality and relevance of those backlinks is the most important factor, not the quantity.

High-quality links build authority and trust, low-quality links have the opposite effect.

A site with hundreds or thousands of low-quality backlinks is helping Google to identify itself as a spammer.

Google factors in the authority of each backlink. Backlinks from high quality "authority" web pages will count far more than backlinks from low-quality pages/sites. Therefore, a page that gets relatively few high-quality backlinks will rank above a page that has a lot of low-quality backlinks. Google may even penalize a page (or site) for having too many poor-quality backlinks.

Google's Battle for Survival

Over the years, Google has had to change and adapt to survive. It has been in a constant battle with webmasters who are eager to manipulate its SERPs. Since the algorithm is based on real factors and properties of a website, site owners have been trying to identify those factors and manipulate them for better rankings. Whenever webmasters find a competitive advantage (sometimes called a loophole), Google tries to quickly plug it.

Let's look at a real example of this struggle.

Over a decade ago, webmasters found out that Google used the Meta Keyword tag as a major ranking factor. What did they do? They began stuffing this tag with keywords to rank well for those terms. What did Google do? It started to ignore the Meta Keyword tag, effectively closing that loophole.

I would like to point out that I do believe Google still looks at the Meta Keyword tag, but not as you might think. I think the company uses it to help identify spammers. Any page that has a Meta keyword tag stuffed with dozens, or even hundreds, of keywords, is clearly doing something underhand or at least trying to.

Here is another example of a loophole being closed.

A few years ago, webmasters found out that by using a domain name that was the keyword phrase they wanted to rank for, the site would get a massive ranking boost in the SERPs. This type of domain is called an Exact Match Domain (EMD). In September 2012, Google released the "EMD Update" which removed that unfair ranking advantage. Hundreds of thousands of EMD sites dropped out of the Google top 10 overnight, which saw an end to a large industry that had profited in buying and selling EMDs.

Today, EMD sites are rarely seen in Google.

The battle between spammer and search engine continues to rage on to this day. Spammers find loopholes, and Google plugs them.

In September 2011, Google CEO Eric Schmidt said that Google had tested over 13,000 possible algorithm updates in 2010, approving just 516 of them. Although 516 may sound a lot (it's more than one update a day), it certainly wasn't an unusual year. Google probably updates the algorithm at least 500-600 times every year. Most of these updates will be minor, but Google does roll out major changes every now and again. We'll look at the most important ones in the next chapter.

The one thing all Google updates have in common is that they are designed to improve the search results for the people that use the search engine – your potential visitors.

Panda, Penguin, and Other Major Updates

We could go back to the very beginning to see all the changes and updates that Google has made, but I want to focus on those changes that have happened since 2011. These are the ones that have changed the way we do SEO today and I think it is important that you know the history as it helps you make decisions on which SEO strategies to avoid.

Changes in 2011

This was a huge year in SEO terms, shocking many webmasters. In fact, 2011 was the year that wiped out a lot of online businesses. Most deserved to go, but quite a few innocent victims got caught in the carnage, never to recover.

At the beginning of the year, Google hit scraper sites (sites that used bots to steal and post content from other sites). This was all about trying to attribute ownership of content back to the original owner and thus penalize the thieves.

On February 23, the Panda update launched in the USA. Panda (also called "Farmer") was essentially targeting low-quality content and link farms. Link farms were basically collections of low-quality blogs that were set up to link out to other sites. The term "thin content" became popular during this time; describing pages that really didn't say much and were there purely to host adverts. Panda was all about squashing thin content, and a lot of sites took a hit too.

In March the same year, Google introduced the +1 button. This was probably expected bearing in mind that Google had confirmed it used social signals in its ranking algorithm. What better signals to monitor than its own?

In April 2011, Panda 2.0 was unleashed, expanding its reach to all countries of the world, though still just targeting pages in English. Even more signals were included in Panda 2.0. Maybe even user feedback via the Google Chrome web browser. Here users had the option to "block" pages in the SERPs that they didn't like.

As if these two Panda releases weren't enough, Google went on to release Panda 2.1, 2.2, 2.3, 2.4, 2.5, and 3.1, all in 2011. Note that Panda 3.0 is missing. There was an update between 2.5 and 3.1, but it is commonly referred to as the Panda "Flux". Each new update built on the previous, helping to eliminate still more low-quality content from the SERPs. With each new release of Panda, webmasters worried, panicked, and complained on forums and social media. A lot of websites were penalized, though not all deserved to be; unavoidable "collateral damage" Google casually called it.

In June 2011, we saw the birth of Google's first social network project, Google Plus.

Another change that angered webmasters was "query encryption", introduced in October 2011. Google said it was doing this for privacy reasons, but webmasters were suspicious of its motives. Prior to this query encryption, whenever someone searched for something on Google, the search term they typed in was passed on to the site they clicked through to. That meant webmasters could see what search terms visitors were typing to find their pages using any web traffic analysis tool. Query encryption changed all of this. Anyone who was logged into their Google account at the time they performed a search from Google would have their search query encrypted. This prevented their search terms from being passed over to the websites they visited. The result of this was that webmasters increasingly had no idea which terms people were using to find their site.

In November 2011, there was a freshness update. This was to supposedly reward websites that provided time-sensitive information (like news sites), whenever visitors searched for time-sensitive news and events.

As you can see, there was a lot going on in 2011, but it didn't stop here.

Changes in 2012

Again, 2012 was a massive year for SEOs and webmasters. There was a huge number of prominent changes, starting with one called "Search + Your World" in January. This was an aggressive measure by Google to integrate its Google+ social data and user profiles into the SERPs.

Over the year, Google released more than a dozen Panda updates, all aimed at reducing low-quality pages from appearing in the SERPs.

In January 2012, Google announced a page layout algorithm change. This aimed at penalizing pages with too many ads, very little value, or both, positioned above the fold. The term "above the fold" refers to the visible portion of a web page when a visitor first lands on it. In other words, whatever you can see without the need to scroll down is above the fold. Some SEOs referred to this page layout algorithm change as the "Top Heavy" update.

In February, Google announced another 17 changes to its algorithm, including spell-checking, which is of interest to us. Later in the same month, Google announced another 40 changes. In March, there were 50 more modifications announced, including one that made changes to anchor text "scoring".

Google certainly wasn't resting on its laurels. On April 24, the Penguin update was unleashed. This was widely expected, and webmasters assumed it was going to be an over-optimization penalty. Google initially called it a "Webspam update", but it was soon named "Penguin". This update checked for a wide variety of spam techniques, including keyword stuffing. It also analyzed the anchor text used in external links pointing to websites.

In April, yet another set of updates were announced, 52 this time.

In May, Google started rolling out "Knowledge Graph". This was a huge step towards semantic search (the technology Google uses to better understand the context of search terms). We also saw Penguin 1.1 during this month and another 39 announced changes. One of these new changes included better link scheme detection. Link scheme detection helped identify websites that had built their own links to gain better rankings.

In July, Google sent out "unnatural link warnings" via Google Search Console, to any site where it had detected a large number of "unnatural" links. To avoid a penalty, Google gave webmasters the opportunity to remove the "unnatural" links.

Think of unnatural links as any link the webmaster controls, and ones they probably created themselves or asked others to create for them. These would include links on blog networks and other low-quality websites. Inbound links such as these typically used a high percentage of specific keyword phrases in their anchor text. Google wanted webmasters to be responsible for the links that pointed to their sites. Webmasters who had created their own sneaky link campaigns were able to do something about it. However, if other sites were linking to their pages with poor quality links, then Google expected webmasters to contact the site owners and request removal of the bad link(s).

If you have ever tried to contact a webmaster to ask for a link to be removed, you'll know that it can be an impossible task. For many webmasters, this was an impractical undertaking because the unnatural link warnings were often the result of tens or hundreds of thousands of bad links to a single site. Google eventually back-tracked and said that these unnatural link warnings may not result in a penalty after all. The word on the street was that Google would be releasing a tool to help webmasters clean up their link profiles.

When you think about it, Google's flip-flopping on this policy was understandable and just. After all, if websites were going to get penalized for having too many spammy links pointing to their pages, then that would open the doors of opportunity to criminal types. Dishonest webmasters looking to take down their competition would simply need to point thousands of low-quality links to their pages using automated link-building software.

In July, Google announced a further 86 changes to its algorithm.

In August, the search engine giant started to penalize sites that had repeatedly violated copyright, possibly via The Digital Millennium Copyright Act (DMCA) takedown requests.

For those who might not be familiar with this, the DMCA is a controversial United States digital rights management (DRM) law. It was first enacted on October 28, 1998, by the then-President Bill Clinton. The intent behind DMCA was to create an updated version of copyright laws. The aim was to deal with the special challenges of regulating digital material.

Ok, moving on to September 2012, another major update occurred, this time called the EMD update. You'll remember that EMD stands for Exact Match Domain and refers to a domain that exactly matches a keyword phrase the site owner wants to rank for. EMDs had a massive ranking advantage simply because they used the keyword phrase in the domain name. This update removed that advantage overnight.

In October of that year, Google announced that there were 65 algorithm changes in the previous two months.

On October 5, there was a major update to Penguin, probably expanding its influence to non-English content.

Also in October, Google announced the Disavow tool. This was Google's answer to the "unnatural links" problem. It completely shifted the responsibility of unnatural links onto the webmaster by giving them a tool to disavow or deny any responsibility or support for those links. If there were any external links from bad neighborhoods pointing to your site, and you could not get them removed, you could now disavow those links, effectively rendering them harmless.

Finally, in October 2012, Google released an update to its "Page Layout" update. In December, it updated the Knowledge Graph to include non-English queries for the more common languages. This drew an end to the Google updates for that year.

Changes in 2013

In 2013, Google updated both Panda and Penguin several times. These updates refined the two different technologies to try to increase the quality of pages ranking in the SERPs. On July 18, a Panda update was thought to have been released to "soften" the effects of a previously released Panda, so Google obviously watched the effects of its updates, and modified them accordingly.

In June, Google released the "Payday Loan" update. This targeted niches with notoriously spammy SERPs. These niches were often highly commercial, which offered great rewards for any page that could rank highly. Needless to say, spammers loved sites like these. Google gave the example of "payday loans" as a demonstration when announcing this update, hence its name.

August 2013 – Hummingbird – Fast & Accurate?

Hummingbird was the name given to Google's new search algorithm. It was not part of an existing algorithm or a minor algorithm update, but an entirely brand-spanking new algorithm that was unboxed and moved into place on August 20, 2013 (though it was not announced to the SEO community until September 26).

This was a major change to the way Google sorted through the information in its index. In fact, a change on this scale had probably not occurred for over a decade. Think of it this way. Panda and Penguin were changes to parts of the old algorithm, whereas Hummingbird was a completely new algorithm, although it still used components of the old one.

Google algorithms are the mathematical equations used to determine the most relevant pages to return in the search results. The equation uses over 200 components, including things like PageRank and incoming links, to name just two.

Apparently, the name Hummingbird was chosen because of how fast and accurate these birds were. Although many webmasters disagreed, Google obviously thought at the time that this reflected its search results – fast and accurate.

Google wanted to introduce a major update to the algorithm because of the evolution in the way people used Google to search for stuff. An example Google gave was in "conversation search", whereby people could now speak into their mobile phone, tablet or even desktop browser to find information. To illustrate, let's say that you were interested in buying a Nexus 7 tablet. The old way of finding it online was to type something like this into the Google search box:

"Buy Nexus 7"

However, with the introduction of speech recognition, people have become a lot more descriptive in what they are searching for. Nowadays, it's just as easy to dictate into your search browser something like:

"Where can I buy a Nexus 7 near here?"

The old Google could not cope too well with this search phrase, but the new Hummingbird was designed to do just that. The old Google would look for pages in the index that included some or all the words in the search phrase. A page that included the exact phrase would have the best chance of appearing at the top of Google. If no pages were found with the exact phrase, then Google would look for pages that included the important words from it, e.g. "where" "buy" and "Nexus 7".

The idea behind Hummingbird was that it should be able to interpret what the searcher was *really* looking for. In the example above, they are clearly looking for somewhere near their current location to purchase a Nexus 7.

In other words, Hummingbird was supposed to determine searcher "intent" and return pages that best matched that intent, as opposed to best matching keywords in the search phrase. Hummingbird is still around today and tries to understand *exactly* what the searcher wants, rather than just considering the words used in the search term.

On December 2013, there was a drop in the authorship and rich snippets displayed in the SERPs. This was a feature where Google displayed a photo of the author and/or other information next to the listing. However, Google tightened up its search criteria and removed these features from listings.

Changes in 2014

In February 2014, Google updated its page layout update.

In May the same year, Payday Loan 2.0 was released. This was an update to the original Payday Loan algorithm and was thought to have extended the reach of this algorithm to international queries.

Also in May, Panda was updated. It was called Panda 4.0.

Changes in 2015

The Mobile-friendly Update

On April 21, Google began rolling out an update that was designed to boost mobile-friendly web pages in the mobile search results.

To help webmasters prepare for the update, Google provided a web page where webmasters could test their site to see if it was mobile-friendly or not. You can find the mobile-friendly testing tool here:

https://www.google.com/webmasters/tools/mobile-friendly/

To use this tool, you simply enter your web page URL and wait for the results. Hopefully, you will see something like this:

The mobile-friendly update:

1. Only affects searches carried out on mobile devices.
2. Applies to individual pages, not entire websites.
3. Affects ALL languages globally.

This update makes a lot of sense. If someone is searching on a small screen, Google only wants to show web pages that will display properly on such devices.

Changes in 2016

On the 23rd of February, Google made some big changes to the SERPs, removing the right-hand column of adverts and placing a block of 4 adverts at the top of the SERPs.

For any given search term, organic results were now pushed down the page. Above the fold, most searchers only saw the paid advertising links.

On May 12th, Google rolled out a second mobile-friendly update that essentially reinforced the first and made mobile sites perform better on mobile search platforms.

On the 1st of September, another animal joined Google's ranks. The "Possum" update was thought to target local search rankings, increasing the diversity of the local results, but also preventing spam from ranking. Local businesses that had previously found it difficult to rank for a city's results, simply because they were just outside the limits of the city, now found it easier.

On 23rd September, Google announced Penguin 4.0. This was a long-awaited (and anticipated) update by the SEO community. Penguin 4.0 is real-time and a core part of the algorithm. That means that any pages caught by Penguin, can be fixed, and those penalties reversed as soon as the page is re-indexed and reassessed by Penguin. With previous iterations of Penguin, webmasters had to wait months (or even years) to see if their SEO fixes reversed the Penguin penalty.

Changes in 2017

In January, Google started to roll out an update that would impact pages that had intrusive popups or other "interstitials" ruining the mobile experience. Essentially, anything that covered the main content on mobile devices and required attention (e.g. a click) to dismiss it, was targeted.

In April, it appeared that HTTPS websites were favored over the insecure HTTP sites.

In October, Google introduced Google Chrome warnings for insecure websites. That wasn't an algorithm update but I felt it was important bearing in mind what I wrote in the previous paragraph.

We also saw a reduction in the number of featured snippets in the search results, with an increase in knowledge panels.

Changes in 2018

In March 2018, Google rolled out the Mobile-First index. This change meant that instead of indexing desktop versions of pages for the search results, Google started using the mobile versions of the web pages. Why? Because of problems searchers had on mobile devices when the desktop and mobile versions of a page were vastly different.

In July 2018 Google started showing all non-HTTPS sites as "not secure" in the Chrome browser.

In August, Google rolled out a big core update which has been nicknamed the "Medic" update. This update affected a lot of health-related sites (hence the name). There have been suggestions that this update targeted sites that made money by recommending products that could be "dangerous" to health or livelihood.

That brings us up to the current time, as I am writing this book. As you can see, Google has been very active in trying to combat the spam thrown at it. The two major updates that changed everything were Panda and Penguin. Together, these two technologies weed out low-quality pages, and pages that have been engineered to rank highly in the search engines.

Anyone who builds a website will want it to rank well in Google. Without having a high-profile presence in the SERPs, a site won't get much traffic, if any at all. If that happens, webmasters WILL try to boost their rankings, and the traditional way is by working on the "on-page SEO" and inbound links. This is where webmasters and Google collide.

Google wants the best pages to rank at the top of the SERPs for obvious reasons. So, Google rewards the pages that deserve to be at the top, rather than pages that webmasters force to the top using SEO (much of which Google collectively calls "Webspam").

What this means to you is that you must deliver the absolute best quality content you can. You need to create content that deserves to be at the top of the SERPs and is likely to attract links from high-quality sites in your niche. Content is not only King now, but it has always been King. The difference now is that Google algorithms are so much better at identifying great content. It's no longer easy to take shortcuts and use underhanded tactics to trick the algorithms as it once was.

Fortunately for you, Google offers a lot of advice on how to create the type of content it wants to show up in the SERPs. In fact, it created "Webmaster Guidelines". These web pages tell you *exactly* what Google wants, and just as importantly, what it doesn't want. We'll look at these shortly, but first a question.

Where Do All of These Updates Leave Us?

Today, optimizing for specific keyword phrases has not just become difficult because of Panda & Penguin. It has also become less effective in driving traffic if those phrases do not match the *intent* of the searcher at Google.

Out of all the Google updates, the one that had the biggest influence on my own SEO was Penguin. Google sent Penguin into places that no SEO professional ever imagined it would dare.

Many SEOs will remember April 24 2012, as the day the world of SEO changed forever. It was also the day that inspired me to release the first edition of this book, entitled **"SEO 2012 & Beyond – SEO will never be the same again"**. Google created such a major shift in the way it analyzed web pages that I now think in terms of Pre-Penguin and Post-Penguin SEO, and that will likely come across in this book.

SEO Today

Today, SEO is very different from what it was just a few years ago. Google has put a number of measures in place to combat the manipulative actions of webmasters.

Ask a bunch of webmasters to define the term SEO and I bet you'll get a lot of different answers. Definitions will vary depending on the type of person you ask, and even when you ask them. SEO before Google introduced the Panda update was easy. After the Panda update, it was still relatively easy, but you needed to make sure your content was good. After Google released the Penguin update, SEO suddenly became a whole lot harder.

In 2019, phrases you'll hear being used by SEO experts will include:

1. On-page SEO
2. Off-page SEO
3. Link building, Authority & Trust
4. White hat SEO
5. Gray hat SEO
6. Black hat SEO

We've looked briefly at the first three of these, so let's quickly define the last three using a diagram.

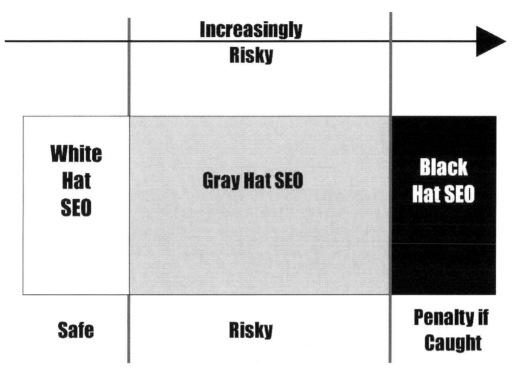

In the diagram above, you can see that we have three forms of SEO:

1. **White Hat SEO** – approved SEO strategies for getting your page to rank well. Google offers guidelines to webmasters which spell out approved SEO strategies.

2. **Black Hat SEO** – these are the "loopholes" that Google is actively seeking out and penalizing. They include a whole range of strategies from on-page keyword stuffing to backlink blasts using software to generate tens of thousands of backlinks to a web page.

3. **Gray Hat SEO** – Strategies that lie between the two extremes. These are strategies that Google does not approve of but are less likely to get your site penalized than black hat SEO. Gray hat tactics are certainly riskier than white hat SEO, but not as risky as black hat.

If you think of this as a sliding scale from totally safe "White Hat" SEO to totally dangerous "Black Hat" SEO, then you can imagine that as you move to the right with your SEO, you are more likely to get yourself into hot water with Google (at least in the long term). As you move more to the left with your SEO, you are more likely to be safer with Google. Google's tolerance level is somewhere in the gray hat area but being pushed more and more to the left with each passing month.

Let's re-draw that diagram:

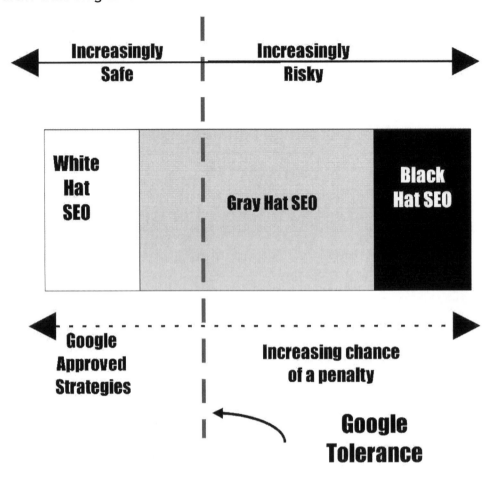

The "increasingly risky" horizontal arrow has been replaced with a movable Google Tolerance line. This tolerance line can move from left to right depending on the site being ranked. Generally, for all new sites, the tolerance level is very close to the White Hat boundary, and this is what you need to be mindful of. More established and trusted site will see that tolerance line moving to the right.

Webmasters who use techniques which are further to the right of their tolerance line risk losing their rankings.

Let's consider the importance of trust.

Trust Vs No-trust

The Google tolerance line will slide left or right depending on the site that is being ranked. For a site that has proven its worth, meaning Google trusts it a lot; we might see the diagram look like this:

A "Trusted" Site

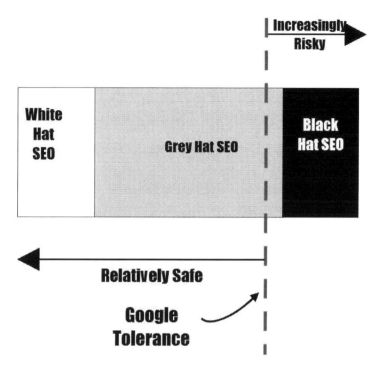

Yet for a new site or one that has no track record to speak of, the diagram will probably look a lot more like this.

A "Non-trusted" Site

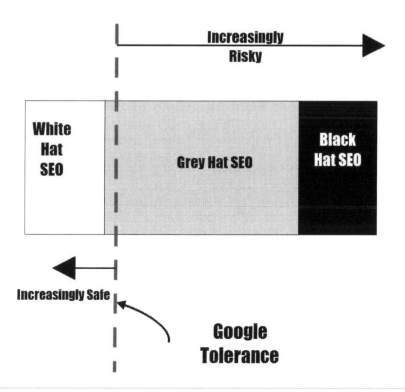

The only difference here is in the location of the "tolerance line".

In other words, Google is a lot more tolerant of sites which have built up authority and trust than it is of new sites or sites which have not been able to attain a decent level of authority or trust.

A high authority site with lots of trust can withstand a certain amount of spammy SEO without incurring a penalty (see later when we discuss "negative SEO"). In other words, the more authority the site has, the more it can get away with.

A new site, on the other hand, would be quickly penalized for even a small amount of spammy SEO.

Webmasters Living in the Past

A lot of webmasters (or SEO companies vying for your business) may disagree with my take on modern-day SEO, and that's fine. The more people that just don't get it, the less competition there is for me and my clients.

I am sure you can still find people who will say this is all rubbish and that they can get your pages ranked for your search terms (depending on the level of competition of course) by heavily back-linking the page using keyword rich anchor text.

The process they'll describe is eerily similar to the process I told you about in the section on how we ranked pages before 2010. It'll go something like this:

1. Keyword research to find high demand, low competition phrases.
2. Edit your web page so that it uses the desired phrase several times.
3. Get lots of backlinks using that keyword phrase as anchor text (the clickable text in a hyperlink).
4. Watch your page rise up the SERPs.

If you don't care about your business, then follow that strategy, or hire someone to do it for you. You might get short-term gains, but you will eventually be penalized and lose all your rankings. Google will catch up with you, and probably sooner rather than later. I have seen spammy link building tactics catapult a web page to the top 3 in Google, only to find the listing gone 24 hours later.

To lose all your rankings on Google does not take a human review, though Google does use paid human reviewers. The process Google created for this is far more "automated" since the introduction of Panda and Penguin. Go over the threshold levels of what is acceptable, and the penalty is algorithmically determined and applied.

The good news is that algorithmic penalties can just as easily be lifted by removing the offending SEO and cleaning up your site. However, if that offending SEO includes low-quality backlinks to your site (especially to the homepage), things become a little trickier.

Remember the SEO expert you hired that threw tens of thousands of backlinks at your site using his secret software? How can you get those backlinks removed? In most cases, you can't. Google does provide a "Disavow" tool that can help in a lot of instances and I'll tell you more about that later in the book. In extreme circumstances, moving the site to a brand new domain and starting afresh may be the only option.

In the rest of this book, I want to focus on what you need to do to help your pages rank better. I will be looking mainly at white-hat strategies, though I will venture a little into gray hat SEO as well. Don't worry, I will tell you whether a technique is risky, so you can choose to avoid it. I won't be covering black-hat SEO at all. It's just not a long-term strategy. Remember, Google can and will move the goal posts without any notice, leaving you out in the cold. Is it worth risking your long-term business plans for short-term gains?

OK, let's now get started with the four pillars of modern SEO.

The Four Pillars of SEO

I have been doing SEO for over 15 years and have always concentrated on long-term strategies. That's not to say I haven't dabbled in black hat SEO because I have, a little. Over the years, I have done a lot of experiments on all kinds of ranking factors. However, and without exception, *all* the sites I promoted with black hat SEO have been penalized; every single one of them.

I don't want to talk about the SEO strategies that will eventually cause you problems, so I'll concentrate on the safer techniques of white hat SEO.

I divide modern, safe SEO, into four pillars:

1. Quality content
2. Site organization
3. Authority
4. What's in it for the visitor?

These are the four areas where you need to concentrate your efforts, so let's have a look at each of them in turn.

1. Quality Content

Before we begin, let me just say that a lot of SEO "experts" still disagree with me on the need for quality content as a major ranking factor, even after Panda, Penguin & Hummingbird. They will often cite exceptions in the search engines where pages rank well for competitive terms without much on-page content or with content of very little value. Exceptions do exist, but these can usually be explained in terms of page authority being the main ranking factor keeping the page at the top.

Without authority, unworthy pages can get forced to the top with black hat SEO, but not for long. Remember, bounce rates and time spent on a site are important indicators to Google. Poor content cannot hide in the top 10. Search engine users essentially vote out content that falls short on quality. They do this by their actions or inactions. They vote by the length of time they stay on any site or page, and whether they visit any other pages while on that site.

Additionally, Google looks at what a visitor does once they hit the back button and return to the SERPs. Do they refine their search (indicating they did not find what they wanted), or move on to something new (indicating they did)?

If you are one of those people who question the need for quality content, then I encourage you to watch a video I recorded before you read the rest of this book. You can view it here:

https://ezseonews.com/lsi-still-important

It's quite an eye-opener.

Before we look at how we can ensure our content is high quality, let's consider the topics your visitors want to see, and how we can get an idea of what people are searching for.

The Content Your Visitors Want to See

The most important part of creating website content is deciding what your visitors want to see. One of my favorite ways of generating content ideas is to spy on my competitors to see what they are adding to their website.

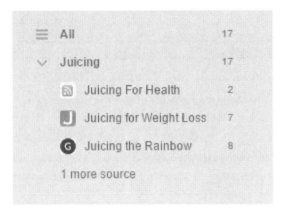

An easy and free way of doing this is to subscribe to your competitor's RSS feed, and then monitor that for new content.

If you collect RSS feeds from several competitors, you can group them together and follow all sites as a single feed using a service like Feedly. Feedly then notifies you of any new content, across all the sites, as it's updated.

You can see from the above image how I have added three feeds from three different websites, all related to juicing, into a collection I aptly named "Juicing". If I click on the "Juicing" item in the menu, it shows me new content from all those feeds in the collection:

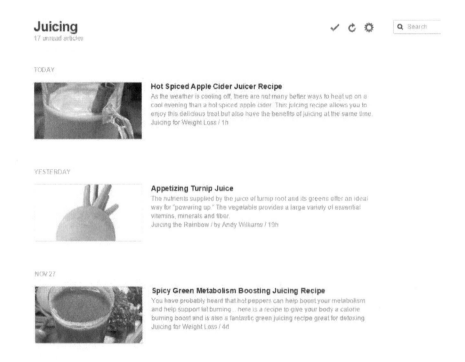

This really is a great way to find new content ideas. Let your competitors do the research to find out what their readers want, then apply their ideas to your own site. Another upside of this is that you can be the first to comment on their new articles, and that can lead to more traffic to your site.

You can extend this method by using Google Alerts to monitor keywords in your niche. For example, if you had a website about bee colony collapse, you could set up an alert at Google for that. So whenever new items appear in the SERPs that relate to bee colony collapse, you get notified right away. Notifications can be sent via email, or they can be included in RSS feeds, which you can then add to your Feedly account. Once set up, you have your finger firmly on the pulse in your niche, and any breaking news gets delivered to you right away, ready for your own "breaking news" article that you can post on your site. Share any new story via social media, and you can quickly find these articles attracting both backlinks and traffic.

Finally, a paid tool I highly recommend you look at is called BuzzSumo:

https://buzzsumo.com/

This tool is one that I use to find popular content in my niches.

Just to show you what it can do, if I type in "juicing", here are the results that are returned:

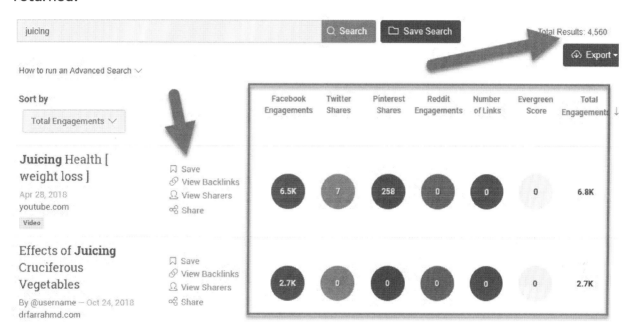

BuzzSumo returned 4,560 articles on juicing, with lots of data about each one. Of particular interest is the number of social interactions each article has. An article with a lot of Facebook or Twitter interest is obviously a piece of content you should be looking at.

Buzzsumo (paid version) also allows you to see some of the users that shared each piece of content, and those web pages that link to the content. How useful is that for backlinking?

The biggest issue with Buzzsumo is the price. It's not cheap and probably beyond the budget of most people starting out with their online business. There isn't really a good cheaper alternative that I know of, but even if you can't subscribe, you can still use it for a few searches each day to find the most popular content for free. You just won't get all the other data that comes with that tool.

These tools are great, but it is also a good idea to know what people are searching for at Google. That is where keyword research tools are useful.

Keyword Research - Using Google Keyword Planner

I was a little reluctant to talk about keyword research tools as a way of finding content ideas, for one simple reason. Armed with the data from a keyword research session, the temptation to create "Webspam" is too hard to resist for many. Keyword research tools are one of the main reasons Google has had to go to extreme measures to clean up its search results of poor, thin content.

For years, the process employed by many internet marketers was the same:

1. Do keyword research.
2. Find keywords that are searched for a lot, have low competition and are commercial terms that are expensive to advertise on Google AdWords.
3. Write a page of content around each of these profitable keywords.
4. Slap up Google Adsense on the page.

That was the recipe for many people to make big money online. A single web page ranking high in Google could make 10s or even 100s of dollars a day with Google Adsense clicks. You can see why the temptation was there to get as many pages online as possible, and some webmasters literally put up millions.

With that said, keyword research is still a valuable way to find out what people want. Like so many things, it's how you use the data that will decide whether Google sees you as a great content creator or web spammer.

Google's own keyword research tool is free to use, but it does have the odd annoyance. I'll show you how to overcome those.

Firstly, Google wants users of its keyword tool to use its advertising platform (Google AdWords). Therefore, you may find it difficult to sign up without being forced into creating ads or entering a credit card. Don't panic, here are the instructions to sign up without having to create ads or add a credit card.

Set Up a Keyword Planner Account Without an AdWords Campaign

Search Google for Google Keyword Planner and you should find it easily enough:

Keyword Planner - AdWords - Google
https://adwords.google.com/ko/KeywordPlanner/Home ▼
to continue to Google Ads. Email or phone. Forgot email? Listen and type the numbers you hear. Type the text you hear or see. Not your computer? Use a ...

When you land on that page, you will be asked to log in to your Google account. This is where the problem lies. If you have already set up a Keyword Planner account using your email address, you are stuck and will need to create an ad campaign to use the planner. The solution is to create a brand new Gmail address and use that instead.

When you log in to the Keyword Planner site, you'll be redirected to the **Getting Started** screen. Look for the link to **Skip the guided setup**, and click that:

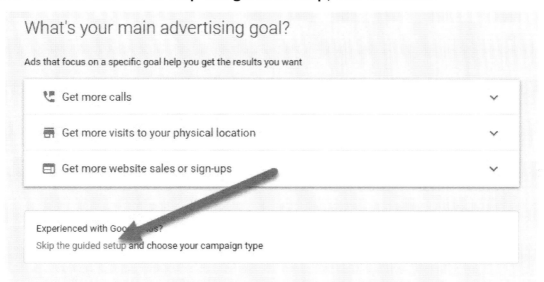

On the next screen, Google will try again to hook you into setting up an ad campaign. Here is the screen:

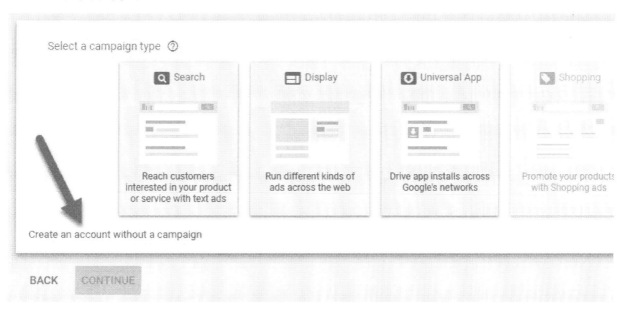

Click the link to **Create an account without a campaign**.

On the next screen, click the **Submit** button:

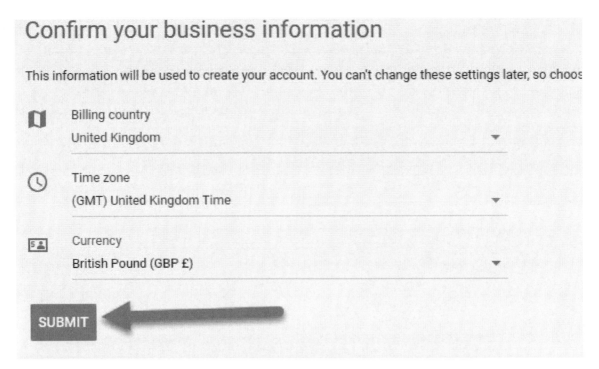

And now click the **Explore Your Account** button.

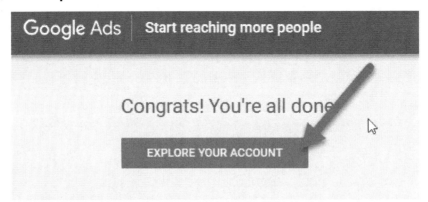

You are taken into your account. To start the Keyword Planner, click on the **Tools** menu and select **Keyword Planner**.

Let's take Keyword Planner for a spin.

Load up the Keyword Planner, and let's see what it can (and cannot) do. On the opening screen, click the **Find new keywords** button:

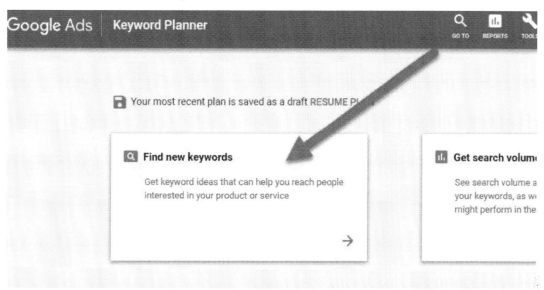

Enter a keyword that you want to explore, and click the button to get started.

Let's assume that I have a technology site and I want to write some articles about the new **Samsung Note 9**. That is the term I entered as my search term.

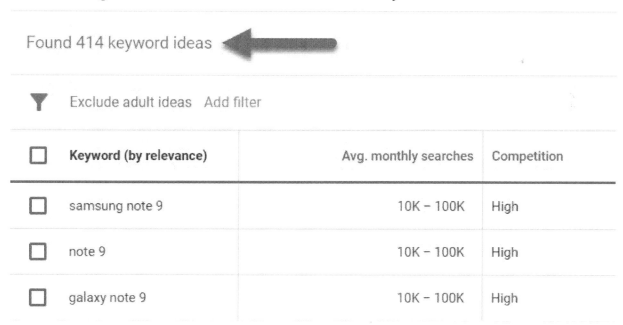

Google Keyword Planner found 414 keywords related to this term.

You can click any column header to order your results by that column. Since we are looking for high demand keywords, let's order our keywords by average monthly searches (click that column header).

	Keyword	↓ **Avg. monthly searches**	Competition	Ad ir
☐	samsung s9	100K – 1M	High	
☐	samsung galaxy s7	100K – 1M	High	
☐	samsung galaxy s9	100K – 1M	High	
☐	galaxy s9	10K – 100K	High	
☐	iphone 9	10K – 100K	High	
☐	mobile phone deals	10K – 100K	High	
☐	galaxy note 9	10K – 100K	High	

But those demand figures...

This brings us to the second major issue with the Google Keyword Planner. Average monthly searches is a range, and a wide range at that.

But I have a fix for that too. Users of Google Chrome and Firefox can install an extension called Keyword Everywhere. Not only does this fix the Keyword Planner range issue, but it gives us some very powerful tools.

Do a Google search for the **Keyword Everywhere** extension and install it for your web browser of choice. You'll need to enter an email address during the install, and Keywords Everywhere will send you an email link to get your API key. You'll need the API key to use their software.

Once installed, you'll have a new button in the toolbar of your browser. That button opens up a menu, and an on/off switch so you can turn the extension off when not being used.

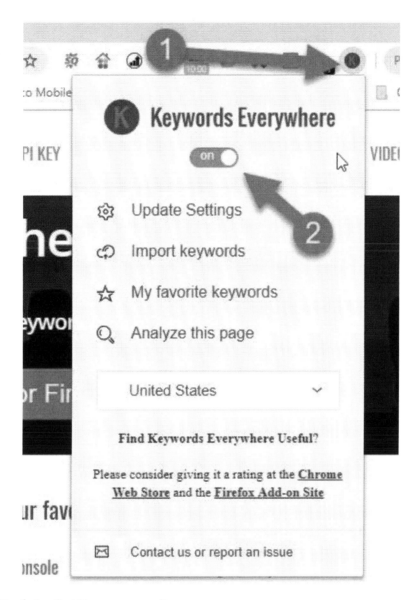

Click on the **Update Settings** menu item.

In the API key box, paste in the API key they gave you and click on the **Validate** button.

Once done, you can close the Keywords Everywhere settings and head back to the Google Keyword Planner.   Log out and then back in again.

Repeat the search you did earlier.   Do you notice the difference?

Keyword (by relevance)	Vol	CPC	Comp	Avg. monthly searches
samsung note 9 ⭐	1,900	$1.30	0.93	10K – 100K
note 9 ⭐	3,890	$1.19	0.75	10K – 100K
galaxy note 9 ⭐	200	$1.63	0.99	10K – 100K
samsung galaxy note 9 ⭐	910	$0.88	0.99	10K – 100K
samsung 9 ⭐	3,210	$1.34	0.98	1K – 10K
samsung galaxy note ⭐	201,000	$0.53	0.94	1K – 10K
samsung galaxy 9 ⭐	1,000	$1.30	1	1K – 10K

You've still got the same columns you had before, but you also have three new ones added by Keywords Everywhere.

Vol - The number of monthly searches made for that keyword.

CPC - The cost per click of that keyword.

Comp - A number between 0 (easy) and 1 (hard) for the competition you will face if you want to rank for that keyword.

Keywords Everywhere has added back the detail that Google stripped out in previous updates to the keyword planner.

A great option you have with Keywords Everywhere is to save all of the keyword data to your "favorites". Look at the lower right of the screen:

You'll get this button on all screens that show Keywords Everywhere data (we'll come on to these in a moment). Notice also that you can save the data as a CSV file, meaning easy import into Excel or a similar spreadsheet program.

If you do click **Add All Keywords**, you'll only get those keywords that are currently visible, so scroll to the bottom of the page and select 500 from the **Show Rows** option. You can then scroll through fewer pages of keywords to add them all to your favorites.

To view your favorites, select **My favorite keywords** from the menu:

The Keywords Everywhere favorites table will open, showing you all of the keywords you have added. The columns can be ordered by clicking the column title. So, for example, you can see which keywords cost the most for advertisers:

	Keyword	Volume	CPC	Competition	Volume (US)
☐	upcoming samsung galaxy note	10	$15.12	0.16	10
☐	samsung galaxy release date	1,300	$6.48	0.17	720
☐	samsung note phone release dates	40	$6.23	0.42	30
☐	note 9 release date	49,500	$5.53	1	1,000
☐	galaxy 9 note release date	260	$5.21	1	170
☐	galaxy note release	70	$4.98	0.55	50
☐	the galaxy 9	210	$4.94	0.99	170

The Keyword Planner is Only the Beginning

I can see from the data on Google's Keyword Planner that there is a huge demand for content on the Samsung Note 9. However, I want to get a better idea of what type of content might be in demand. Keywords Everywhere can come to the rescue again. It doesn't just work with Keyword Planner. It also adds keyword data to a lot of other tools, like Google Search:

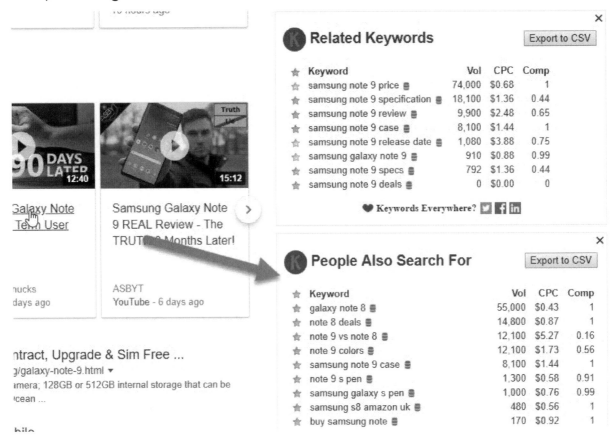

You can see a complete list of sites that get the Keywords Everywhere treatment in the settings screen:

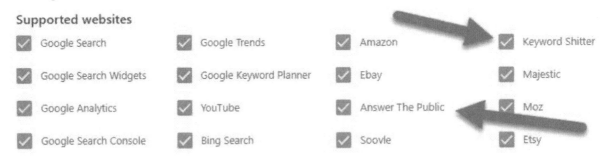

As you can see, this plugin will add keyword data into your Google Analytics and Google Console screens. However, there are two that I really like when doing keyword research. They are called **Keyword Shitter** and Answer the Public. Do a Google search to find them.

The first of those keyword tools spits out keywords at a rapid pace, and Keywords Everywhere provides useful data about each phrase. Go and try it.

Here is a snapshot of the phrases returned from that tool:

```
970 - 1544
samsung note 9 flip cover case
samsung note 9 credit card case
samsung note 9 case designer
samsung note 9 case disney
samsung note 9 case drop test
samsung note 9 digital case
samsung note 9 otterbox defender case
samsung galaxy note 9 case otterbox defender
samsung galaxy note 9 heavy duty case
whitestone dome samsung galaxy note 9 case
samsung note 9 case etsy
esr samsung galaxy note 9 case
element case samsung note 9
samsung note 9 case from samsung
samsung note 9 case flip
samsung note 9 case for sale
samsung note 9 folio case
samsung note 9 fabric case
samsung note 9 carbon fiber case
samsung note 9 case jb hi fi
samsung galaxy note 9 folio case
best case for samsung note 9
case for samsung galaxy note 9
otterbox case for samsung note 9
leather case for samsung note 9
lifeproof case for samsung note 9
```

I actually stopped the tool after a minute or so as it keeps on finding new words. I also filtered out only those phrases that contain the word Samsung. So that's 970 keyword phrases that might be useful.

Keywords Everywhere works hard on that page too, finding all the supply and demand data. You can see that as you scroll down the page:

```
samsung note 9 [1,900/mo - $1.30 - 0.93] ☆
samsung note 9 price [33,100/mo - $1.07 - 0.93] ☆
samsung note 9 case [170/mo - $0.68 - 1] ☆
samsung note 9 review [3,600/mo - $2.87 - 0.37] ☆
samsung note 9 deals [0/mo - $0.00 - 0] ☆
samsung note 9 specs [433/mo - $1.71 - 0.31] ☆
samsung note 9 price uk [0/mo - $0.00 - 0] ☆
samsung note 9 ee [0/mo - $0.00 - 0] ☆
samsung note 9 release date uk [0/mo - $0.00 - 0] ☆
samsung note 9 contract [0/mo - $0.00 - 0] ☆
samsung note 9 fortnite [0/mo - $0.00 - 0] ☆
samsung note 9 vodafone [40/mo - $0.83 - 0.78] ☆
```

One thing I like to do with keyword lists like the one from Keyword Shitter is to collect them all in a text file and use Google Keyword Planner to analyze them for CPC, impressions and potential clicks. In other words, get Google to tell me which of the keywords are the most commercial in nature.

Let's see how this works. To demonstrate, I'll grab those 970 keywords from the Keyword Shitter.

On the Keyword Planner site, go up to the Tools menu and select Keyword Planner to start a new session. From the opening screen, select **Get search volume forecasts**:

Now paste in the keywords from Keyword Shitter and click **Get Started**:

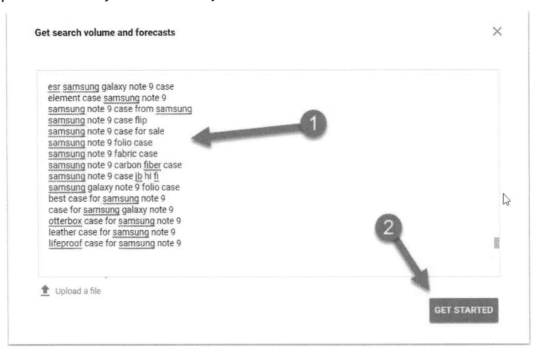

Google Keyword Planner will now go away and find data about your keywords:

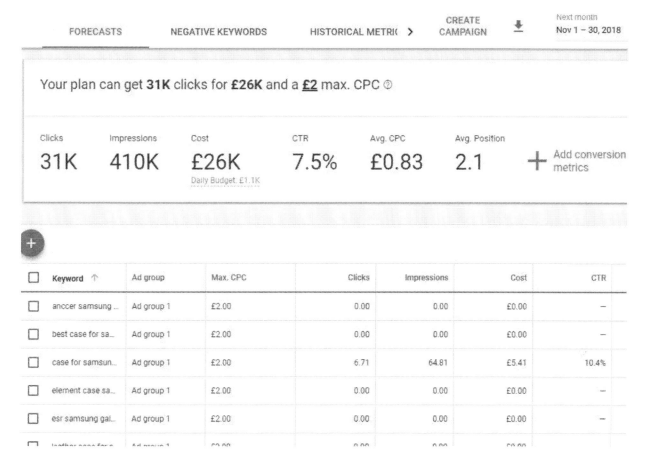

The data in the table is designed for AdWords advertisers, so provides data about the potential cost per click, CTR, Impressions, etc. of these keywords. This can be very interesting data to look through as it highlights the more commercial keywords (the ones advertisers are already bidding on).

Answerthepublic.com

This is a great tool for finding content ideas and it works with Keywords Everywhere. A quick search for Samsung Note 9 returned keywords in three categories: Questions, Prepositions, and Comparisons.

This tool found 50 questions that people ask about the Samsung Note 9:

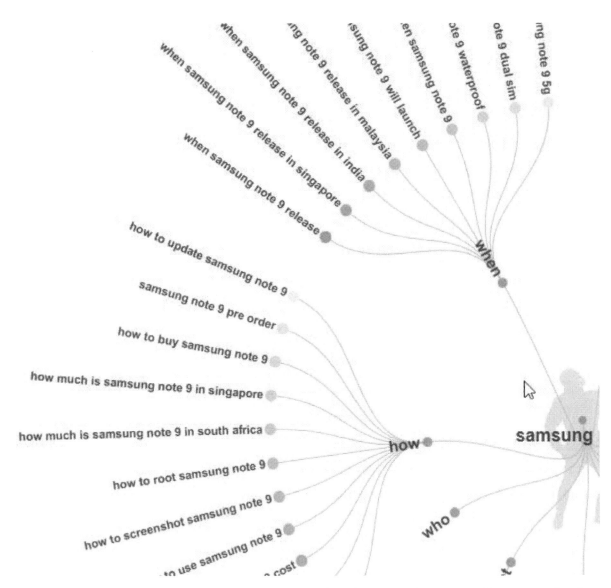

I love these visual diagrams, but you can see the data as plain text if you prefer by switching from **Visualization** to **Data**:

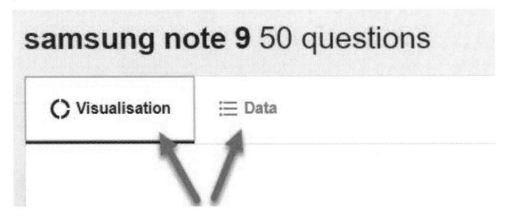

Some of these questions provide excellent ideas for articles on the phone and represent real questions asked by real searchers.

The prepositions section provides further content ideas. These are search phrases about the Samsung Note 9 that include words like can, to, without, near, with, for, and is.

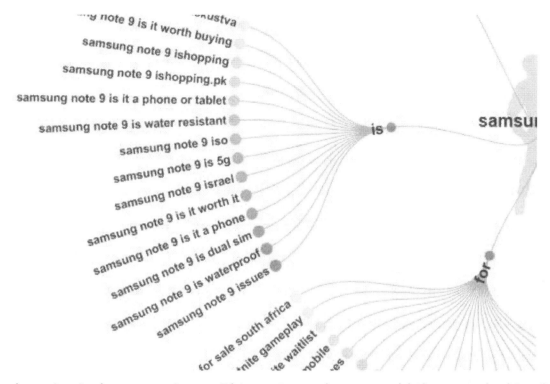

The final section is the comparisons. This again can be pure gold if you are looking for content ideas. These are search phrases that include words like versus, and, like, vs, and or:

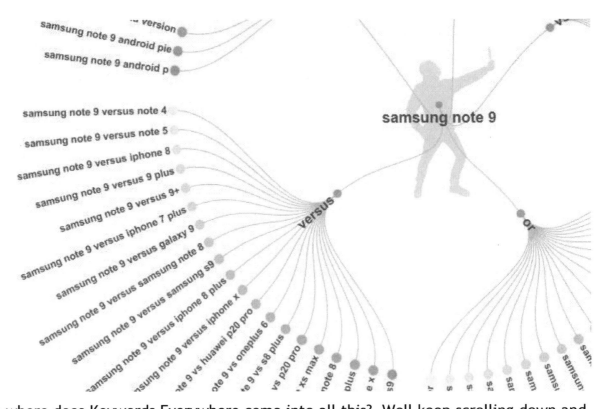

So where does Keywords Everywhere come into all this? Well keep scrolling down and you'll see a list of all keywords at the bottom of the page:

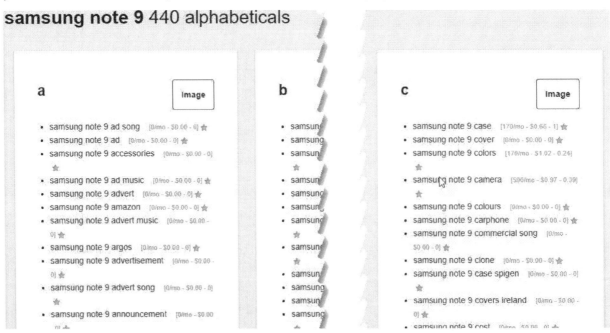

And don't forget that **Add All Keywords** button at the bottom of the page if you want to save all of this data.

Another Keyword Planner Example - Weight Loss

Let's pretend we are in the weight loss niche and looking for content ideas with the Keyword Planner. If necessary, click on the Tools menu and select Keyword Planner to get started. Make sure Keywords Everywhere is running.

Click on the **Find new keywords** button and enter **weight loss** in the search box. Click the **Get Started** button to retrieve keywords.

At the very top of the table, I can see the exact phrase that I typed in:

	Keyword (by relevance)	Vol	CPC	Comp
☐	weight loss ☆	368,000	$1.92	0.91
☐	how to lose weight *	450,000	$1.07	0.33
☐	how to lose weight...	450,000	$1.52	0.83
☐	lose weight ☆	246,000	$1.71	0.57

The exact term "weight loss" is searched between 368,000 times per month according to Keywords Everywhere. I can also see that competition is high (lots of advertisers bidding on this phrase) at 0.91 (this is a value between 0 and 1). The average CPC is $1.92.

What does that mean?

If someone searches Google for "weight loss" and Google shows my advert, it wants me to agree to pay up to $1.92 if that person clicks on my ad. That's $1.92 PER CLICK!

Ads can appear in the search results, or on partner sites (and pretty much anyone can be a partner through the AdSense program). Imagine you had a weight loss site and added AdSense to monetize it. If there are advertisers willing to pay $1.92 per click, then every time a visitor to your site clicked this type of advert, you would make a "commission" equal to the lion's share of up to $1.92. Can you see why people started creating pages around specific keyword phrases?

There are a lot of other keywords in this niche that could potentially pay a lot more per click:

	Keyword		Volume	CPC	Con
☐	most healthy way to lose weight		30	$11.98	
☐	before after weight loss		5,400	$11.10	
☐	surgical weight loss		720	$10.31	
☐	weight loss surgery		49,500	$9.94	
☐	weight loss camp for adults		1,600	$9.75	
☐	medical weight loss programs		1,300	$9.36	
☐	dotties weight loss		590	$9.10	
☐	healthy ways to lose weight quickly		90	$8.44	
☐	weight loss programs for men		1,900	$8.18	
☐	effective weight loss program		320	$8.06	
☐	weight loss retreat		2,900	$7.27	
☐	dotties weight loss zone		2,400	$6.93	

Can you see why focusing on specific keywords can be so tempting?

You will see a lot of keyword ideas generated by Google. These keywords are taken straight from Google's keyword database, and let's face it, Google knows what people are searching for, so while the data is not 100% accurate (Google would never want to give us all the facts), they are reliable enough to determine in-demand topics.

Looking down the keywords I've generated and filtered for "weight loss", I can see a few good content ideas:

1. Fast weight loss / Rapid weight loss (always popular in the pre-summer months).
2. Weight loss supplements (though this could be a whole category of content on a weight loss site, with different articles exploring different supplements). We also have weight loss pills related to this search.
3. Weight loss surgery.
4. Diet Plans (again this could be a major category on a weight loss site).
5. Diets that work.
6. Medical weight loss gets a lot of searches, though there will be a lot of related search phrases like gastric surgery, gastric bypass, bariatric surgery, etc.

If you find an area that you would like to look into further, just change the search term at the top of the page. You can enter several words if you like:

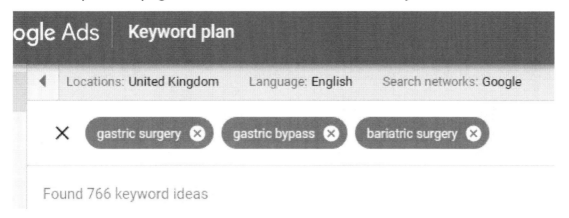

When you click the **Get Results** button, you'll get to see the data for those specific phrases:

	Keyword	Vol	CPC	Comp
☐	obesity surgery centre ☆	40	$2.45	0.54
☐	weight loss surgery houston ☆	480	$37.00	0.85
☐	bypass surgery procedure ☆	720	$0.81	0.09
☐	laparoscopic weight loss surgery ☆	140	$5.07	0.66
☐	laparoscopic gastric bypass ☆	720	$12.80	0.23
☐	gastric bypass and pregnancy ☆	320	$6.96	0.15

.. as well as all of the related terms generated by the Google keyword tool.

This new set gives me more ideas for content, like:

Keyword	Volume	CPC
gastroplasty	1,900	$16.28
does gastric bypass work	90	$15.52
weight loss surgery before and after	720	$14.01
weight loss surgery financing	260	$12.26
most effective weight loss surgery	140	$11.13
gastric bypass definition	590	$10.15
sleeve surgery	12,100	$9.49
types of gastric bypass surgery	260	$9.00
cheap gastric bypass surgery	90	$8.64

Look at those CPCs!

Each of these phrases on their own could be the inspiration behind an article. It is important to remember, though, that you **WILL NOT** be writing an article targeting the keyword phrase itself. These phrases are just the seeds for content ideas. You need to get inside the head of the person typing these phrases into Google and decide why they are typing the phrase?

For example, looking at all of the keywords that mention "complications" is interesting:

Found 26 keyword ideas

Show broadly related ideas | Exclude adult ideas ⊗ | Keyword text contains complication ⊗ | Keywo

Add filter

Keyword	Vol	CPC	Comp
☐ bariatric surgery complications ☆	880	$4.36	0.29
☐ sleeve gastrectomy complications ☆	390	$2.95	0.11
☐ gastric sleeve complications ☆	2,400	$8.19	0.34
☐ gastric bypass surgery complications ☆	390	$8.02	0.35
☐ gastric bypass complications ☆	1,300	$5.99	0.2
☐ gastric band complications ☆	260	$3.29	0.23
☐ complications after gastric bypass surgery ☆	70	$6.95	0.3
☐ roux en y gastric bypass complications ☆	390	$5.72	0.18
☐ lap band complications ☆	590	$3.04	0.24

I'd imagine (though I could be wrong), that the people searching for this phrase are likely to be the potential patients or their families/friends trying to be prepared for all eventualities. In other words, how safe is it? Are complications common?

My initial idea for content might be to find real people who had been through the operation and interview them about the procedure. With the internet, it is relatively easy to find people who are happy to talk and share experiences.

I'd ask them things like:

- How did the operation go?
- How long was the recovery time?
- What, if anything went wrong?
- How have you found eating since the operation?
- Any words of warning to prospective patients?
- If there was one thing you wished you'd known before the operation, what would it be?

I'd be tempted to find some people that were very happy with the operation and the results, and others that had problems. You could put both sides of the story forward, and offer statistics on how likely someone was to face complications.

So, I started with a keyword phrase idea of **gastric bypass complications**.

That is where my approach differs from a lot of old-school SEOs.

Rather than try to rank for that specific phrase as they would, I used the phrase as an idea for a piece of content and wrote about the TOPIC.

My article is likely to rank for that exact phrase (as well as hundreds of other phrases), even if I don't necessarily have the exact phrase on my page. Why? Because the way we theme pages will mean we are including all of the related theme words and phrases that Google expects to see in an authoritative article on that topic. Not only that but with such an interesting and visitor-focused article, it is likely to get a lot of shares and backlinks, which in turn will help it rank.

So, forget the old ways of writing keyword-focused content.

Find phrases that people are looking for, and then try to get into their heads to find out why they are searching for those phrases. Once you can answer that, you can create content that will compete in Google, excite your visitors, attract likes, shares, and most importantly, backlinks!

So, you have ideas for content and you know what people are searching for at the search engines. The next step is to get a little advice from Google.

What Google Tells Us About Quality Content

Google's Webmaster Guidelines offer advice to webmasters. They tell us what Google considers "good content", and what it considers as spam. Let's take a quick look at what the guidelines say about website content.

1. Create a useful, information-rich site

This one should be obvious. Create content that your visitors *want* to see.

2. Think about the words people use to search

...and try to incorporate them into your pages.

This guideline is one that I think may soon disappear, but it is still there as I type this. One of the points of Google's Hummingbird was to be able to lump together closely related terms so that Google could understand the searcher's intent. After Hummingbird, there was no need to include specific phrases on your page, as Google would look at the combined words on the page and be able to determine relevancy to any search term (whether it appeared on the page or not).

Also, from an SEO point of view, focusing on keywords usually results in a web page optimized for the search engines at the expense of the visitor's experience. Google openly labels that type of page as Webspam.

The best advice (which you will understand if you watched the video earlier in this chapter) is to think about the words people use to search, the synonyms of those words, and the searcher's intent. Questions you will want to ask include: what is the searcher looking for exactly? What words, phrases, and topics, does my page need to satisfy that intent?

We will look at all of this in more detail later in the book.

3. Try to use text instead of images for important names, content, or links

Google's crawler does not recognize text in images, so if there is an important word or phrase that you need Google to know exists in any part of your page, use text. If it must be an image for whatever reason, then use the ALT tag to create a description of the image which includes that phrase.

A great example of using text instead of images is in links on your site. Links are currently the most important factor in SEO, so the more the search engines know about the nature of a link the better. If you are linking from one page on your site to another about "purple furbies", then use **purple furbies** as the link text. This will tell Google that the page you are linking to is about purple furbies. These internal links also help rank a page for a specific term. Internal links are a safer way to get keyword rich anchor text into a link (something that is not so safe coming from other websites). You will see more about this in the section on "back-linking" later in the book.

4. Make <title> and ALT attributes descriptive

The <title> tag of your page is one of the most important areas in terms of SEO. Try to get your most important keyword(s) in there, but do not stuff keywords into the title. The title tag has two main objectives; one is to entice the searcher to click through from the search engines, and the other is to tell Google what your page is all about.

We talked about click-through rates (CTR) earlier in the book and looked at how important a factor they are in modern SEO. If you find a page has a low CTR (something you can check in Google Search Console), then tweak the title to see if you can make it more enticing to searchers. You then need to monitor the CTR of the page in the coming days and weeks. Just know that better titles (ones that match the searcher's intent) will attract more clicks in the Google SERPs than ones that don't.

NOTE: A page listed in the search results also contains a short description under its title. If your Meta Description includes the search term that was typed in at Google, then it is likely to be used as the listing description. If the search phrase is not present in the meta description, Google may choose a snippet of text from your web page that does include the search phrase.

It is also possible to optimize the Meta Description for better CTR, but this is not an exact science since Google may not be using that as the listing description. We'll look at this later.

Images have ALT tags. Their primary purpose is to help people who have images turned off, for example, people with impaired vision. Often, they will use text-to-voice software to read pages, so your ALT tags should help them with this. An ALT tag should describe the image to those users in a concise way. It is also a great place to insert a keyword phrase or synonym if it is 100% relevant, but NEVER use ALT tags just as a place to stuff keywords.

5. Make pages for users, not search engines

This is probably the most important point in all the Webmaster guidelines.

In the past, many webmasters created pages to please the search engines, giving their visitors little thought. Today, that is a fast track to low rankings.

Whatever you do in 2019 and beyond, don't just create content for the search engines in the hope of ranking better and building more traffic. Pleasing algorithms over people is an old tactic that no longer works. Instead, you need to create the content that your audience wants to see, read and interact with. Keeping your visitors happy makes Google happy. When you please the search engine giant, your authority and traffic will build in a safe, natural, and more sustainable way. When we come to look at backlinking, we'll discuss a type of page that you can create specifically to attract backlinks. These can give your sites massive boosts in authority which will make all pages on the site rank more easily.

6. Avoid tricks designed to manipulate your rankings

Google offers you a rule of thumb. If you are comfortable explaining what you are doing to a Google employee or one of your competitors (who could report you to Google), then you are probably doing things the right way. Another great test is to ask yourself whether you would do what you are doing if search engines didn't exist.

7. Make your website stand out in your field

No matter what niche you are in, and no matter what keywords you want to rank for, you ultimately have 10 other pages competing with you. They are the 10 web pages at the top of the Google SERPs. That's where you want to rank, right? Therefore, you need to ignore all the other pages ranking on page two and beyond. Your focus is only on the top 10 slots of page one.

The questions you need to be ever mindful of are:

How can I make my page stand out from these competitors? And, how can I make my page better, more engaging, different and valuable?

Google needs to see that your page adds to the top 10 in a unique way, and not simply covers the same information. In other words, you want to rise above being just another rehashed page on the same topic.

Google Tells Us to Avoid the Following

1. Automatically Generated Content

In an effort to build websites faster, webmasters have created a variety of tools, including some that can actually create content for you. Any content generated like this is very poor in quality and considered spam by Google. You should avoid any tool or service that offers to auto-generate content at all costs. This will get your site penalized or even completely de-indexed (removed from Google's SERPs).

Some webmasters go as far as having all the content on their site automatically generated (and updated) from stuff on other websites, e.g. using product data feeds (and RSS feeds). This way they get to populate their web pages effortlessly, but their site has no unique or original content of its own. The only time using data feeds is a good idea, is if you own the feed. Therefore, the contents will be unique to your own site. An example would be an e-commerce site using a product feed.

2. Creating Pages with Little or No Original Content

Great content is King, and that means it must be unique and well written. The term "thin page" describes a web page that has little or no original (and useful) material. These are pages which don't offer much value to the visitor. They include pages with very little written content (word count) or pages that might have a lot of content but it's not original or in any way useful. Being original is also more than just having a unique article that passes a Copyscape check (Copyscape is a free plagiarism tool that lets you check articles for uniqueness). Truly original content also means offering new ideas, thoughts, and insights; things not found on the other pages in the top 10.

3. Hidden Text

Some webmasters make sections of text on their web pages invisible. This typically includes keyword rich text using lots of related terms the webmaster hopes to rank for. It's not hard to make text invisible to the visitor. All you must do is use the same color font as the page background, i.e. white text on a white background. However, if you try to hide text from Google this way, you're on a hiding to nothing. This technique used to work several years ago, but today it will more than likely get your site penalized.

Hidden links also come under the umbrella of hidden text. This was a tactic used in the past to spread link juice around, maybe by linking a full stop (period) to another page to make it rank better.

There are several other ways to hide text on a web page (e.g. using CSS), but Google is on to all of them.

Simple advice: Don't!

4. Doorway Pages

This term refers to pages that are set up to rank for a single specific keyword phrase. They are highly optimized for that phrase, and their sole purpose is to rank high for the chosen search term. Traffic is then typically (though not always) funneled to another page or site from the doorway page.

5. Scraped Content

Scraped content is the content copied from other websites. Spammers often do this to add more material to their own websites, quickly, and with very little effort.

Scraping can involve grabbing entire articles or just parts of another web page. Scraping tactics also include copying someone else's content and then swapping out synonyms to make the stolen content appear unique.

Even pages that embed podcasts or other shared media like YouTube videos, for example, can be considered scraped content unless the webmaster adds their own unique commentary or thoughts to the page that embeds the media. A web page should offer value to a visitor, and that includes a unique experience. A good test if you are embedding content from another site is this. Strip out any "scraped content" and then see what you have left. Is it STILL a valuable and useful resource?

6. Participating in Affiliate Programs Without Adding Sufficient Value

One of Google's algorithm changes targeted web pages that were heavy on adverts. Google reasoned that too many ads on a page make for bad user experience. Therefore, ads should be secondary to the main content, and must not dominate the page.

Another thing you need to be aware of is how to properly run reviews sites if that's your thing. Your reviews need to be totally unique and contain original thoughts and ideas. Your reviews must also contain information that is not available on the merchant site or other affiliate sites. You need to be adding something totally unique, that no other review has.

If you simply go to Amazon and use their product description and user comments, then your page is not only scraped content, but it also fails to add enough value. Reviews need to have original thoughts, ideas, and suggestions, to be of any importance. After all, why would someone want to read your review when they can read all the exact same information on Amazon or the manufacturer's own site?

A good test is to strip out all the adverts and scraped content from a page (even if you re-wrote it in your own words), and then see whether the page still offers sufficient value to the visitor.

7. Stuffing Pages with Keywords

Some webmasters stuff additional keywords into their page. Quite often, you will see a list of keywords on the page, maybe in the form of a "related terms" section, or a list of US states, as two examples.

Another common way of stuffing keywords is to re-use a specific word or phrase several times to inflate its keyword density. Keyword density is the percentage of times a keyword appears on a web page compared to the total number of words on the page. It often leads to unnatural, forced, or grammatically incorrect language.

Google offers this example as an explanation:

"We sell **custom cigar humidors**. Our **custom cigar humidors** are handmade. If you're thinking of buying a **custom cigar humidor**, please contact our **custom cigar humidor** specialists at **custom.cigar.humidors**@example.com."

As you can see, that is totally unnatural and not easy to read, yet this is exactly the sort of trash that used to dominate the SERPs of yesteryear.

Stuffing pages with keywords was clearly done for the search engines and not the visitors. Try it and your page/site will get a slap from Google. Like so many other black-hat tactics, this used to work once, but not anymore.

8. User-generated SPAM

A good example of user-generated spam includes the comments posted on your site. If you accept comments, and you should, make sure you moderate them. In addition, only accept legitimate comments that add to the "conversation" you started on the page. Never approve comments that simply attempt to stroke your ego with things like "Great blog", or comments that ask totally irrelevant questions like, "Hey, great WordPress theme, what is it?" Only approve comments that raise legitimate points or ask legitimate questions about your article. Trash anything that's non-specific or mark it as SPAM if it's obvious.

Another type of user-generated content that you need to be careful with is guest posts. If you accept articles from other people and post them on your site, you must never accept any content that is below your own standards. I would also suggest you never allow authors to place external links in the body of an article, and definitely not using keyword-rich anchor text.

If the author wants to include a link back to their website, only allow it in the author's bio section at the end of the article. If the link is to a true, well-known authority site, then it can be dofollow. If the site in the link is not a well-known authority site, I'd recommend you nofollow the link. If the author won't write for you without a dofollow link, then offer them a dofollow link to their social profile instead. Linking out to Facebook or Twitter is always going to be safe.

These guest post linking rules are tough, and several students have complained that if they follow my guidelines, they won't get people to write guest posts because there is very little in it for the writer. And therein lies the problem. The writer is only giving you content in exchange for a link. When the link back is the motive, then we need to be careful. Is the content quality going to be good enough? Can we be sure they are not outsourcing the content writing to a cheaper source that may be plagiarizing existing works?

What I tell these students is that if they don't follow these guidelines, they won't have a site to accept guest posts because it could very quickly get penalized for linking to a "bad neighborhood". If your site reaches authority status in your niche, then writers will benefit from the exposure. They'll get referral traffic from your visitors, something they would not have otherwise received.

Some General Content Guidelines

There are several types of content that you can add to your website. These include articles, product reviews, quizzes, videos, etc. However, no matter what type of content you are creating, it must adhere to the following three points:

1. Create for the visitor, not the search engines. That means it needs to read well and have no visible signs of keyword stuffing.
2. Add value to the top 10 SERPs (if you want to rank in the top 10, your page must be seen as adding something unique to that collection of pages).
3. Give your visitors what they want. Create the content they want to see. Give your visitors a reason to stay on your site, return to your site, and recommend your site to others.

To put it simply, all the content on your site has to be the best that you can make it.

A good rule of thumb, as suggested by Google, is this:

Would your content look out of place published in a glossy magazine?

If you ever hire ghost-writers, be sure to proofread their content before publishing. Make sure that it's **factually & grammatically** correct and does not have any spelling mistakes.

As you read through the content that you intend to publish on your website, ask yourself these questions:

- Is it content that your visitors will find useful?
- Is there information in there that your visitors are unlikely to know, and therefore find informative?
- If it's a review, does it sound overly hyped up? Are both sides of the argument covered, i.e. positives and negatives? Is there information in the review that is not available on the manufacturer's website or other affiliate sites? Does the review offer a different way of looking at things which may help the buyer make a better-informed decision prior to purchase?

Real Examples of Poor Content

Here is the first paragraph of an article I found online a few years ago. I'm sure you can guess what the author was trying to optimize the page for.

Understanding Pomegranate Juice Benefits

Some people may not be that knowledgeable about pomegranate juice benefits but it is actually a very effective source of Vitamin C. The pomegranate fruit contains a lot of healthy nutrients and you can get a lot of good immune system boosters out of pomegranate juice benefits. It can actually provide around 16% of the required amount of Vitamin C that adults need to take on a daily basis. Pomegranate juice benefits also include Vitamin B5 as well as the antioxidant element of polyphenols and potassium.

You won't find this page in Google anymore, and it doesn't take a rocket scientist to figure out why ;)

It's not too difficult to guess the main phrase the author was targeting, is it? In fact, it reminds me of Google's "do not do" example we saw earlier about custom cigar humidors.

"Pomegranate juice benefits" sticks out like a sore thumb. In fact, in a relatively short article (just 415 words) that phrase appeared 17 times. That's a key phrase density of 4%.

How many people think a key phrase density of 4% is OK or natural? Is repeating the same phrase so many times in one piece normal? Yet even 4% was moderate in the heyday of trash articles.

So, what is a natural keyword density?

Let me whisper the answer.

Natural density of a keyword phrase is whatever density occurs naturally when an expert in their field writes an article without considering or paying any attention to, keyword density.

If you look back at that pomegranate paragraph, there is an even bigger sin. Look at this sentence:

*"The pomegranate fruit contains a lot of healthy nutrients and you can get a lot of good immune system boosters out of **pomegranate juice benefits**."*

It doesn't make sense at all.

It should finish with "...out of pomegranate juice", but the webmaster took the opportunity to stuff in that main key phrase again, making the sentence nonsense.

This is a very clear indicator that the author was stuffing that phrase into the article to help it rank higher for that phrase.

Let's look at another example.

Below is an example of a badly written article where theme phrases have been repeated solely for the search engines. This was an example that I found a few years ago, but while old, it still shows the point. Ignoring the quality of the information in this piece, let's just look at an example of keyword stuffing:

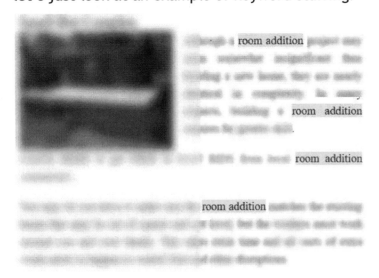

I have highlighted one phrase that occurs 4 times in a very short space of time. That phrase appears on the page 17 times in total, with the plural version appearing 5 times. The word "room" appears 25 times and "addition" appears 19 times. The total article length is around 1000 words.

The phrase "room addition" sticks out because it is a little awkward to read, unnatural even when you read the text around it (which is just fluff and padding anyway). This looks a lot like a doorway page designed to rank for a single high demand, high-profit keyword. This page does still exist in Google but has changed over the years. At the time I found this page, Google Keyword Planner confirmed it was a phrase that advertisers were paying good money for:

	Save all	Search terms (1)		
	Keyword	Competition	Global Monthly Searches ?	Approximate CPC (Search) ?
☐	room addition ▾	High	60,500	€2.67

This is a few years old now, but at the time the phrase had 60,500 monthly searches and costs advertisers around 2.67 Euros PER CLICK.

The webmaster was using AdSense advertising on the page, and that further confirms to me that he was creating doorway pages. These types of pages exist for the search engines, and their only purpose is to rank well for single, high-profit keywords.

Funnily enough, the site that hosts this article used to be a site that Google showed off as a quality AdSense/Affiliate website. This was probably because of its spectacular earnings in the AdSense program. Despite that, this site was later penalized during the initial rounds of Panda and Penguin; something which caused a lot of webmasters to conclude that Google does not like affiliate sites. After all, an affiliate site that the search engine giant once showcased as a shining example ended up getting a Google slap.

My view on this is that Google simply does not like poor or spammy content. This site was lucky to get away with its shabby articles for as long as it did, and most probably never got a real in-depth human review.

When Google introduced Panda and Penguin, automated quality checks became the norm. This meant that EVERY site could now be thoroughly checked for quality. These new checks obviously identified the page above, along with other pages on the same site, as low-quality content, and therefore in violation of the Google guidelines. Looking through a lot of the earlier content on that site, I'd agree that it was penalized for good reason. Today, while a lot of the doorway style pages remain, it's great to see that this webmaster has tried hard to update his content to make it more useful. His site has recovered to a certain degree and he still uses Google Adsense ads on the site to monetize the site.

The sad thing is that this type of article may have ranked well before Panda and Penguin came along. Why is that sad? Because web searchers had to put up with this kind of rubbish constantly. It's not the kind of stuff they were searching for, but it was often the kind of stuff they got, nonetheless.

Today, no amount of sneaky black hat techniques could get this page into the top 10, at least not for the long-term. That is the difference between pre- and post-Panda/Penguin SEO. It's the reason this page no longer exists in Google, or in fact online. The webmaster has closed the site down, presumably after it stopped being profitable.

As I write this, if I do a Google search for **pomegranate juice benefits**, only ONE web page in the top 10 contains the term on the page. That page uses the term once in 2,836 words (a density of just 0.035). How's that for a natural density?

As I mentioned earlier, with Hummingbird, the need to include a specific phrase on the page (to rank for that phrase) has gone. That is why I suggested Google's advice about including the words people search for on your site is outdated and may disappear from the Webmaster Guidelines.

The lesson to learn from this is to throw keyword density rules out of the window.

Go and search Google for **pomegranate juice benefits**. How many of the top 10 pages include that phrase in the title? After reading the preceding section, you are probably not surprised to see that none of them do. What may surprise you is that only two pages out of the top 100 have that phrase in their title!

Try it for yourself. Enter any search term that isn't a brand name or product name. You will see that, in general, the top 10 search results in Google list far fewer pages containing the actual search term. This number has decreased over the years (I've kept an eye on it since the first version of this book in 2012).

Okay, so the question is this: how is Google able to decide how to rank web pages for the term "pomegranate juice benefits", or any other search term if they are not looking for that actual phrase in the content?

To Google, "Pomegranate juice benefits" means the same as "health benefits of pomegranate juice" and "health reasons for drinking pomegranate juice". There is no need to distinguish one from another, as they mean the same thing.

If someone searches for any of those phrases (or synonyms of those phrases), Google could display the same set of pages if it wanted to, knowing that the searcher's intent was "to find out how pomegranates could help improve their health". The individual phrases are unimportant. The theme is what Google needs to work out.

- Google understands the searcher's intent.
- Google understands the theme of every web page.
- Google can match the two.

OK, let's consider another important test for your web content.

Does Your Article Sound as If an Expert Wrote It?

The reason I ask is that when somebody who really knows their subject writes an article, they will use a certain "niche vocabulary". That is, they will use words and phrases that define the topic of the article.

You can read an article I wrote several years ago discussing this. It's called "Niche Vocabulary - why poor content can't hide in Google".

http://famousbloggers.net/niche-vocabulary-poor-content-google.html

You will see in that article, that if the content does not contain its niche vocabulary, then it's unlikely to rank well in Google, even when it includes the actual target key phrase.

Every Article You Write Will Have Its Own Niche Vocabulary

Articles on related topics may well use a lot of the same niche vocabulary, but they will also contain other words and phrases that define the topic more specifically.

Let's look at an example of this.

To carry out a test, I found a number of words in the top 10 pages of Google ranking for the term epilepsy. These words appeared on many of the top 10 pages ranking for that term. These are what I call theme words (or niche vocabulary), i.e. words that commonly appear in articles written on the topic.

Here are the theme words I found for the term epilepsy:

Age, aid, anti, brain, cause, children, control, develop, diagnosis, diet, doctor, drugs, epilepsy, epileptic, guide, health, help, home, information, ketogenic, life, living, log, medical, medications, part, plan, research, seizure, seizure-free, seizures, side, special, support, surgery, symptoms, take, term, test, time, treatment, types, unit, and work.

I then chose two sub-niches in the epilepsy fields to see if these words appeared on those pages as well. These sub-niches were:

1. Epilepsy treatment
2. Ketogenic diet for epilepsy

Both terms are highly related to epilepsy. Just for reference, the ketogenic diet is a high-fat, adequate-protein, low-carbohydrate diet used primarily to treat difficult-to-control epilepsy, mostly in young patients. Since both terms talk about epilepsy, they both should contain a lot of the epilepsy niche vocabulary.

First, let's have a look at the top-ranking pages for the term **epilepsy**. Here is a screenshot showing the number one ranked article with the theme words that I found earlier highlighted in the text:

sturbed **brain** activity that **cause** changes in attention or behavior. s
es, incidence, and risk factors **epilepsy** occurs when permanent ch
cause the **brain** to be too excitable or jumpy. the **brain** sends out
ds. this results in repeated, unpredictable **seizures**. (a single **seizure**
en again is not **epilepsy**.) **epilepsy** may be due to a **medical** cond
ffects the **brain**, or the **cause** may be unknown (idiopathic). comm
psy include: stroke or transient ischemic attack (tia) dementia, such
se traumatic **brain** injury infections, including **brain** abscess, menin
ds **brain** problems that are present at birth (congenital **brain** defe
occurs during or near birth metabolism disorders that a child may be
enylketonuria) **brain** tumor abnormal blood vessels in the **brain** ot
age or destroy **brain** tissue **epilepsy** **seizures** usually begin betwee
ut they can happen at any **age**. there may be a family history of **sei**
psy. **symptoms** **symptoms** vary from person to person. some pec
le staring spells, while others have violent shaking and loss of alertne
re depends on the **part** ▉▉▉ **brain** affected and **cause** of **epilep**

You can only see a small section of the article here as it's quite long. Even so, I'm sure you will agree that the theme words used are obvious throughout the piece.

Let's repeat this, but this time using the number one ranked article for the term **epilepsy treatment**:

with the introduction of **dilantin** (warner-lambert), has been a triumph of mode
e. the **development** of newer **medications**, **especially** tegretol (ciba-geigy) a
eckitt & colman) has meant that **epilepsy** can be suppressed in most patients
serious or annoying **side** effects. this is not to say that every patient can be full
led, or that **side** effects do not occur. a continuing effort is being made by
onal pharmaceutical companies to find safer, more effective **treatment** ▉▉
y. new **drugs** are not cascading onto the market however, for the high cost of
h, **development** and marketing (about a$150 million for any new drug) is an
nt disincentive. how do **drugs** prevent **seizures**? strange to say, most of the
sed in treating **epilepsy** today were discovered to have **anti-epileptic** prope
ce. we have used these **drugs** with great benefit for years without really know
y **work**. however, a more systematic search for new **anti epileptic** ▉▉ s is r
ay, based on **research** progress in understanding how neurones transmit
s to each other, and our increasing knowledge of the structure and function of
ne which surrounds each neurone. the **messages** that one neurone sends to th
ditated by releasing neurotransmitter chemicals, can either excite the neurone
ine, or can inhibit its electrical activity. the identification of gamaa-amino butyri

Once again, we see the theme words sprinkled throughout the content, as we would expect since this article is also about epilepsy.

Let's now look at the final example, which is the **ketogenic diet**:

ketogenic diet was then gradually forgotten as new anticonvulsant medications developed. the ketogenic diet has recently been 'rediscovered' and is achieving increasingly widespread use. its modern day role as alternative management for c with difficult-to-control epilepsy is currently being re-defined. the ketogenic di a 'fad' or a 'quack diet', but rather is an alternative medical treatment child difficult-to-control epilepsy. the ketogenic diet should only be used under the supervision of a physician and a dietician. background fasting to achieve control seizure was described in both the bible and during the middle ages, but it was (during the early 1920s that scientific papers first appeared describing the benefici effects of prolonged fasting for children whose epilepsy could not be controlle few medications then available. these papers claimed that starvation, drinking on for 10 to 20 or more days, could result in control seizure for prolonged peri time. during this era, when the metabolic effects of diabetes were also being stud was noted that the biochemical effects of fasting could be mimicked by eating a d

This too has the same theme words for epilepsy sprinkled throughout its content.

Since all these articles have epilepsy "theme words" sprinkled within them, they could all theoretically rank for the term epilepsy. Google will know these articles are about epilepsy because they contain epilepsy-related words and phrases.

In addition to the core set of epilepsy-related theme words, each of these articles also contains **a slightly different set of theme words** which help to define what area of epilepsy they are discussing. We could show this by finding theme words specific to each of the three articles. We would see words and phrases with a different emphasis popping up (though there would still be a core of epilepsy-related words).

To illustrate this further, I found a number of "theme phrases" - 2, 3 and 4-word phrases that are common to the top 10 ranked pages for the three terms – epilepsy, epilepsy treatment, and the ketogenic diet for epilepsy.

Here is a table of the results, showing the theme words and phrases appearing in the top 10 pages ranked for each of the search terms:

Epilepsy	Epilepsy Treatment	Ketogenic Diet
activity in the brain atkins diet blood sugar causes of epilepsy epilepsy medication epilepsy medications epilepsy surgery ketogenic diet part of the brain seizure medicines temporal lobe vagus nerve	adverse effects aid for seizures anticonvulsant drug anticonvulsant drugs anti-epileptic drug anti-epileptic medications anti-seizure medications controlling seizures epileptic control epileptic seizures ketogenic diet seizure control seizure medications temporal lobe treatment of epilepsy treatments for epilepsy	anticonvulsant drug anticonvulsant drugs beta hydroxybutyric acid body fat control of seizures control seizures diet controls seizures different anticonvulsants high fat high fat diet high fat intake medical treatment for children protein and carbohydrate seizure control seizure type treatment of seizure while on the diet

This table clearly shows that each of the three search terms has a different niche vocabulary.

All three articles have theme words relating to epilepsy, as we would expect. However, each of the articles also has their own set of theme phrases which help to distinguish the actual sub-niche within epilepsy.

1. The **epilepsy** article has a wide range of theme phrases relating to all aspects of epilepsy.

2. The **epilepsy treatment** article focused more on phrases related to the treatment of epilepsy (no big surprise there).

3. The **ketogenic diet** article had more theme phrases relating to the diet itself and the control of seizures.

Anyone who read earlier versions of this book will recognize the Epilepsy example from those editions. Therefore, the example is a few years old and you may question whether the information is still valid today. For that reason, let's look at a more recent example to check.

I ran an analysis of the top 10 pages ranking in Google for the term "Health benefits of Krill Oil". By the way, at the time of writing, only two pages listed in the top 10 search results had that exact phrase in the title.

Here are the theme words I found on seven or more of the top 10 pages:

Acids, age, animal, balance, benefits, better, blood, capsules, cardiovascular, care, cell, cholesterol, clinical, daily, dha, diet, disease, eat, effects, epa, fatty, fish, flu, food, health, healthy, heart, human, krill, levels, liver, lower, nutrition, oil, omega-3, protein, ratio, red, reduce, research, safe, side, skin, source, sources, studies, study, supplement, supplements, test, and women.

There are 51 words in that list and all 51 show on seven or more of the top 10 pages that rank for the term "health benefits of krill oil".

I also checked for 2, 3 and 4-word phrases found on the same top 10 pages. Here are the ones I found:

Allergic reaction, amino acid, bad cholesterol, benefits of krill, benefits of krill oil, brain health, cardiovascular disease, cell membranes, cholesterol levels, clinical studies, clinical study, cod liver, crp levels, daily dose, dietary supplement, effects of krill oil, experimental animal, eye health, fatty acids, fish oil, fish oil supplement, fish oil supplements, fish oils, food source, free radicals, health benefits, health care, health food, healthy cholesterol, heart disease, heart health, krill oil, krill oil arthritis benefits, krill oil benefit, krill oil daily, krill protein, lose weight, metabolic syndrome, nitric oxide, oil supplement, omega 3, omega-3 fatty acids, omega-3 phospholipid, omega-3 polyunsaturated fatty acids, pain killer, polyunsaturated fatty acids, premenstrual syndrome, rheumatoid arthritis, side effects, source of omega-3, sources of omega-3, triglyceride levels, and weight loss.

The Difference Between Theme Words and Theme Phrases in My Analysis

The difference between theme words and theme phrases is obvious. Theme words contain just one word, whereas theme phrases contain more than one word.

When it comes to Google, finding theme phrases in an article is further confirmation of a theme, but when I am analyzing top ranking pages, I concentrate on the theme words, not the phrases. Why? Because theme phrases often have several variations which essentially mean the same thing and ARE the same thing to Google. An example in the list above would include:

- fish oil supplement
- fish oil supplements

Both mean the same thing. Just because an article contains one and not the other, does not mean the article cannot rank for both.

A much better strategy would be to **place the importance** on the words that make up those phrases (fish, oil, and supplement(s)).

Here is another example:

- omega 3
- omega-3 fatty acids
- omega-3 phospholipid
- omega-3 polyunsaturated fatty acids

Just because an article on krill oil does not specifically use the phrase **omega-3 polyunsaturated fatty acids,** does not mean it hasn't talked about omega-3.

If I concentrate on the words: **omega-3, fatty, acids, phospholipid and polyunsaturated** in my analysis, then I can cover all variations of these phrases.

I hope you can see that there is not much point counting individual theme phrases. The important theme phrases comprise all the important theme words, so this is what I concentrate on when writing authoritative articles.

OK, let's get back to the experiment.

I wanted to see how many of my 51 theme words were being used by pages ranked in the top 100 of Google.

For this analysis, I grouped pages ranking in the following positions:

1-10, 11-20, 21-30, 31-40, 41-50 & 51-60

I wanted to see how well the pages in these positions were themed for my 51 keywords. I analyzed each page individually and then averaged the results out for the group.

Here are those results:

Position 1-10, on average, used 86% of my theme words.

Position 11-20, on average, used 81% of my theme words.

Position 21-30, on average, used 78% of my theme words.

Position 31-40, on average, used 69% of my theme words.

Position 41-50, on average, used 69% of my theme words.

Position 51-60, on average, used 73% of my theme words.

As you can see, all the pages in the top 60 contained a good number of my theme words, with all pages averaging between 69%-86%.

Taking this a step further, I then wanted to see how well those pages ranked further down the SERPs were themed.

I grabbed the URLs ranking at:

100-109, 200-209, and 300-309

Position 100-109, on average, used 65% of my theme words.

Position 200-209, on average, used 72% of my theme words.

Position 300-309, on average, used 62% of my theme words.

So even those web pages ranked down in the 100-300 range are well-themed, containing a good proportion of my 51 theme words.

By the way, the reason I didn't analyze pages ranked lower than 300 is because Google doesn't include more than a few hundred URLs in the SERPs.

Colon Cleanse Capsules, Eye Supplements, Krill Oil and Acai Capsules.

In order to show you the most relevant results, we have omitted some entries very similar to the 381 already displayed.
If you like, you can repeat the search with the omitted results included.

Searches related to health benefits of krill oil

health benefits of krill oil **to the skin**	health benefits **flax seed** oil
health benefits of krill oil **supplements**	krill oil **supplements**
health benefits **yerba mate tea**	benefits of krill oil **pills**
health benefits **fish** oil	**mega red** krill oil benefits

‹ Goooogle
Previous   1 2 3 4

I did a Google search for **health benefits of krill oil**, showing 100 results per page. On page four, the results end with Google telling me that the rest of the pages in the index are similar to these first 381. Therefore, Google only ranked 381 pages for this phrase.

It's very interesting that all the pages included in the SERPs seemed well themed around a core set of theme words, and we can harvest those theme words by analyzing the top 10 results in Google for any given term.

Final Test in My Experiment

It's looking like all web pages ranked in Google for a search term are themed around a core set of relevant words and phrases. Any page that does not cut the mustard doesn't appear in the main set of search results (the 381 pages we saw in the previous screenshot).

Because it's so important to know what Google wants with regards to "quality" content, I had the idea to test this still further. If all web pages really are themed around a group of related words, then I should be able to analyze the pages ranked 300-310 and grab the theme words from those pages, instead of the top 10. If I re-analyze the pages ranked in positions 1-10, 100-110, 200-210 & 300-310, I should find a similarly high percentage of those theme words used in each case.

OK, here's what I did.

I extracted the theme words from the pages ranked 300-310 using Web Content Studio (my own tool that helps webmasters to write better, quality, themed content in a way that mimics natural writers). I then refined the selection, only accepting theme words that appeared on seven or more of those 10 pages. I ended up with the following list of 49 theme words:

Acid, acids, Antarctic, anti-inflammatory, antioxidant, antioxidants, astaxanthin, benefits, blood, body, brain, cholesterol, damage, deficiency, dha, disease, effects, epa, essential, fat, fatty, fish, food, health, healthy, heart, high, inflammation, inflammatory, krill, levels, nutrition, oil, omega, omega-3, phospholipid, powerful, products, protein, rates, red, side, skin, source, supplement, supplements, support, vitamins, and weight.

I then checked these theme words against the pages ranked 1-10, 100-109, 200-209, and 300-309. The results were interesting:

Position 1-10, on average, used 77% of the theme words.

Position 100-109, on average, used 66% of the theme words.

Position 200-209, on average, used 69% of the theme words.

Position 300-309, on average, used 75% of the theme words.

OK, we expected a high percentage of the theme words in those pages ranked 300-309 because those are the pages that I used to collect the theme words. Those pages used an average of 75% of my theme words (remember I chose the words that only appeared on seven or more pages so that percentage sounds about right).

However, look at the pages ranked 1-10. They used a higher percentage of theme words than the pages from which the theme words were collected. The top 10 pages used 77% of the theme words.

The pages ranked 100-109 and 200-209 were no slouches either. They used, on average, 66% and 69% of the theme words.

All of this goes to show that, on average, ALL of the web pages that rank in Google are well themed around a set of "niche vocabulary". That is quite exciting, but also a little scary. If ALL of the pages ranked in Google are well-themed, chances are they are all good quality. Based on this knowledge, how on earth do you beat them into the top 10? Well, that is where you need to give your visitors what they want by making your page "special". In other words, give them something extra, something not offered by the other pages in the top 10. Providing you do this well, you will make Google sit up and take notice of your content.

How to Use This Information to Write Better Content

If you are an expert in the field you are writing about, you will automatically and naturally use the correct and relevant theme words and phrases as you write about the topic, because you need to.

If, however, you are not an expert, then things are a little more difficult. You need to find which words and phrases are important to the topic that you want to write about before you start writing.

As you write the content, the idea is to sprinkle in relevant theme words and include a small number of highly relevant theme phrases too. This will help the search engines identify the topic more easily.

The theme phrases you use on a web page should be the most important ones for that topic. These are the ones which will tell the search engines what that page is all about. Do not, under any circumstances, use theme words or phrases more often than is necessary. For example, don't repeat a phrase 3-4 times simply because you want to rank for that term. Google's Penguin will be straight onto you if you do, and that could see your rankings drop for keyword stuffing or the unnatural use of keywords.

So, with the niche vocabulary being so important, how can we mine this information from the top 10 pages?

Finding Theme Words & Phrases

You have a couple of options when it comes to finding theme words for your content. One option is free, the others paid.

Option 1 - Google SERPs + SEOQuake

This option is 100% free and involves using the Google SERPs together with a browser plugin called SEOQuake (a program, which allows users to view a large number of SE parameters on the fly).

How to use:

1. Install SEO Quake in your browser. There are versions for Firefox, Opera, Safari,

and Chrome.

2. Go to Google and search for the phrase you want to rank for.

3. Visit each of the top 10 pages in turn, and click the SEOQuake button to show the menu:

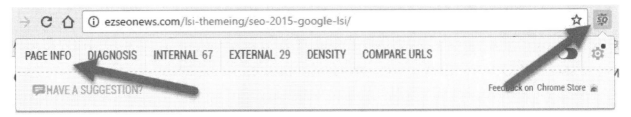

4. Select **Page Info** from that menu.

The resulting **page info** screen includes lists of keyword densities. We're not interested in the density itself, but what that density tells us about the importance of the word or phrase.

Here is a density report for my **health benefits of krill oil** search phrase:

Keywords density

Total number of words: 1495. See all

Keyword	Found in	Repeats
oil	T K H1	28
krill	T K H1	26
omega-3	H1	21
health		8
body		8
fish		7
benefits	T K H1	7
natural		6
products		6
acids	H1	6

It should be no surprise that this top-ranked page includes the words "krill", "oil" and "health" in the top four most used words on the page. Omega-3 which is vital to the health properties of krill oil is also right up there.

You'll also find 2, 3 and 4-word phrases listed lower down the report.

By going through each of the top 10 pages and checking which words and phrases appear on most of them, you can then build up your list of theme words and phrases to include in your own content.

OK, so what about paid options?

Well, first a disclaimer. I created the two paid tools I am going to mention, so the following discussion is about my own tool, and obviously, if you buy, I am the one receiving your money.

Paid Option 1 – Keyword LSI Spider

This tool is a simple spider that will essentially do all the manual work described in the last section, for you. You simply enter a keyword phrase and click a button. The spider checks the top 10 web pages in Google to create a master keyword and phrase list. It then counts how many pages in the top 10 use each keyword. In a couple of minutes, you have a comprehensive list of theme words and phrase being used on the top 10 pages that rank for any keyword you choose.

I ran **is cholesterol bad for you** through it and here are the results it returned:

Key Words:

cholesterol, heart, bad, disease, high, fat, blood, levels, risk, people, hdl, health, body, ldl, years, low, cause, found, diet, foods, life, liver, arteries, attack, total, lower, attacks, research, causes, healthy, women, eat, saturated, fats, types, density, lipoprotein, brain, triglycerides, diabetes, factor, food, walls, children, eggs, medical, plaque, eating, age, test, lipoproteins, cells, vascular, men.

Key Phrases:

cholesterol levels, bad cholesterol, heart disease, high cholesterol, heart attack, total cholesterol, good cholesterol, risk factor, ldl cholesterol, blood cholesterol, heart healthy, low density lipoprotein, two types, hdl cholesterol, saturated fat, blood pressure, trans fats, risk of heart disease, cholesterol lowering, cholesterol level, heart failure, artery disease, dairy products, high density lipoprotein, total cholesterol level, heart disease risk, ldl and hdl, high blood pressure, cholesterol and hdl, hdl good cholesterol, cholesterol in food, heart attack or stroke, saturated fats, triglyceride levels, hdl levels, red meat, dietary cholesterol, fatty acids, heart defects, weight loss, cholesterol numbers, major risk, risk factors, congenital heart defects, attack and stroke, high ldl cholesterol, high blood cholesterol, major risk factor, cause of heart disease, risk for heart disease, saturated fat and cholesterol, risk for high cholesterol, heart attack and stroke

That's quite a comprehensive list.

For readers that are interested in this spider, I have included a link below to a password protected page that allows you to get a discount on the full price of this software.

You can find out more details of what this tool can do, and how I use the results, here:

https://webcontentstudio.com/spider

Password: reader

Paid Option 2 - Web Content Studio

While I feel that Web Content Studio (WCS) is the best tool for web content writers, I do not want this book to be a sale pitch for my own tools. Therefore, I won't go into a lot of detail. Instead, I'll state the main benefits of the tool and send you to the website where you can find out more about it.

Benefits of WCS

The main benefits of using WCS are:

1. Does everything the Keyword LSI spider does, plus a lot more.
2. The speed of finding niche vocabulary. It is faster and has more options than the Keyword LSI Spider.
3. WCS will tell you the most important words and phrases (i.e. the ones that appear on most of the top 10 pages).
4. The WYSIWYG article editor and theme reports tell you how good a job you've done. When you finish your first draft, you can get WCS to analyze the content against the niche vocabulary it collected in the previous step. Any words or phrases not found in your content can be quickly spotted, as well as any word or phrase that may have been used a few too many times.

There are a lot of other features of this tool that you might find useful, but as I said, I don't want this to sound like a sales pitch. I'll leave you to investigate further if you are interested. Besides, I would highly recommend you use the free, manual option, for harvesting niche vocabulary first so you know what is involved.

For more details on the tool itself, visit:

https://webcontentstudio.com/seo

Password: reader

We now know the importance of having niche vocabulary in our content, along with the ways to find it. That will go a long way to making sure the articles you write are quality. Once you get to understand the niche vocabulary in your chosen topic, you can then use it naturally as you compose your content.

There are several on-page factors that you need to get right, so let's take a look at those now.

On Page SEO Factors to Get Right

The Title Tag

The title tag is probably the most important ranking factor on your page in terms of SEO benefits. It is also vital in terms of persuading Google searchers to click on your link in the SERPs. In the source code* of your web page, the title tag looks like this:

<title>Title Goes Here</title>

* Source code is the basic backbone of most web pages (invisible to visitors, or under the hood so to speak). The source code includes a series of tags that instruct the internet browser software how to display the page as well as the actual page content that is visible to the viewer on the front end. The source code is also an essential factor with regards to SEO, as it allows search engine bots to better read your page and page elements.

Search engines look at the words in your title tag to determine what your page is about. Therefore, you should try to get your main keyword phrase into the title. The closer to the beginning of the title tag your keyword is, the better it will serve you.

If I was writing a web page about the health benefits of krill oil, the important phrases in that search terms are krill oil and health benefits.

If I do a search on Google for **health benefits of krill oil,** here are the title tags of the top ten pages ranking for that term.

6 Science-Based **Health Benefits of Krill Oil**

Krill Oil: Uses, Side Effects, Interactions, Dosage, and Warning

12 **Krill Oil Benefits** + Dosage, Reviews & Comparison to Fish Oil - Selfhacked

Health benefits of krill oil: 5 ways the supplement trumps regular fish oil | Fox News

The **Benefits of Krill Oil** | Webber Naturals

Krill oil vs fish oil: Which is better and why?

Are **Krill Oil Benefits** Even Better than Fish Oil Benefits? - Dr. Axe

The 10 Most Incredible **Benefits Of Krill Oil** And Omega-3 Fatty Acids

Review of the **Health Benefits of Antarctic Krill** | Bioriginal

Krill Oil: Benefits, Dangers & Side Effects - Drugs.com

All these pages are from authority sites in the health niche, so they will have a massive ranking advantage over smaller sites. Anyway, the point is that you can still see they've included the main keywords/synonyms in the title tag.

Nine of the ten pages include the phrase **krill oil** in the tag (one just refers to Antarctic Krill, which is used to make krill oil), with seven of them having the phrase near the start of the title. Where possible, always try to get the most important words at or near the beginning of the title tag.

The big omission in those titles is the word "health". Only three of those ten pages includes that word in their title tag. However, all ten of these sites are massive health authority sites, so Google can pretty much assume the benefits refer to health.

Only two pages in the top 10 do not use either the word health or benefit(s). One is WebMD and the other is Medical News Today. Both are huge authority sites that Google trusts for all health-related searches. The way Google has evolved over recent years means it can now accurately determine a searcher's intent. If someone searches for health benefits of krill oil, Google will understand that they are looking for the kind of information provided by that WebMD or Medical News Today article. These sites have earned their reputation.

When creating your title tag, try to write one that not only includes the words that make up your main phrase or concept but something that entices people to click your link when they read the title.

- Keep your title tag to 67 **characters or less**. Any longer than that and it gets truncated in the search results.

- Title tags on every page of your site should be unique. Never use the same title tag on two or more pages.

It is worth monitoring the click-through rates (CTR) for your pages. If the CTR appears low, you can tweak the title tag to see if you can increase the CTR. The Title and Meta Description tags are the two variables you have the most control over in your quest for better CTR in the Google SERPs.

The Meta Description Tag

The Meta Description tag is not as important as the title tag, but you should still create a unique, interesting, and enticing description, on all of your pages. As I mentioned before, if your Meta Description includes the search term, chances are it will be used by Google as the listing description, but not always. Google often tries to find some content on the page itself that better matches the searchers intent.

In the source code of your web page, the Meta Description looks like this:

<meta name="description" content="Description goes here."/>

Here are the Meta Descriptions of the top ten pages ranking in Google for the krill oil term we used earlier. I have included a screenshot of the actual description used by

Google in the SERPs. Where Google has used the Meta Description, I have highlighted it. As you'll see, Google will use content on the page if it thinks it's a better match to the searcher's intent.

1. **Krill oil is high in important omega-3 fatty acids. Here are six science-based health benefits of krill oil.**

   6 Science-Based Health Benefits of Krill Oil - Healthline⊘
   https://www.healthline.com/nutrition/krill-oil-benefits ▾
   8 Dec 2017 - 6 Science-Based Health Benefits of Krill Oil. Excellent Source of Healthy Fats.
   Share on Pinterest. Can Help Fight Inflammation. Omega-3 **fatty acids** like those found in krill
   oil have been shown to have important anti-inflammatory functions in the body (9). Might
   Reduce **Arthritis** and Joint **Pain**. May Help Manage PMS ...

2. **Learn more about Krill Oil uses, effectiveness, possible side effects, interactions, dosage, user ratings and products that contain Krill Oil**

   Krill Oil: Uses, Side Effects, Interactions, Dosage, and Warning - WebMD⊘
   https://www.webmd.com/vitamins/ai/ingredientmono-1172/krill-oil ▾
   Krill oil contains fatty acids similar to fish oil. These **fats** are thought to be beneficial **fats** that
   decrease swelling, lower **cholesterol**, and make blood platelets less sticky. When blood
   platelets are less sticky they are less likely to form clots.

3. **Krill oil is a good source of the omega-3 fatty acids EPA and DHA and can protect against heart disease, treat depression, and help prevent cancer.**
   12 Krill Oil Benefits + Dosage, Reviews & Comparison to Fish Oil ...⊘
   https://www.selfhacked.com/blog/krill-oil-benefits/ ▾
   ★★★★★ Rating: 4.4 - 15 votes
   15 Nov 2018 - **Krill oil** is a good source of the omega-3 fatty acids EPA and DHA and can ...
   more about **krill oil's health benefits** and its comparison to fish oil.
   What is Krill Oil · Components · Health Benefits · Krill Oil vs. Fish Oil

4. **Krill oil is an omega-3 fatty acid providing EPA & DHA. Unlike most omega-3s krill oil naturally contains antioxidant such as vitamin A, vitamin E, and astaxanthin. This means that RoyalRed Krill Oil helps support cardiovascular, eye, brain, and overall health.**

   The Benefits of Krill Oil | Webber Naturals⊘
   https://www.webbernaturals.com/products/krill-oil-benefits/ ▾
   Unlike most omega-3's **krill oil** naturally contains antioxidant such as vitamin A, vitamin E, ...
   Krill Oil helps support cardiovascular, eye, brain, and overall **health**.

5. **For healthy fats, omega-3 fatty acids are some of the best. Fish oil**

supplements offer the nutrient, but could a tiny sea creature provide a better alternative? Dr. Manny talks with the author of "The Thrill of Krill," Dr. Dennis Goodman, to find out.

Health benefits of krill oil: 5 ways the supplement trumps regular fish ...●
https://www.foxnews.com/health/health-benefits-of-krill-oil-5-ways-the-supplement-tru...
1 Jul 2015 - Here are 6 health benefits of krill oil: It promotes cardiovascular health. It reduces inflammation and may prevent arthritis. It enhances neurological development in newborns. It eases PMS symptoms. It has anti-depressive effects. It may improve gastric health.

6. Krill oil and fish oil are popular dietary supplements containing omega-3. Krill oil comes from a small crustacean while fish oil comes from oily fish, such as salmon. Both are shown to increase blood levels of omega-3 and have benefits for health. Learn more about the differences between krill oil and fish oil here.

Krill oil vs fish oil: Which is better and why? - Medical News Today●
https://www.medicalnewstoday.com/articles/321897.php ▾
Jump to Benefits - Benefits of krill oil and fish oil. Krill oil versus fish oil ... fatty acids have been shown to boost a person's overall heart health and reduce ...

7. Not only is krill oil possibly the best source of omega-3, but it has countless other benefits and can support a healthy endocannabinoid system.

The 10 Most Incredible Benefits Of Krill Oil And Omega-3 Fatty Acids●
https://www.honeycolony.com/article/incredible-benefits-krill-oil/ ▾
9 Aug 2017 - Not only is krill oil possibly the best source of omega-3, but it has countless other benefits and can support a healthy endocannabinoid system.

8. Krill Oil information from Drugs.com, includes Krill Oil side effects, interactions and indications.

Krill Oil: Benefits, Dangers & Side Effects - Drugs.com●
https://www.drugs.com › Drugs A to Z ▾
All krill oil sold in nutritional supplements is harvested out of the open ocean, upsetting the natural balance of food supplies for larger marine animals.

9. Krill oil benefits include reduced inflammation; improvements in heart, skin and brain health; stronger bones and joints; and increased weight loss. It may also be associated with a lower risk of certain types of cancer.

Are Krill Oil Benefits Even Better than Fish Oil Benefits? - Dr. Axe

https://draxe.com/krill-oil-benefits/ ▾

28 Feb 2018 - **Krill oil benefits** include reduced inflammation; improvements in heart, skin and brain **health**; stronger bones and joints; and increased weight ...

10. **Author: Mikko Griinari and Inge Bruheim (Clanet Oy, Finland and Olympic Seafood AS, Norway) Abstract Clinical studies demonstrate that krill oil is an effective**

Review of the Health Benefits of Antarctic Krill | Bioriginal

https://www.bioriginal.com/page.../review-of-the-health-benefits-of-antarctic-krill/ ▾

Clinical studies demonstrate that **krill oil** is an effective omega-3 source at a low ... Initial investigations on the potential **health effects** of **krill** protein have been ...

Only three pages (ranked 3, 7 & 9) had their Meta Description tag used for the description in the Google SERPs.

Have a look through the meta descriptions that were used on these pages. Can you see why Google chose not to use most of them? Think about the searcher's intent. Do you think the meta descriptions coded in the web pages are good descriptions for the search term "health benefits of krill oil"?

If you have a page and you know who you want to attract to that page, you need to think about the Meta Description you use. A description that does not fit with the searcher's intent, won't be used in the SERPs.

What you will find is that a lot of these META Descriptions include related words and phrases, like **heart disease, treat depression, prevent cancer, astaxanthin, cardiovascular, eye, brain, omega-3, fish oil**, etc. These are some of the niche vocabularies for the search term, and while it's a great idea to get the most important vocabulary into the Meta Description (and title), too much can shift the focus away from true searcher's intent.

It may or may not be a surprise to you that Google didn't use the actual meta descriptions for most site listings (a lot of webmasters don't realize this). If Google has to create its own, better description, it will pick a description that it believes matches the searcher's intent. Google does this for you. After all, a description that matches the searcher's intent is likely to have a higher click-through rate, so you should benefit.

When you are crafting your titles and Meta Descriptions, my advice is to think about the searcher's intent, and then write titles and Meta Descriptions that complement each other, without necessarily duplicating important words or phrases across the two.

When I write a Meta Description, I always create it at the same time as I do the title tag. I want them to work together to entice the click. I will have a list of the most significant words and phrases in a hierarchy, with the most important ones at the top. Top of my list for this search term would be **krill oil** and **health benefits** (or just benefits if my site was a health site). Lower down my list would be phrases like **lower triglycerides**, **heart health,** and **side effects**, etc. However, I would only use these words in the title or meta description if they perfectly met what I believed to be the searcher's intent.

The most important phrase, in this case, krill oil, would go into both tags. The title would be written to include any other vital keywords related to the search term (like health benefits), while the Description would be used to include some of the niche vocabularies. If there was a very important search term, I might include it in my carefully crafted description, so that the description could be used by Google for search queries involving that phrase.

Combined, the title and Meta Description tags should work together to entice the click.

The Meta Keyword Tag

The Meta Keyword tag is a place where you can list keywords and key phrases related to your web page.

In the source code, it looks like this:

<meta name="keywords" content="Keyword1, keyword 2, etc">

A few years ago, search engines used the Meta Keyword tag as a ranking factor and took notice of the words and phrases inside it. Today, however, the search engines do not give you any boost in rankings for this tag. It is my belief that search engines may use it to spot spammers and award penalties to those who use and abuse it.

Any page that has a keyword stuffed Meta Keyword tag is breaking the webmaster's guidelines and is therefore ripe for a penalty.

I personally do not use this tag on my sites and do not recommend you bother with it either. If you do want to use it, make sure you only include a small number of keywords. Note too, that they must relate to your content, meaning every single word or phrase you include in this tag is actually on your web page (important).

Let's have a quick look at the Meta Keywords used by the top ten sites for the krill oil search term.

1. NONE

2. Krill Oil, effectiveness, satisfaction, ease of use, uses, user ratings, user reviews, side effects, safety, interactions, medical information, medical advice, natural treatment, warnings, products

3. NONE

4. NONE

5. NONE

6. NONE

7. NONE

8. NONE

9. NONE

10. NONE

So, 9 out of 10 pages don't include a Meta Keyword tag, and that echoes my advice. Don't bother. They won't help you rank any higher, but include too many, or include keywords that aren't on your page, and Google could punish you. It's a lose-lose scenario.

Before we leave the title & Meta tags section of the page, I want to give you an important rule.

Every page on your site MUST have a unique title, unique Meta description, and Meta keywords (if you use them).

Pay attention to this rule if you use a Content Management System like WordPress. WordPress can use near identical titles on archive pages.

Headlines on Your Page

As a webmaster, you obviously have control over the headlines you use on your web pages. You have several sizes of headlines, ranging from the biggest H1 header, all the way down to the smallest H6.

In your web page source code, an H1 header looks like this:

<h1>Your Headline Here</h1>

In terms of user experience and SEO, my own rules for using h1 – h6 headlines are as follows:

1. Only ever use a single H1 (the title at the top of your article) on a web page.

2. Use h2 headlines to divide up your content and make it easier to skim read. You can use as many as you need.

3. Use h3 headers to subdivide h2 sections. Again, use as many as you need.

4. I don't recommend you use H4 – H6 tags in your content unless absolutely necessary.

So how does this work in practice?

H1 is the main headline on your page. Because of this, the search engines give keywords in this heading the most attention. In SEO terms, your H1 headline is the one that has the biggest effect on your page ranking. However, just because it helps to rank your page, don't make the mistake of thinking you can use more than one. Only ever use one H1 header and place it at the very top of your page as the opening title.

Try to get the main keyword for the page into the H1 header, preferably near the start of the headline.

As you write your content, break it up with H2 headers. If an H2 section has sub-sections, use H3s for those titles. I rarely use H3 headers on my own pages as H1 and H2s are enough in nearly all cases. Be aware that H2 and H3 have very little effect on rankings, so I don't recommend going out of your way to add keywords to them unless it makes sense to do so.

Incorrectly using headers is unlikely to get you into trouble unless there is clear and obvious keyword stuffing within the headlines. As with anything in SEO, create your content for your users first, search engines second.

The opening H1 headers for the top 10 pages ranking for **health benefits of krill oil** are:

1. 6 Science-Based **Health Benefits of Krill Oil**
2. **KRILL OIL**
3. 12 **Krill Oil Benefits** + Dosage, Reviews & Comparison to Fish Oil.

   This page then uses 11 more H1 headers on the page.

   - What is Krill Oil
   - Components
   - Mechanisms of Action
   - Health Benefits
   - Krill Oil vs. Fish Oil
   - Krill Oil Caveats and Side Effects
   - Sources and Dosage
   - Caution
   - Gene Interactions
   - Reviews
   - Buy Krill Oil

4. **Health benefits of krill oil**: 5 ways the supplement trumps regular fish oil

5. The **Benefits** of **Krill Oil**

6. Is **krill oil** better than fish oil for omega-3?

7. Are **Krill Oil Benefits** Even Better than Fish Oil **Benefits**?

8. 10 Most Incredible **Benefits** of **Krill Oil** And Omega-3 Fatty Acids

9. Review of the **Health Benefits of Antarctic Krill.**

10.   Krill Oil

The page ranked #3 is an odd one in terms of its on-page SEO. It's certainly not something I would recommend, but there is no real attempt to stuff keywords into those h1 headers. Those headlines look like natural titles of the article and given the huge authority status of the site, it's not something that will trouble them with Google. Where they might have a problem is if those 12 h1 headers were stuffed with phrases including "health benefits" and "krill oil".

As you can see from the other 9 pages, the H1 headers all include **Krill Oil** (except for #9 which include "Antarctic krill" instead) in the headline and most mention or imply benefit(s). We've also got other niche vocabulary appearing in these headlines too, but always write your headlines for your visitors.

Image Optimization

When you add an image to your page, the source code (in its simplest form) looks like this:

```
<img src="Image URL" alt="ALT Text"/>
```

You might also have width and height parameters.

The **Image URL** in that code will be the URL to the image (which includes the image filename). Google can read the image filename in this URL, so it makes sense to help Google out and tell them what the image is. If the image is a bottle of krill oil, call the file "bottle-of-krill-oil.jpg". If it's an image of krill in the sea, call it "krill-swimming-in-sea.jpg", or whatever else helps to best describe the image. The opportunity is clearly there to insert a keyword, but don't overdo it. Only insert the most important word or phrase if it helps describe the image.

The other important part of this code is the ALT text. This is the text shown in browsers when images are turned off (not visible to the user). It's also the text that is read by text-to-speech software, often used by those with sight impairment. Use the ALT tag to describe the image with these users in mind. You can put a keyword in there, but again, only if it is needed.

You may want to experiment by creating a different filename and ALT tag for an image. However, be careful. If Google thinks you are stuffing keywords into these tags, it won't end well for you. I tend to make the filename for the search engine and the ALT tag for the visually impaired visitor.

Spelling & Grammar

Poor spelling and grammar on your site reflect badly on you. It certainly won't help the trust factor and can lead to higher bounce rates and less time spent on the site. For no other reason than this, it's a good idea to check both.

Google views spelling and grammar as quality signals. The odd mistake won't make a difference, but pages with lots of errors will probably not rank too well in the long-term. For example, a serious site like a business site, or one that offers advice about health or finance, is unlikely to rank for anything if it is littered with spelling and grammatical mistakes.

In the old days of SEO, webmasters often included spelling mistakes in their content to try to rank for those misspelled words and phrases. Today, Google autocorrects when you misspell a search term at google.com. And besides... With Google today, the misspelled version of the word would mean the exact same thing as the correctly spelled word.

Links on the Page

Your web pages will include links to other web pages. These web pages may be on the same site (internal links) or point to pages on a different website (external links).

Over the course of time, web pages may be moved or get deleted. It is important, therefore, to check links periodically to make sure they don't become broken or dead.

The most common broken links on a page tend to be external links since we have no control over pages run by other webmasters. They can remove or rename their pages without notice, and when they do, your link becomes broken.

Fortunately, there is a good tool that can check for broken links on your site. It's called Screaming Frog SEO Spider. This tool has a free version as well as a paid version. The free version is suitable for smaller sites. We'll be using this tool extensively in the second half of this book when we carry out a full SEO audit.

Internal links on your site can also get broken if you rename a page, or delete one. I use a lot of internal linking on my sites to help visitors navigate and to help Google spider or crawl, my content. Changing a filename of a page could break dozens of links, or hundreds if you run a large site.

But what about linking out to other websites? Is that a good or bad idea?

Well, linking out to other websites is natural. Think about writing a research paper for a minute. It's natural to cite other papers if you've benefited from information in them, and you do that by listing those references at the end of your paper.

Similarly, when you create an article for your site, it's natural to "cite" other web pages by linking to them. These might be pages you used for research or pages you found interesting and relevant to your own content. In other words, they are pages that you think your visitors would appreciate.

The one thing you need to be aware of is that links to other web pages are votes for those pages. If those other pages are spammy or low-quality, those links can hurt you. As far as Google is concerned, when you vote for a "bad neighborhood", you are associated with that bad neighborhood. In other words, be careful where you link.

If you need to link to a page that you don't necessarily endorse for various reasons, you can do it. Google recognizes something called the **nofollow** tag, and when used inside a link, Google will essentially ignore that link.

The source code of a link with the nofollow tag looks like this.

<a href="Theothersite.com" rel="nofollow">The Other Site</a>

I tend to use the "nofollow" tag for all outbound links unless the site I'm linking to is a recognized high authority site within my niche. In these cases, I'll leave the nofollow code out because I want Google to associate my site with these authority sites. In other words, I'm telling Google "I endorse this site".

While we are on the subject of "nofollow", if you allow visitors to comment on your content (recommended), then make sure their links are all "nofollow". That includes any link used in the comment itself, and any URL included as part of the submission.

Note that the "nofollow" approach to comments will probably mean you get fewer comments than a site that leaves the links as "dofollow". This is because a lot of blog commenters have an agenda. They only see comments as a way of getting links back to their own website.

Leaving comment links as dofollow simply to attract more links, is SEO suicide. There are software tools out there that can search the web for blogs that have dofollow comments and you'll quickly find your site targeted by comment spammers. You'll get dozens and then hundreds of outbound links to pages you have no control over, and no idea of quality or reputation. In time, a Google penalty will follow as it sees you linking to all these bad neighborhoods.

The way you should approach comments is simple. Look to attract comments from those people who genuinely want to join the conversation, even if it means they don't get a dofollow link.

The Content Search Engines Want to See

I've said it before and I'll say it again… **Write for the visitors, not the search engines.**

When we create web content, we should be trying to provide outstanding content for the visitor. We should be trying to create the content that is the best match for the searcher's intent. Great content will always have the upper hand in the ranking wars.

But what if I told you that there is some content that search engines want to see that is not created for the visitor. It's created specifically for the search engines. Indeed, visitors on your web page will be totally unaware that this content exists. And this hidden content is endorsed by all the major search engines (and many social networks).

The content I am referring to is called Structured Data, or Schema.

Although it is beyond the scope of this book to fully cover Schema and structured data, I do want to give you enough information to help you get started in adding structured data to your own website.

What is Structured Data?

Search engines want to fully understand what your web pages are about because it helps them accurately rank your content in the SERPs. While most search engines are great at analyzing the words on a page to find topic or theme, you can help them even more by providing specific information in a standardized language that search engines can understand.

Structured data (also called schema markup) provides this extra information.

Structured data simply means data (or information) that has been organized in a specific way (structured).

The structured data can include information about a web page, e.g. author, title, description, rating, ingredients, cooking time, video length, etc. At its discretion, Google can then use this data to add more value to the search results. Here is an example showing how Google used structured data embedded in a web page to highlight review data:

A2 Hosting Reviews | 2018 Web Hosting Reviews●
https://www.a2hosting.co.uk/reviews ▾
★★★★★ Rating: 5 - 452 votes - Starting from US$3.92
A2 Hosting specializes in a number of services featuring a number of customers who use each of these solutions. Read web hosting reviews from these actual ...

Linux Hosting Reviews : Top Ranked Linux Web Hosting●
https://www.a2hosting.co.uk/linux-hosting/reviews ▾
★★★★★ Rating: 5 - 447 votes
Read Linux Hosting **Reviews** From Real A2 Hosting Customers. 20X Faster Service Is Just One Of The Reasons We're A Top Ranked Linux **Web Hosting** ...

Notice the listings in the SERPs have star & number ratings, number of votes, and even starting prices. These are called **rich snippets**, where the word "rich" refers to anything that is not normally found in a normal listing (blue title, green URL and black description).

Rich snippets like this are created by Google using structured data that these webmasters embedded into the web page.

Here is a snippet of that structured data from the source code of the first page:

```
<script type="application/ld+json">
    {
        "@context": "http://schema.org/",
        "@type": "Product",

            "name": "Shared Hosting",

        "description": "Host your sites on our high performance solutions featuring our 20X faster Turbo Server option.",
        "brand":{
            "@type": "Brand",
            "name": "A2 Hosting"
        },
        "offers":{
            "@type": "AggregateOffer",
            "priceCurrency": "USD",
            "lowprice": "3.05"
        }


        ,"aggregateRating": {
            "@type": "AggregateRating",
            "ratingValue": "5",
            "bestRating": "5",
            "ratingCount": "452"
        },
        "review": [
```

The arrow points to the structured data that specifies the rating value and count. You can see that value is used in the rich snippet.

The box drawn around the description highlights another important point. Just because you add the structured data, doesn't mean Google will use it. If you look back at the screenshot showing the rich snippets in the SERPs, Google didn't use that description in the rich snippet. Google also does not have the latest "lowprice" of $3.05 (the SERPs snippet shows prices starting from $3.92) so this structured data may have been updated since the last Google crawl of this page.

The structured data embedded on this page gives Google more information that it can use at its discretion to enhance the listing in the SERPs. It also helps Google better understand the content on the page, which in turn, helps it rank the page more accurately.

Do a search for chocolate brownie recipes and you'll see more great examples of rich snippets, including the carousel:

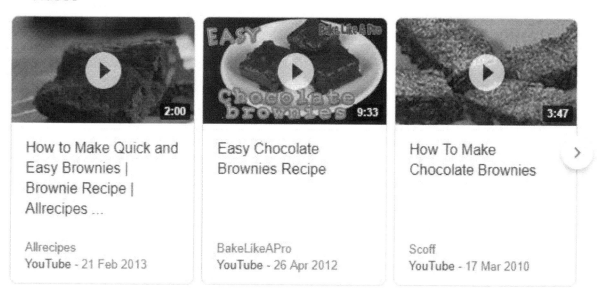

Here is another example where the site has its own search box embedded directly in the SERP listing:

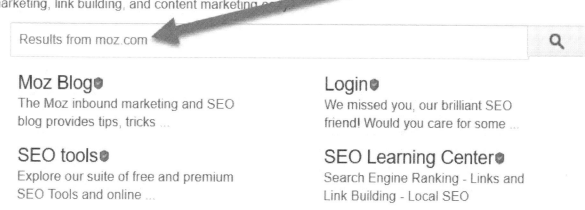

And what about this one showing tour dates:

Celine Dion Tickets | Celine Dion Tour Dates 2018 and Concert ...

https://www.viagogo.com/Concert-Tickets/Rock-and-Pop/Celine-Dion-Tickets ▾

Celine Dion tickets now available from $97.00 as of 11 Dec 2018 - viagogo, world's largest ticket marketplace - All tickets 100% guaranteed!

Fri, 28 Dec   Caesars Palace - Colosseum, Las Vegas, USA
Sat, 29 Dec   Caesars Palace - Colosseum, Las Vegas, USA
Mon, 31 Dec   Caesars Palace - Colosseum, Las Vegas, USA

To see more examples of how Google uses structured data, see these pages:

https://developers.google.com/search/docs/guides/search-gallery

https://webmasters.googleblog.com/2016/05/introducing-rich-cards.html

Rich snippets (and something called rich cards on mobile devices) show information for articles, recipes, products, ratings, videos, etc. If you have the structured data on your page, Google can use it to enhance your listing.

You won't get higher rankings in the SERPs because you include the structured data, but rich snippets in the SERPs can increase click-through rates (CTR), and as we've already seen, higher CTR can improve your rankings. Look at this screenshot and tell me which listing draws your attention:

Celestron's 9.25" Schmidt Cassegrain – A Planetary ... - Damian Peach
www.damianpeach.com/c925review.htm ▾
Fig01: The author's C9.25 telescope on German Equatorial Mount read for a night ... In this review I will examine this telescope (of which I have used throughout ....

Celestron C9.25 XLT Optical Tube Assembly - CG5 / Vixen / Sky ...
https://www.firstlightoptics.com › Telescopes › Celestron › Optical Tube Assemblies ▾
★★★★★ Rating: 5 - 1 review - £1,359.00 - Out of stock
Celestron C9.25 XLT Optical Tube Assembly - CG5 / Vixen / Sky-Watcher. Celestron ... Product Info; Specifications; Q&A; Customer Reviews (1). Generally ...

Celestron 9.25: A Good Scope But No Real Mystery - Schmidt ...
https://www.cloudynights.com › ... › Telescopes › Schmidt-Cassegrains (SCTs) ▾
17 Oct 2006 - Recent Reviews ... Celestron 9.25: A Good Scope But No Real Mystery ... A C9.25 has a proportionately longer optical tube than other SCTs.

Want to buy Celestron Advanced C9.25-SGT? | Frank - Telescope Planet
https://www.telescopeplanet.co.uk/celestron-advanced-c9.25-sgt ▾
Celestron Advanced C9.25-SGT The Celestron Advanced C9.25 telescope offers unparalleled quality optics at a very reasonable price. The telescope is the big ...

Structured Data (SD) should be an integral part of your SEO as it can be read (and used) by search engines, Facebook, Pinterest, etc.

Who will benefit from implementing structured data?

If any of the following are true, then you should be implementing structured data on your website.

1. If organic search traffic is important to you.
2. You want your pages to stand out in the SERPs
3. You have multiple articles related to key terms and you want them to stand out as a carousel in the SERPs.
4. Your pages include reviews, job listings, local business, events, products, courses, e-commerce.

Implementing Structured Data

I don't want to confuse you, but there is more than one way to implement structured data. However, we are only going to talk about the method that Google prefers, which uses a taxonomy called schema.org, and the JSON-LD programming language. For WordPress users that don´t want to learn even the smallest amount of programming, don't panic. I'll be looking at a Wordpress plugin that can implement structured data for you.

To add structured data, we need to know the rules that govern the structure.

In its simplest form, structured data is a set of variable/value pairs.

Remember this:

```
<script type="application/ld+json">
    {
        "@context": "http://schema.org/",
        "@type": "Product",

        "name": "Shared Hosting",

        "description": "Host your sites on our high performance solutions featuring our 20X faster Turbo Server option.",
        "brand":{
            "@type": "Brand",
            "name": "A2 Hosting"
        },
        "offers":{
            "@type": "AggregateOffer",
            "priceCurrency": "USD",
            "lowprice": "3.05"
        }

        ,"aggregateRating": {
            "@type": "AggregateRating",
            "ratingValue": "5",
            "bestRating": "5",
            "ratingCount": "452"
        },
        "review": [
```

That code shows variable/value pairs. Let's zoom in on an example:

```
,"aggregateRating": {
    "@type": "AggregateRating",
    "ratingValue": "5",
    "bestRating": "5",
    "ratingCount": "452"
},
"review": [
```

This code is the structured data, or Schema, that defines the "Aggregate Rating". The aggregate rating has several variables, each with a value.

So, the ratingValue variable is assigned the number 5.

The ratingCount (number of individual ratings that make up the rating value) is 452.

The variable names shown in that code are critical. If you don't use the exact variable name, the code won't be understood. As webmasters, we need to know what variables are available to us, and what values those variables accept. That is where the taxonomy we referred to a moment ago comes in.

In 2011, Google, Bing, Yahoo!, and Yandex, got together to create a standardized list of attributes and entities which they all agreed to support, and which became known as Schema.org (yes it's a website). Schema.org is the taxonomy of "things" we can add to our structured data.

OK, so let's have a quick recap.

1. Structured data consists of things, and things have properties.
2. Schema.org is a taxonomy of all things and their properties.
3. Google specifically recommends that we use schema.org and a programming language called JSON-LD for creating the structured data code we embed in our web pages.
4. Schema.org is, therefore, our #1 resource for creating our own structured data.

Got it?

Well, there is a fly in the ointment... Google!

Google also has its own guidelines in addition to what you'll find at Schema.org. You can create your structured data according to schema.org, but if you don't also implement Google's own guidelines, then the search giant can apply a penalty to your pages/site. You can find these guidelines here:

https://developers.google.com/search/docs/guides/sd-policies

The good news is that most of Google's guidelines are only there to prevent webmasters abusing the system, e.g. creating structured data that does not accurately reflect the contents of the page.

JSON-LD

Earlier we mentioned that structured data is coded using the JSON-LD language. JSON-LD is the code used to pass the data to the search engines.

Obviously, programming in JSON-LD is beyond the scope of this book, but we can create JSON-LD structured data using the Google structured data helper.

https://www.google.com/webmasters/markup-helper/?hl=en

This tool allows you to markup your site, then capture the JSON-LD that you need to add to your page.

Try it out. Go to that site.

Find a URL on one of your websites and select the type of schema you want to create, then paste in the URL:

Structured Data Markup Helper

Website	Email

This tool will help you add structured-data markup to a sample web page. Learn more

To get started, select a data type, then paste the URL or HTML source of the page you wish to mark up below:

- ● Articles
- ○ Events
- ○ Movies
- ○ Software Applications

- ○ Book Reviews
- ○ Job Postings
- ○ Products
- ○ TV Episodes

- ○ Datasets
- ○ Local Businesses
- ○ Restaurants

1

2

3

URL	HTML

https://fishyfats.com/health-benefits/health-benefits-fish-oil/   **Start Tagging**

Click the **Start Tagging** button to start.

Your page will load up in a split screen, with the data items on the right, and your web page on the left. You can now use your mouse to highlight information on your web page. When you do, you'll get a popup menu allowing you to tag the data you just highlighted. In this example I've highlighted the title, and will select **name** from the menu:

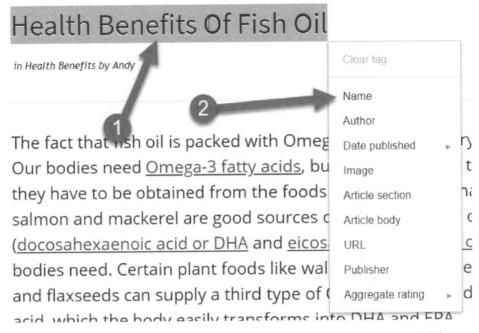

When you click a menu item, that data value is written to that variable over on the right of the screen:

Markup as much information as you can about your page. If there is any information that you want to markup, but it is not physically found on the page (so you cannot highlight it), click the **Add Missing Tag** button at the bottom. You can then manually enter the data:

When you are done marking up your page, click the **Create HTML** button, top right:

On the next screen, make sure you have JSON-LD selected from the drop-down box, and your valid JSON-LD code will be listed below:

Structured data as JSON-LD Markup

Add the script block below to the head section of your html:

```
<!-- JSON-LD markup generated by Google Structured Data Markup Helper. -->
<script type="application/ld+json">
{
  "@context" : "http://schema.org",
  "@type" : "Article",
  "name" : "Health Benefits of Fish Oil",
  "author" : {
    "@type" : "Person",
    "name" : "Andy"
  },
  "datePublished" : "2016-10-16",
  "image" : "https://fishyfats.com/wp-content/uploads/2016/03/krill-miracle.jpg",
  "url" : "https://fishyfats.com/health-benefits/health-benefits-fish-oil/"
}
</script>
```

This code can now be inserted into the web page. There are various ways to insert the code into a web page. If you are familiar with Tag Manager, you can use that. Or, you can paste the code directly into the HTML of your page, test it, then move onto the next page you want to markup.

Testing Markup

You can test your structured data over on Google's structured data testing tool.

https://search.google.com/structured-data/testing-tool

When you arrive at that URL, you are given the choice of testing a URL or a code snippet. If you have entered the structured data into your webpage already, test the URL. Your page will be analyzed, and the results shown:

Detected	0 ERRORS	0 WARNINGS	4 ITEMS
hentry	0 ERRORS	0 WARNINGS	1 ITEM
Organization	0 ERRORS	0 WARNINGS	1 ITEM
BreadcrumbList	0 ERRORS	0 WARNINGS	1 ITEM
Article	0 ERRORS	0 WARNINGS	1 ITEM

You are looking for a clean bill of health. That means 0 errors.

Each of those entries in the results table represents a different bit of structured data on your web page. Depending on how your site was built, you may have structured data already present in your web pages. If you use WordPress, then WordPress itself will add some for you, and so will some plugins.

The page above has structured data related to:

1. Hentry (added by WordPress).
2. Organization (Added by the Yoast SEO plugin)
3. Breadcrumblist (Added by the Yoast SEO plugin)
4. Article (added by the JSON-LD we just created).

You can click on any of these entries to expand the structured data. So, clicking on **Organization** shows me the structured data for that "thing":

Troubleshooting with Google Console

The old interface (you can still switch to it) of the Google Search Console has a section that can help you with your structured data. You'll find the structured data tools under the **Search Appearance** menu.

The structured data screen will highlight any problems with the structured data on your site.

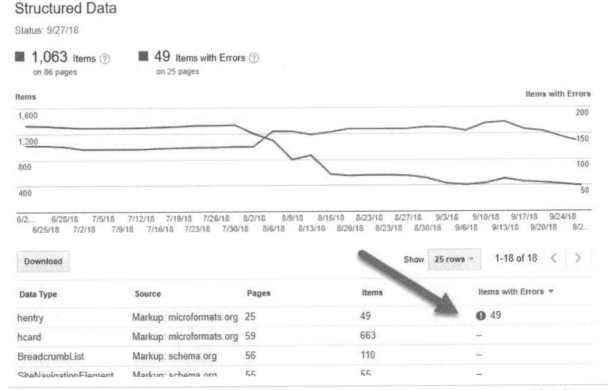

Clicking on the lines that contain errors will open a more detailed view. You'll get to see the URLs with structured data errors, as well as the errors themselves.

If you click the URL, a dialogue box opens with more details as well as a button to test the structured data on the live page:

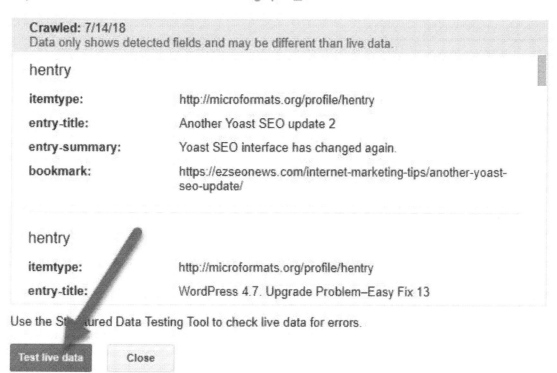

You may find that when you test your live page the schema validates fine. That's because it has been fixed since Google last saw it. It will remain in the error list until

Google re-spiders the page and finds the valid schema in place.

We have only really scratched the surface in terms of manually adding structured data to a website, but as far as manual methods go, we've covered all we are going to in this book. As you have seen, there are a lot of rules you must follow, and these rules can change without notice. I don't personally want the hassle or the time-suck of having to check Schema.org and Google guidelines every time I add structured data to a web page. Therefore, my own preferred method of adding structured data is with a WordPress plugin.

The plugin I use is called Schema Pro and I want to quickly show you how that works.

Schema Pro WordPress Plugin

The main reason I love this plugin for structured data is that it is updated regularly. When Schema.org is updated, this plugin gets updated. It means I can concentrate on more important things and leave the plugin to handle my structured data requirements.

You can find details of the plugin here:

https://ezseonews.com/schemapro

I am going to set up some structured data using this plugin on a test site of mine.

Schema Pro Settings

Once installed and activated, the plugin adds a menu under the settings menu in the left sidebar of your dashboard.

I prefer the Schema Pro settings in a different place and you can do that in the configuration menu:

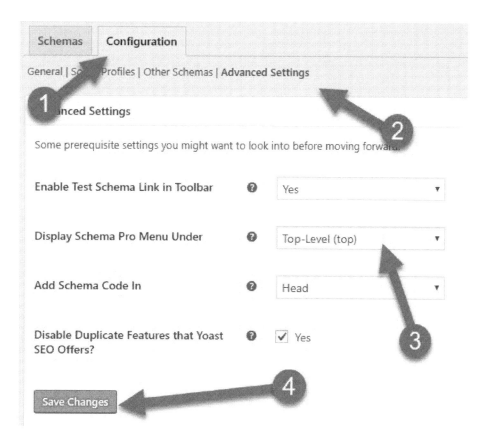

Choosing the **Top-Level (top)** option moves the Schema Pro settings to its own top-level menu, high in the sidebar menu:

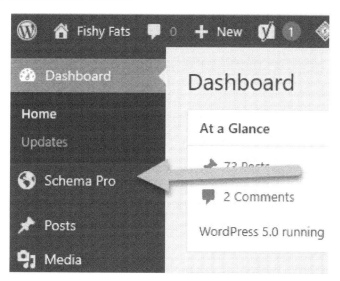

While we are still in the **Configuration** tab, it's worth setting up a couple of other things. On the **General** tab, you can enter information about your site:

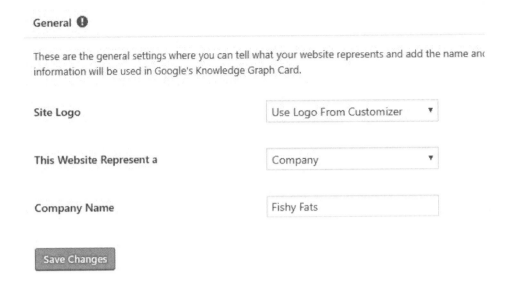

Whatever you add here will be added to the structured data of your web pages. In the screenshot above, my pages will now have structured data values for site logo, site type, and company name.

On the social profiles tab of the settings, add in any social media pages you have set up for the site:

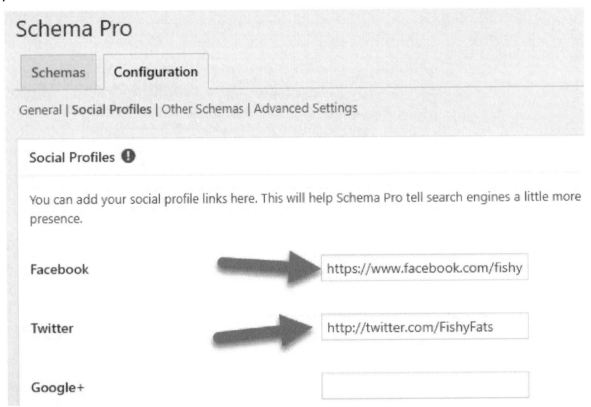

On the **Other Schema** settings tab, you can assign more structured data:

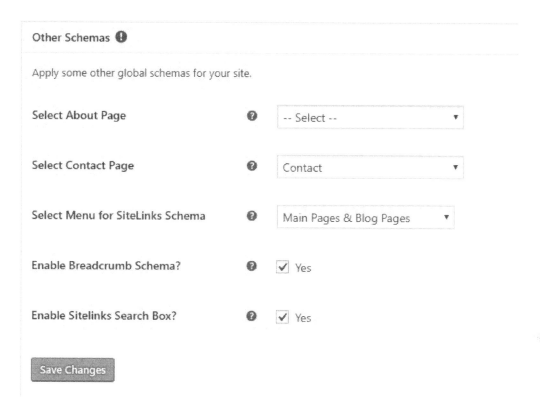

Again, all this data you are entering now is converted into JSON-LD and added to your pages automatically. You can test the schema that is being added to pages by visiting your site while logged into your Dashboard. The Schema Pro plugin adds an entry to the WordPress admin bar:

Clicking that link will open the current web page in the Structured Data Testing Tool, so you can see the new structured data and confirm it is OK:

Adding Specific Schema

With the general settings done, we can now start adding schema for specific pages. Click onto the **Schema** tab, and click the **Add New** button:

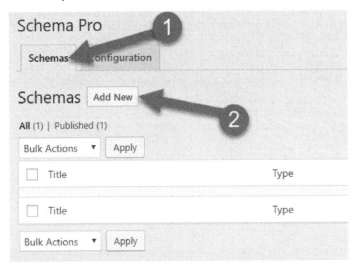

The screen that loads will give you a choice of the schema type you want to create:

After clicking the **Next** button, you'll be asked where on your website the new schema should be integrated:

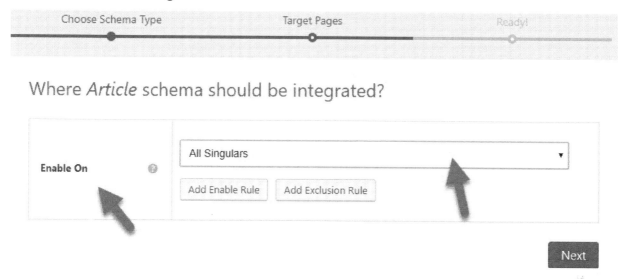

You make your choice by selecting from the drop-down box:

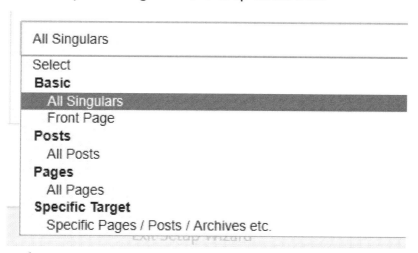

In my case I want this schema applied to **All Posts**.

Note that the last entry, **Specific Target**, allows you to select specific posts, archive pages (tag, category), or pages. For example, if you want to apply the schema to just one or two posts, you can. You also have the power to add **exclusion rules** which prevent the schema being added to pages based on your criteria.

You can add multiple "enable" and "exclusion" rules to target specific pages and sections of your site. E.g. You can set up review schema and have it applied to all posts in the review category.

When you are done, click the **Next** button.

You'll get confirmation that your schema has been set up:

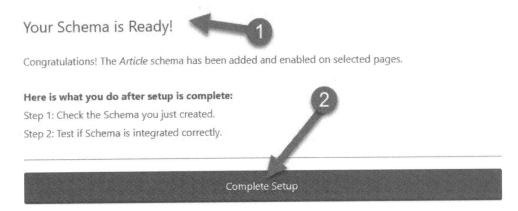

Click the **Complete Setup** button to enter the **Edit Schema** screen:

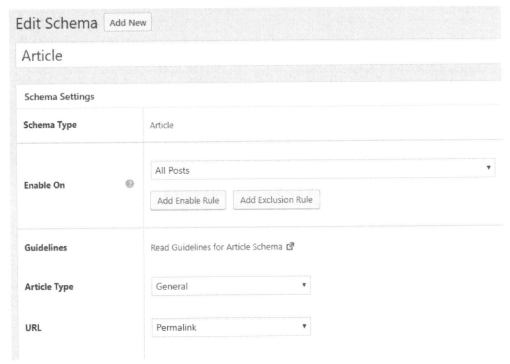

This screen allows you to edit the schema, including the enable/exclusion rules if you need to. The schema is set up by selecting options from drop-down boxes.

Whatever is selected in the drop-down box is used to create the structured data for each post. Think of the options in the drop-down boxes as variables, which will change for each post.

For example, if you have the **Title** variable selected for the **Headline** property, each post will use its own title for the Headline schema.

Most of these options will be correctly selected for you, but you can change or override the default settings. For example, for the **Publisher Name**, the plugin selected **Site Title** in the structured data (which makes good sense):

Clicking the drop-down box allows me to make a different selection if I want to, including **Fixed Text**, where I can type in any text I like:

Another useful option in the drop-down box is **New Custom Field**. In this case, you can choose the value at the time you publish the content. A good example of this is the **Image** field which is essential to article schema. It is set to **Featured Image** by default, but if a post does not have a featured image assigned, it will result in a structured data validation error. See the second arrow in the following screenshot:

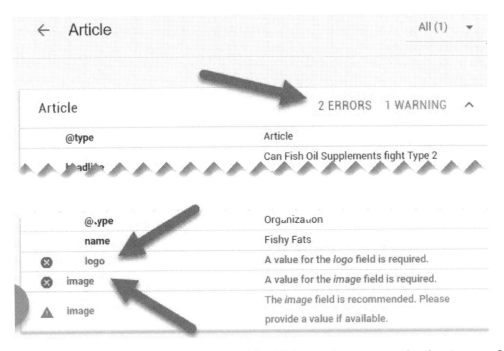

By changing the image to **New Custom Field**, I'll be able to specify the image for each post at the time I publish the post (directly on the edit post screen):

By selecting an image at the time of publishing, the image error will be resolved. However, there is still another error in that error report. The logo. That one is easily fixed by assigning a Site Icon in the Site identity settings of my theme:

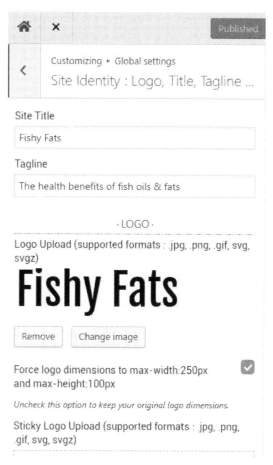

Then on re-checking my structured data:

There is so much more this plugin can do for you. However, I am going to leave it there. If you decide to buy the plugin, you'll have full access to the plugin documentation to help you.

Before finishing this chapter, I wanted to mention that there are some free structured data plugins. I tried the ones I could find and found some basic functionality issues with all of them. Make sure you check these if you decide to use a free plugin:

1. The free versions were limited and you had to upgrade to a paid version to get some essential features.
2. Since the free versions are free, there is no guarantee that these plugins will be updated when Schema.org changed. Having your structured data plugin updated automatically with the latest information is something that really is worth paying for.

There is a lot to learn with structured data and I could only scratch the surface in this chapter. It is something that I think you need to be using as an SEO, so let me finish by listing some of the more important resources.

Schema & Structured Data Resources

1. Schema.org - The taxonomy Google recommends.
   https://schema.org/
2. Google Structured Data Guidelines:
   https://developers.google.com/search/docs/guides/intro-structured-data
3. Structured data testing tool:
   https://search.google.com/structured-data/testing-tool
4. Google Search Console:
   https://www.google.com/webmasters/tools/home?hl=en
5. Markup helper
   https://www.google.com/webmasters/markup-helper/?hl=en

2. Site Organization

What Google Tells Us About Site Design

Google gives us a lot of information about site design, which we should consider as best practices. Put another way, Google knows how the search engine works, and therefore knows the site design elements that work best.

Google lists all these Standards in its Google Webmaster Guidelines, but let's go through some of the important points here.

1. Create a Sitemap

Google wants you to create a sitemap and submit it in the Google Search Console, and I recommend you do this. If you are using WordPress, there are many plugins which can create sitemaps automatically for you.

Google also suggests that you have a sitemap for visitors as it helps guide them to relevant parts of your site. I think this is less important than a sitemap for the search engines since a good navigation system on the site (plus a good search facility) will easily replace the need for a visitor sitemap. It is my experience that users would rather use an intuitive navigation system, one that effortlessly guides them around the site's pages, than a long list of hyperlinks in a sitemap.

2. Make Sure Your Site Has a Clear Hierarchy

We'll look at the hierarchical structure of the site soon, but for now, just know that Google expects EVERY page on your site to be reachable through a static link on another page (not necessarily the sitemap). I'd go one step further in suggesting that every page on your site should be no more than two clicks from the homepage, and the more important pages no more than one click away from the homepage.

3. Keep Links on a Page to a Reasonable Number

Search engines can spider every link on a page, even very long ones, so I can only assume this guideline is for the benefit of users. If you have certain "calls to action" that you want visitors to make, the fewer links (and other distractions) there are, the better.

4. Dynamic Pages Vs Static Pages

Dynamic pages often contain the "?" character before some parameters. Google suggests you try to make static pages rather than dynamic pages, though if you must use dynamic pages, try to keep the parameters to a bare minimum.

5. A Robots.txt File?

The Robot.txt file is a kind of gatekeeper, controlling who or what gets through to your web pages. They set the rules for your site, e.g. stopping search engine spiders from crawling specific pages; preventing them from appearing in the SERPs.

A robots.txt file sits in the root folder of your site and basically contains a series of allow or disallow commands telling spiders/crawlers which pages they can and cannot access. Google suggests that if you have pages on your site that you do not want spiders to crawl, then use a robots.txt file. If, on the other hand, you want the spiders to crawl every page on your website, then do not create a robot.txt file, not even a blank one.

For WordPress users, my advice is to check out yoast.com for the latest advice on robots.txt files:

https://yoast.com/wordpress-robots-txt-example/

The free Yoast SEO WordPress plugin allows you to easily control which pages Google shows in its search results, and which pages it doesn't. It's a plugin that I highly recommend for all WordPress users.

6. Check Your Site in Different Browsers

Unfortunately, different web browsers can display a page very differently. It is, therefore, wise to check your site in a range of different browsers to make sure it looks good for everyone, irrespective of what browser they are using. You might not be able to get your site looking perfect in every single web browser (there are a lot of them around these days) but you want it to at least look good in the top six, namely Google Chrome, Mozilla Firefox, Microsoft Internet Explorer, Microsoft Edge, Opera, and Apple Safari).

Do a Google search for **browser compatibility testing** and you'll find free tools to make this testing easier and quicker.

You must also check in mobile browsers. A responsive theme is a must-have these days. Responsive themes adjust how your site displays, depending on the browser resolution of the visitor. At the time of writing, between 45%-60% of my own site visitors (for a variety of sites) are coming in on mobile devices. The Statista website states that in 2018, 52.2% of searches were on mobile phones. That is a lot of traffic to lose if you don't have a mobile-friendly website.

For WordPress users looking to switch to mobile-friendly site design, I highly recommend that you find a responsive theme. Most new themes these days are mobile-responsive but do check with the theme creator.

Most responsive theme will load quickly, look great, and keep mobile users happy, without compromising the experience of desktop visitors.

7. Monitor Your Site Load Times

Site visitors will not hang around if your pages take a long time to load. Therefore, don't add unnecessary bloat to your pages. Create light, fast-loading pages with optimized images to make sure they load as quickly as possible. Page load speed is certainly a factor used in the Google algorithm, and although it is not a major one, it is still worth noting.

Two great free services you can use to test your own page load times are:

1. Page Speed Insights from Google.
2. GTMetrix

You can find both tools easily by searching Google. Both provide a lot of information and you'll probably end up preferring one over the other. My personal favorite is GTMetrix. You can create a free account there and keep historical page load data.

So those are the important guidelines on site structure. I'll give you a few of my own recommendations shortly, but for now, I recommend you head on over to the Google Webmaster Guidelines and familiarize yourself with them all. Seriously, they'll help to keep you on the right side of Google.

A Note About Exact Match Domain Names

An exact match domain (EMD) is one that uses the main keyword phrase you are targeting as the domain name, e.g. buyviagraonline.com (if you wanted to target "buy Viagra online"). Typically, EMD websites target very few keywords, placing all their eggs firmly in the "EMD phrase" basket.

On September 28, 2012, Google released an update that aimed to reduce the ranking ability of poor quality EMDs.

 **Matt Cutts**
@mattcutts

New exact-match domain (EMD) algo
affects 0.6% of English-US queries to a
noticeable degree. Unrelated to
Panda/Penguin.

RETWEETS	FAVOURITES
359	42

2:03 pm - 28 Sep 2012

This news didn't come as a surprise to the more switched on SEOs because two years earlier, Google's Matt Cutts announced that the company would be looking at why EMDs ranked so well when he spoke at Pubcon, Las Vegas, in November 2010.

The problem with EMDs today is that Google scrutinizes them more closely. This means there's always an added risk of them receiving penalties, whether they deserve it or not.

One thing that makes a lot of EMDs stand out is the high percentage of backlinks that use the exact same keyword phrase as the anchor text. The problem for EMD owners is that using one phrase over and over is largely unavoidable. This is because it's the name of the website, and therefore creates many of the same-looking links pointing back to the page.

Because of this, I recommend you look for a brandable domain name instead and try to find one that people will remember easily. The only type of EMD that I would say is OK, is one that represents a brand name. For any other commercial terms, don´t even think about it.

Good Site Structure

The way you structure your site is extremely important, not only for the search engines but also for human visitors. Good organization, coupled with a clear and intuitive navigation system is not only practical, but it's also vital.

From a human point of view, it makes sense that content on a similar topic can be accessed from the same section of the site. For example, if you have a website selling bicycles, then all the mountain bikes should be grouped together, all the road bikes in another section, and maybe bikes for children in yet another part of the site.

If a young, 22-year-old mountain bike rider came to your site, he or she should be able to browse the mountain bike stuff without seeing road racers or children's bicycles distracting their viewing.

If you're using WordPress as a site builder, then organizing your site like this is extremely easy. You simply create a category for each section and assign posts to the most logical category. While it is possible to assign a post to more than one category, I recommend the one-post to one-category approach. This makes for a tighter organization (a better silo) and serves the webmaster, the site visitor, and the search engines, better. If you need to categorize your articles further, e.g. having all 26-inch frame bikes on the same page, then use tags as a tool for the frame sizes. We will look at tags a little later.

This type of "silo" structure works very well for the search engines because it helps them categorize your content. Think of a site that has reviews on the following bikes and accessories.

- Allen Deluxe 4-Bike Hitch Mount Rack
- GMC Denali Pro Road Bike
- GMC Denali Women's Road Bike
- GMC Topkick Dual-Suspension Mountain Bike
- Hollywood Racks E3 Express 3-Bike Trunk Mount Rack
- Kawasaki DX226FS 26-Inch Dual Suspension Mountain Bike
- Mongoose Exile Dual-Suspension Mountain Bike
- Pacific Stratus Men's Mountain Bike
- Topeak Explorer Bike Rack
- Victory Vision Men's Road Bike

If you were to put these into related group (silos), those silos would look something like this.

Silo 1 - Mountain Bikes

- GMC Topkick Dual-Suspension Mountain Bike
- Kawasaki DX226FS 26-Inch Dual Suspension Mountain Bike
- Mongoose Exile Dual-Suspension Mountain Bike
- Pacific Stratus Men's Mountain Bike

Silo 2 Road Bikes

- GMC Denali Pro Road Bike
- GMC Denali Women's Road Bike
- Victory Vision Men's Road Bike

Silo 3 Car Racks

- Allen Deluxe 4-Bike Hitch Mount Rack
- Hollywood Racks E3 Express 3-Bike Trunk Mount Rack
- Topeak Explorer Bike Rack

To illustrate how this looks in graph form, the overall structure of the site would now look like this:

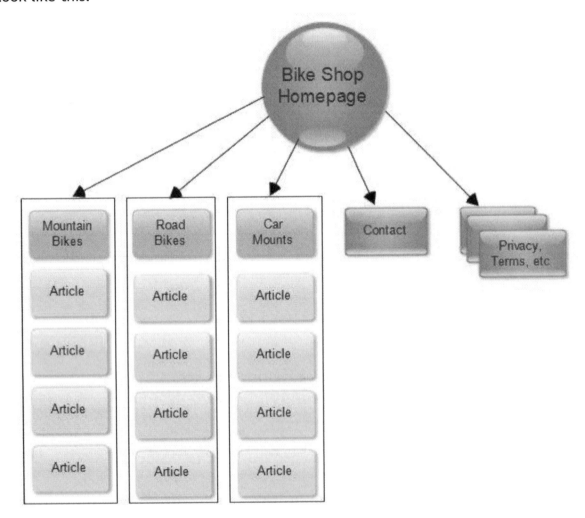

Keeping your site tightly organized into silos makes it easier for your site visitor and the search engines.

Internal Links

One of the most overlooked pieces of the SEO puzzle is internal linking. This not only helps the search engines to spider your pages more easily, but it also helps visitors find other related content within your site.

If your site is built using a content management system, there should be plugins that can help with this.

For example, Wordpress users can download the free "Contextual Related Posts Plugin", which will automatically create a related posts section at the end of every article on your site.

https://wordpress.org/plugins/contextual-related-posts/

Here is an example of a "Related Posts" section on a web page:

Related Posts

> Curcumin, the powerful antioxidant found in Turmeric
Turmeric contains an active ingredient called Curcumin. This active agent has amazing health benefits.

> Turmeric as a powerful antioxidant
Turmeric contains curcumin, a powerful antioxidant. In this video, Dr. Mercola discusses the benefits and properties of curcumin.

This example shows related posts in the sidebar of the site. However, a great place to include them is at the end of an article, or even embedded between paragraphs. That way, when your visitor has finished reading one article, they immediately see a list of related articles that might also interest them. This helps to keep visitors on your site for longer.

Linking Pages on a Site Together

Another form of internal linking, which I think is extremely important, is contextual linking. This is when a link is located within the body of your content.

For instance, if you are writing an article about the "GMC Topkick Dual-Suspension Mountain Bike", you might like to compare certain features of the bike to the "Mongoose Exile Dual-Suspension Mountain Bike". When you mention the name of the Mongoose Exile bike, it would help your visitors if you linked that phrase to your Mongoose Exile review. This would also allow the search engines to find that article, and help them determine what it's about, based on the link text.

This type of internal linking helps to increase indexing of your site, as well as the rankings of individual pages.

In addition, Google tolerates (dare I say likes) internal links (to the same domain) with keyword-rich anchor text. Just check out a few Wikipedia pages to see how it uses contextual linking between its pages. This is in stark contrast to how Google views keyword-rich anchor text from one site to another site. These can easily get you penalized.

A few years ago, I ran an experiment to investigate the effects of internal linking on the ranking of the homepage of a niche site of mine. My goal was to see if I could improve its rank for a chosen phrase with nothing but internal linking. I analyzed the entire site and found that there was a total of 957 links to the homepage from other pages on the site.

637 of those backlinks used the phrase "home" as the anchor text.

319 backlinks used the name of the site.

1 other backlink used a different phrase.

Rather than change the anchor text of these internal links, which were very "natural", I added 17 new contextual links in a natural way. I varied the anchor text so that there were an additional 7 anchor text phrases being used to link to the homepage. These anchor text phrases were all relevant to the term I was targeting.

To cut a long story short, here is the graph showing my rank in Google during this experiment:

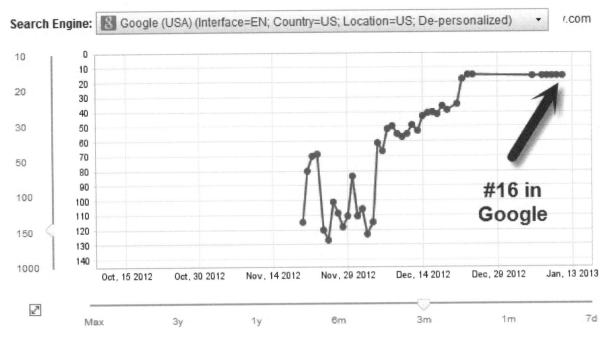

The page started at #190 in Google before the experiment started, which you don't see at the start of that graph because of the scale I used.

That was back in 2012. In 2019, you need to be a little bit more careful with this style of "manipulation". I still use it when I want to improve the rank of a new page, but I am very careful. Every link must be natural, and rather than linking with specific keyword phrases I am targeting, I'll usually link with the title of the article I am linking to. Since the title contains keywords, this helps, but this type of link using the title as anchor text is also extremely natural if you think about it.

Tags - Another Way to Categorize Your Content

Tags are another way to categorize content if you are running a WordPress (or similar content management system) site.

When you write a post, you can include a number of these tags, which further helps to categorize the piece.

For example, if you wrote a post about the "Dyson DC 33 Animal" vacuum cleaner, you would probably put it in the "Dyson" category, as that is the most logical "navigation label" for your visitors.

However, you might also want to offer your visitors an easy way to find vacuums that use the Dyson Ball technology or contain a HEPA filter. So rather than have a separate category for "Dyson Ball" and another for "HEPA filter" (and put the DC33 Animal in all three categories), a better way would be to create tags for this extra classification.

Here are some "tags" you might use on the vacuum site:

- Upright
- Dyson Ball
- Pet hair
- HEPA filter
- Bagless

These tags will help to categorize the posts within the Dyson category, along with every other brand name category on your site.

WordPress creates a page for each of these tags, and each of these tag pages can actually rank quite well in Google.

Let's look at an example.

These four vacuums all have HEPA filters:

1. Eureka Boss Smart-Vac Upright.
2. Hoover Windtunnel
3. BISSELL Cleanview Helix Upright Vacuum Cleaner
4. Miele S2 Series Lightweight

The first vacuum will be in the Eureka CATEGORY with all other Eureka vacuums.

The second vacuum will be in the Hoover CATEGORY with all other Hoover vacuums.

The third vacuum will be in the Bissell CATEGORY and, the fourth vacuum will be in the Miele CATEGORY.

All four vacuums are tagged with "HEPA filter", so will also appear on the HEPA Filter "tag page".

Additionally, the first three vacuums would also appear on the "Upright" tag page.

When people visit your site, they'll be able to narrow down their choice by Brand (using category navigation), or by looking for specific features (using tags to navigate).

A Word of Warning!

I advise you to use tags wisely and sparingly. Don't tag every post with hundreds of tags. Think about your tags carefully and only include the most relevant ones for each post.

The Use and Misuse of Tags

A lot of people do not really understand the significance of tags and see them as a "keyword list" like the Meta Keywords tag. To that end, they create long tag lists for each post. Here is a screenshot of some tags assigned to one post I saw:

Tags: advantages disadvantages of solar power, advantages of a solar panels, advantages of solar cell panel, are MONOCRYSTALLINE sollar pannels good, best mono solar panel price, best quality monocrystaline solar panels, bestpv panels mono or poly, buy pv panels monocrystalline, compare monocrystalin policrystalin photovoltaic, compare monocrystalline and polycrystalline, compare monocrystalline and polycrystalline pannel, compare pollycrystalline vs. monocrystaline modules, crystal cells for solar panels, crystal solar, crystalline si solar efficiency, crystalline solar best, crystalline solar cell technology, crystalline solar cells cost, crystalline solar panels, crystalline solar plate cost, crystalline solar pv module, csun mono-crystalline panels, describe 2 advantages of solar cells, difference between mono and polycrystalline, difference between monocrystalline, difference monocrystalline polycrystalline solar, difference solar panels polycrystalline &, disadvantage to many solar panels, ecokes monocrystalline, ecokes photovoltaic panels, ecokes solar panel, electricity, energy, how i get Monocrystalline silicon, how many rating monocrystalline cell, how Monocrystalline cells are made, how to produce monocrytaline silicon, http://www.monocrystal photo cells/, is monocrystalline better than polycrystalline, is monocrystalline PV best, LUXOR Solar Mono Crystal Dickschichtmodule, maker of monocrystalline panels, mon vs poly efficiency, mono and poly crystalline, mono crystalline pv panels, mono or poly solar panels, mono silicon solar panels, mono solar panel dimensions, mono solar power, mono v poly solar panels, mono versus poly crystalling panels, mono vs poly crystalline panels, mono vs. multicrystalline solar panel, Mono-

This was actually only about 25% of the total tags listed on that page. It just kept scrolling down and down. In SEO terms, this is bad practice. Very bad!

To understand why long tag lists are a bad idea, let's look at what happens when you create a post.

When you publish a post (article) on your blog, WordPress will put that same post onto several

pages of your site, including:

1. A page specially created to show the post (the main page).
2. The category page.
3. The author page.
4. For every tag assigned to the post, that post will appear on the corresponding tag page. So, if you tag a post with 25 tags, it means that post duplicates across 25 tag pages.

Can you see how that one post now duplicates on multiple pages of your site?

Duplicated Content on a Site Is NOT Good!

Another big problem with using too many tags occurs when only one post uses a particular tag. In that case, the tag page will only have the one article on it, meaning it is almost identical to the main post page created by WordPress for that article.

How to Use WordPress Tags Properly

Get into the tag mindset. Before you use a tag on a post, think about the tag page that will be created for that post.

Your article will appear on each of those tag pages you tag it with. So, when you create a new tag for a new post, ask yourself whether you will use this tag on other, relevant posts. The rule of thumb is to never create a tag if it is unlikely to get used by several other posts on your site.

Here is what I suggest you do:

During the design stages of your site, make a list on a piece of paper of all the tags you want to use (you can add/edit this list as you build out your site, but at least have a list you can refer to). As you create posts on your site, refer to the tag list you wrote down, and use only tags on that list. By all means, add new tags over time, but make sure the tags are going to be used more than once. Don't create a tag that will only ever be used for a single post on your site. Remember, **tags are a way to classify groups of related posts**. Also, only use a few of the most relevant tags for each post.

Finally, never use a word or phrase for a tag that is (or will be) the same as a category name. After all, WordPress will create pages for each category as well; so, think of tags as an "additional" categorization tool at your disposal.

Modifying Tag Pages?

Quite often, you will find that your tag pages are getting traffic from Google. I have found that the tag pages often rank very well for the chosen tag (as a keyword phrase).

I like to modify my tag pages (and category pages) by adding an introductory paragraph to each one. Create a tag, then go in and edit it. You'll find a box labeled **Archive**

Intro Text. Use that to write an introduction to the tag page.

When created this way, the tag pages have an introduction, followed by a list of all related articles (those tagged with that tag). This helps to make your tag pages unique, but it also allows you to add more value to your site.

Used properly, tag pages can work for you. Used without thought, tag pages can increase duplicate content on your site and therefore increase your chances of a Google penalty.

3. Authority

What Is An "Authority" Site?

If you go over to the Free Dictionary website and search for authority, there are many different definitions. The highlighted definition (4a) below is spot on:

au·thor·i·ty (ə-thôr′ĭ-tē, ə-thŏr′-, ô-)

n. pl. **au·thor·i·ties**

1.

    a. The power to enforce laws, exact obedience, command, determine, or judge.

    b. One that is invested with this power, especially a government or body of government officials: *land titles issued by the civil authority.*

2. Power assigned to another; authorization: *Deputies were given authority to make arrests.*

3. A public agency or corporation with administrative powers in a specified field: *a city transit authority.*

4.

    a. An accepted source of expert information or advice: *a noted authority on birds; a reference book often cited as an authority.*

    b. A quotation or citation from such a source: *biblical authorities for a moral argument.*

To make your website an authority site, it must be an **"accepted source of expert information or advice"**.

A well-organized site with excellent content is a great start (the first two pillars of good SEO). However, those two pillars are not enough to make your site an authority. The reason for this is because no one would have heard about you or your fabulous site just yet, and that means zero votes (and little traffic).

Your site (or your own name if YOU personally want to be the authority) must be well-known in your niche.

So how do you get to be well-known?

Answering that is the easy part. You need to put your site's name and your own face out there and on as many relevant, high-quality places as you can, with links pointing back to relevant pages on your site. In other words, you need "quality" backlinks.

Getting backlinks used to be easy, but with Penguin on the prowl, backlinks can quickly get you penalized if you follow the wrong advice. This is especially the case if your site is relatively new or doesn't have much authority yet.

There is another aspect of this that I want to discuss before we go into details on back-linking, and that is linking out from your site to authority sites within your niche. We are all part of a huge web of interlinked websites. If you find information on another website that you use on yours, it makes sense that you credit the other website with a link back to that information.

Let's look at an example of this.

Think about a search engine trying to evaluate your page on the Atkins Diet. Don't you think that links to other people's studies and medical references would make your page more useful to your visitors? It would if your content was also excellent. It would help instill confidence in your visitor by giving them additional value.

When you write content for your website, don't be afraid to link to other authority sites if they have relevant information that expands on what you've referenced in your own article. Don't use "nofollow" on links to well-known authority sites either, as that just tells the search engine you:

(a) Don't trust the site you are linking to, or
(b) You are trying to hoard the link juice on your own site.

I recommend you set these links to open in a new window or tab, so you don't lose your visitors to these other websites. What you may even decide to do is have a reference section at the end of your post, with active hyperlinks pointing to other authority sites. This helps your visitor because they can read the entire post without distraction.

In short, do link out to other authority sites, but only when it makes sense and you think it will help your visitor.

OK, that's outbound links sorted.

Links Coming into Your Site

Backlinks to a website are a very important part of the Google algorithm. It's the main reason webmasters build links to their own websites; to help them rank better. However, there is something very important that you need to know about link building. It's not something that most SEO books or courses will tell you. Here's what they don't want you to know:

Google doesn't want you building links to your site.

In fact, we can probably state this a little more strongly.

Google HATES you building links to your site and may penalize you if caught.

Google is on the warpath against "Webspam" and "link schemes". This includes "unnatural" links. Any link that was created purely to help your page rank higher in the SERPs is considered as an **unnatural link**.

An unnatural link is one where you, as the webmaster:

1. Choose the link text.
2. Choose the destination page.
3. Choose which page the link appears on.
4. Choose where on the page the link appears.

Is every link you have built to your site unnatural? Possibly, but it's not quite that clear-cut.

Google sees any link you build for the sole purpose of increasing your rank in the SERPs as unnatural. Any link that you create and would have created even if the search engines did not exist, is not unnatural. It's a fine line, and obviously open to interpretation.

An example of this is if you write an article for an authority site and put a link to your site in the author bio. This is considered a natural link. You are the expert that wrote the article and people may want to find out more about you. You would put that link in there even if there were no search engines. Google recommends you add the "nofollow" tag to this type of author bio link.

I know... You won't get any link juice if you do. But didn't you say you would add that type of link even if search engines did not exist? The "nofollow" tag proves that to Google. By not adding the "nofollow" tag, you are leaving yourself open to a penalty later if Google cracks down on this.

As I mentioned a moment ago, the term "unnatural" is used by Google to describe those links you created specifically to boost the position of your page in the SERPs. However, the penalties for crossing that line can be severe and even innocent links can cause problems if Google deems the motive was primarily a ranking one.

If Google finds links that you created to your site with the sole purpose of helping it to rank better, it will ignore those links at best. However, Google may decide to penalize your site if there are lots of them. It's easy for Google to dismiss a few links here and there, but not so easy if there are hundreds or thousands of them.

You need to bear this in mind as you build links to your web pages.

It can be tempting to use black hat strategies for building links. There are many people out there who will show you proof that keyword-rich anchor text links still work (usually just before selling you a link-building tool or service). What they don't show you is what happens to that page in the medium to long-term. This type of link building can still give good results in the short-term, but only until Google catches you. In 2019 it's Google's automated software that hunts you down, and it's very efficient.

In this book, I'll show you the absolute best way to get natural, powerful links, back to your web pages. But first, let's consider the benefits of link building.

An Overview of Link Building & Its Benefits

Here is the general concept of link building:

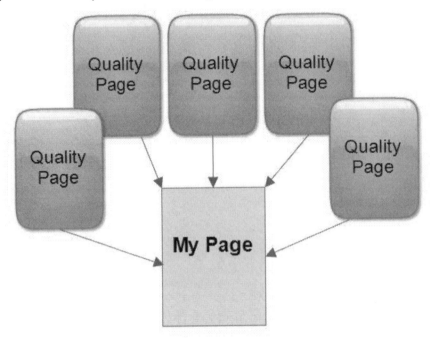

As you build quality links to a page it gains authority, which then allows it to rank more easily in the SERPs. As pages on your site gain authority, the domain authority of the entire site increases. As domain authority increases, all pages on the site can rank more easily in the SERPs.

This means that by focusing on building links to a handful of pages on your site, you can increase domain authority, which in turn makes it easier for ALL pages on the site to rank.

The Linking Page Relevancy

Some people will tell you that it doesn't matter whether inbound links are on pages related to your page or not. That may have been the case several years ago, but it's certainly not the case now.

If you had a website on "breeding goldfish" with 100 inbound links, yet 95% of those links were found on pages about:

- Prescription drugs

- Viagra
- Auto maintenance
- Wedding speeches
- Golf Equipment
- Other, unrelated pages

What is that telling the search engines?

I think Google would look at those backlinks and conclude you were involved in link schemes designed to help your pages rank better. As we saw earlier, Google's webmaster guidelines tell us that this is a quick road to a penalty.

If the search engines want to use inbound links as a measure of authority, then obviously the most authoritative links you could get would be from quality pages that were on the same/related topic to the page they linked to.

With Google Penguin, this may be even more important as Google appears to be giving less weight to the anchor text and more weight to the actual THEME of the web page (or site) that the link is on. Therefore, look for links from pages and sites that are relevant to your own niche, and look for quality sites to get your links.

Always consider quality as a priority in every backlink you get. The backlink should be on a quality page on a quality site. The page on your site should also be quality.

What I have described here is perhaps a little scary. If bad backlinks can get your site penalized, then what is to stop your competitors from building poor quality backlinks to your site? Well, this does happen, and Google calls it **negative SEO**.

Is Negative SEO Real?

Negative SEO is a term that refers to webmasters/SEOs who build poor quality links to a competitor's website to get it penalized. Many SEOs agree that since Penguin, negative SEO tactics have become a reality. I think it was a reality even before Panda, and one of my own tests proved that to me.

At the start of 2011 (before Panda), I began some aggressive back-linking to a site of mine that was several years old. I wanted to use this as a test, so I set up about 150 blogs using automation software. My plan was to use these blogs to build links to my site. I controlled these blogs so I controlled the backlinks from them. I had the power to delete the links if I needed to, and that was important for my experiment.

Once everything was in place, I began submitting content to the 150 blogs. Each piece of content contained a contextual backlink to a page on my test site.

I monitored 85 keywords that I wanted to rank for.

The rankings climbed for several weeks, and so did my traffic. My test pages ranked in the top 10 of Google for 60 of the keywords, with a large proportion in the top three.

Suddenly, it was over. I woke up one morning to find that Google had penalized my site. In fact, all 85 keywords dropped out of the top 100, rendering them totally useless.

After these keywords had been out of the top 100 for eight weeks, I began phase two of my experiment. I deleted all 150 blogs. In doing so, I deleted the spammy backlinks in one hit.

Over the next month, things began to improve slowly. Pages started climbing back into the top 100 to the point where I ended up with 64 of the 85 phrases back in the top 100. Around 42 pages were back in the top 30, and 12 were back in the top 10.

My rankings obviously did not return to the same level as they were immediately before the penalty was applied. My pages had only ranked that well because of those backlinks I had built. My rankings after the recovery were similar to the rankings before the start of the experiment. I think this experiment clearly shows what negative SEO could/can do.

I know the penalty was algorithmically applied and not via a human reviewer. Whenever a human reviewer penalizes a site (called a manual action), you must submit a re-inclusion request after you've cleaned up the problems. I didn't have to do that. Once I had removed the backlinks, the rankings returned.

If your site gets penalized today, the chances are it is an algorithmic penalty like in my experiment. If you are unsure, login to the Google Search Console and check your messages. If Google took manual action against your site, it will have informed you.

In late 2016, Penguin became a real-time algorithm. This means that any Penguin penalty on your site can be overturned much more quickly (it used to take months). If you get penalized and you suspect it was Penguin, clean up the site (and/or backlinks) and wait for everything to be re-spidered. Penguin will re-evaluate your site, and rankings can return immediately. In 2019, fixing the issues can remove the penalty, which is great news.

So, what exactly happens when you point a bunch of poor backlinks at a web page?

Poor Backlinks

Here is a diagram showing poor backlinks to a page:

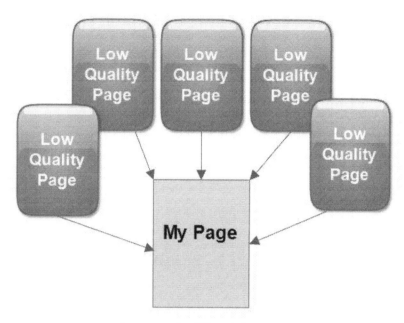

Search Rankings
DECREASE

In this model, poor backlinks may get your page penalized. The result will be a likely and sudden drop down the rankings.

Poor backlinks include:

- Backlinks on low-quality pages. These include any page that does not offer much value or has no real purpose other than to provide a backlink.

- Backlinks on Spammy websites. Any website in a bad neighborhood should be avoided.

- Backlinks on off-topic and irrelevant pages.

- Large numbers of backlinks all using identical, keyword-rich anchor text.

The point to take home from this is to concentrate on backlinks from good quality, authority sites, and I'll show you how.

The Type of Backlinks You Should Get

First and foremost, go for quality backlinks every time, not quantity.

For your site to become a real authority, it needs incoming links from other authority websites. Since Google Penguin, I no longer recommend using any type of automated link building tool.

Before you start link building, you need to get your page/site ready for quality links. I recommend you ask yourself this question:

Do you believe your page deserves to rank well based on the **quality of the content**?

If not, then trying to get backlinks and boost your authority may be a waste of time. Remember, poor content cannot hide in Google, so to rank high, and maintain those rankings, you need to have high-quality content on your site.

But...

Creating great content is not enough.

A lot of people will tell you:

"Build it and they will come!"

That sounds great, but, it doesn't work unless your site already has good authority. You can create the absolute best content on the planet, and publish new ground-breaking content on a weekly basis, but get no traffic. The reality is, you need to get some authority, and authority comes from backlinks. However, without high-quality content on your site that others can link to, you won't get other sites willing to link yours.

The fact is, you won't get traffic without great content, but great content won't get traffic without authority, which requires great content.

Got it?

If you prefer, you can think of it this way.

Great content + Authority = Traffic

Got it now?

Great!

Focus on Gaining Site Authority Because...

Authority will help all pages on a site rank better.

For a page to rank well on your site, you need to make sure it **deserves** to rank well (in terms of content and your site/author authority).

For example, you write a page on the "health benefits of vitamin D".

Do you think your page deserves to rank above medical sites where the authors are medical doctors and trained nutritionists? Google clearly wants to show the most useful and accurate information it can to its customers (web searchers), and that probably means choosing a medical authority site over yours (truer than ever after the Medic update in August 2018), even if your content happens to be better. You cannot compete on the authority level unless you are an authority on the "health benefits of vitamin D" yourself. That is the way it should be because we all want to find the best and most relevant information when we search online.

How might you gain authority in this area? Well, you could quite simply write articles on vitamin D and have them posted on numerous authority health sites, establishing yourself as an authority. With a link back to your site in the author bio box, your name and site will eventually become recognized as an authority, by association.

A better way to quickly boost authority is to create an epic piece of content on your site and invite links to your content from other authority sites. This may sound like an impossible strategy, but later in the book, I'll explain how you can get it to work.

To increase your authority, I would suggest you:

1. Only look to get links from authority sites that are relevant to your niche.
2. Try to be EVERYWHERE. Whenever someone is searching for information in your niche, make sure they constantly see your name or site cropping up.

No discussion about backlinks would be complete without talking about anchor text.

Backlink Anchor Text?

A lot has changed in the last few years.

You used to optimize a web page by including the main keyword phrase in the page title, URL, H1 header and several times in the content. We'd then point lots of backlinks to the page using the main keyword phrase as the anchor text of the backlink.

Google used to reward this type of inbound link "optimization".

Since Penguin, that type of optimization is more likely to get your page/site penalized.

If you check out the Google Webmaster Guidelines, you'll see this as an example of a "link scheme":

Links with optimized anchor text in articles or press releases distributed on other sites. For example:

There are many wedding rings on the market. If you want to have a wedding, you will have to pick the best ring. You will also need to buy flowers and a wedding dress.

Google has been cracking down on keyword-rich anchor text links for some time. This type of back-linking used to be the norm and no one thought anything of it. However, when we look at those links now, they really do look spammy, don't they?

But it's not just keyword-rich anchor text that causes you backlink problems. Google's tolerance for all types of link spamming has shifted dramatically over recent years.

With the release of the Disavow Tool in late 2012, Google effectively made webmasters responsible for ALL links that point to their website. That means natural links, links the website owners built themselves, and even those links built in negative SEO campaigns by competitors. As the webmaster, it was now YOUR job to deal with all links to your site, good and bad.

Back in 2013, a study was released showing this tolerance shift. The study showed that:

1. When the Penguin was first released, Google did not penalize sites even when 90% of incoming links were spammy.
2. By June 2012, Google would only tolerate 65% spammy links before issuing a penalty.
3. By October 2012, Google's would only tolerate 50% spammy links before issuing a penalty.

That was 6 - 7 years ago! How much further has Google's tolerance shifted? How low is this percentage now? It's anybody's guess, of course, but I recommend you avoid building any links that use keyword-rich anchor text.

Perhaps the good news is the fact that Google seems to be paying less attention to inbound anchor text and more attention to the topic of the page that is linking to yours.

For example, if your page is on "Health benefits of curcumin" and you got a link from a page about curcumin or turmeric, then that link would be a valuable one, irrespective of the anchor text used to link to your page.

With that in mind, I'd suggest trying to make your links look as authoritative as possible. Think about how academic literature links to another article. They'll use the title of the other article or the bare URL. They might also use the journal name and edition to help find the document. If you were writing a guest post for another website with the intention of linking back to your own site, instead of doing this:

> Curcumin has shown remarkable <u>anti-cancer properties</u> not only in stripping the cancer cells defenses to make them more visible to the body's natural immune system, but also in cell apoptosis.

...where **anti-cancer properties** is a phrase you are targeting, do something like this instead:

> Curcumin has shown remarkable anti-cancer properties not only in stripping the cancer cells defenses to make them more visible to the body's natural immune system, but in an article "<u>Curcumin initiates cancer cells death</u>", the author describes experimental results showing cell apoptosis occurring.

Do you see how natural this looks to a visitor? This looks like a recommendation to read more information on the topic. It looks like something to help the visitor rather than just something used to score points from a search engine. This type of link looks more authoritative, more natural to Google, AND it will be extremely valuable to your site.

If you submit articles to other sites for back-linking, then I recommend the following:

1. If you can, use contextual links like the one above, where the link uses the article title (or URL). The reader will be in no doubt what the destination page is all about.

2. Place a link to a homepage or social media channel in the author's resource box. Once again, no keyword-rich anchor text. Nofollow links in the author bio, as requested by Google. If you have a contextual link to your site in the article, leave that as dofollow, and link to a completely different site in the author bio box (e.g. social profile).

In 2019, we need fewer backlinks to rank well, but they need to be from relevant, quality web pages. Google gives MORE weight to quality links. Quality over quantity every time.

What About Existing Keyword-Rich Backlinks?

My suggestion, if you have lots of keyword-rich anchor text links to your site, is as follows:

1. Try to change the anchor text from keywords to page titles/URLs or site name.
2. For backlinks on poor quality websites, remove the links altogether. If you cannot get the links removed, consider disavowing them if they are on poor-quality sites.
3. Build more quality backlinks from authority websites that relate to your niche.

If you are choosing the anchor text, use page titles, headline text, site name or bare URLs. By building better links to your site, you may be able to over-power the poorer links.

4. If you have thousands or even hundreds of thousands of poor backlinks to your site, the disavow tool may be the best approach. In some cases, moving your site to a new domain may be the only option, but you'll then need to start building your site authority from scratch, so this really is a last resort.

A lot of website owners identify keyword phrases they want to rank for. If link quality and anchor text can easily cause you problems, how do you go about ranking for your chosen phrases?

Ranking for a Main Keyword Phrase

Several years ago, it was easy to identify a high-demand phrase we wanted to rank for and create a page (with backlinks) to rank for that phrase.

Effectively, each page focused on a single phrase. It's what Google now calls a doorway page strategy, and it no longer works.

As we've already seen, Penguin penalizes if it thinks you've over-optimized the on-page or off-page factors for a page. It is now very hard to optimize a page safely for a specific term.

You can see this if you do a Google search. Many of the pages that rank for any given term do not contain that term in the title. Some don't even include it on the page.

For example, if I search Google for the term **honey bees dying**, only six pages in the top 100 of Google include that exact phrase in the title. Most don't even include that phrase on the web page itself.

In 2019, pages don't rank well in Google because of the exact keyword phrases they include. Pages rank well because of the way they are themed around that exact keyword phrase.

In our honey bees dying example, pages will include the words and phrases that Google would expect to be in an authoritative article about honey bees dying. We covered all of this in the section on writing content around a theme, but it's good to mention it again to emphasize its importance.

If you want to rank for a specific phrase, this is the method I recommend:

1. Search Google for your keyword phrase.
2. Find the theme words used on pages that rank at the top.
3. Write an "epic" post on the topic and theme it with the relevant niche vocabulary. Make sure the page is unique and adds more value than the other pages in the top 10. In other words, make sure it deserves to be in the top 10.

4. Get backlinks to your new page from other authority sites in the niche.
5. Use internal linking to the new page with a variety of link text, including the target phrase.

That's it, my five-step process for ranking a page for a specific keyword phrase. As your site gets more authority, ranking will become easier for all your new content on the site.

The benefit of this strategy is that you'll also rank for hundreds of long-tail keyword phrases.

OK, so where can you look for backlinks?

The Best Backlinks

The very best backlinks you can get to your site are the ones you do not create yourself. These are backlinks from other sites that you did not personally request. In other words, another webmaster links to your site because they think it's worthy and offers value to their visitors. Obviously, you don't have any say in the anchor text that is used in these links. These are natural votes and are extremely powerful.

The **ideal backlinks** to your site would have the following properties:

1. The link is on a high authority site.
2. The page containing the link relates to the page it links to.
3. The page containing the link is a high-quality page, with high-quality content.
4. The link is in the body of the article (contextual).
5. There are very few outbound links (to other websites) on the same page.
6. The page your link appears on has a lot of human interaction (social shares, comments, etc.).
7. You do not control the backlink.

That's quite a list, and you may be thinking those kinds of links are impossible to get. I won´t lie to you, it takes work, but I do have a plan.

How to Get High Quality, Authoritative Backlinks

The best chance you have of getting those "Holy Grail" backlinks is to develop epic content that acts as **"Link Bait"** and then use email outreach to try to get links to it.

The fact is that creating link bait is not enough. You need to actively solicit links to it.

Getting quality backlinks is a two-step process.

1. Develop an epic piece of content.
2. Promote that Content and ask for links with an outreach campaign.

In step two, you need to promote that content to the types of people that **have the power to** link to it or promote it to their own audience. People who have a website in your niche with the power to link to yours, and those with a large social following, are called **influencer**

Think about this for a moment. Not everyone has a website, so not everyone has the power to add a link to yours. The average website visitor will be there to read your content but won't link to it. The average website visitor is not an **influencer.**

The fact is, if people are not linking to your content, you either:

- Don't have good enough (or the right) content, and/or
- You haven't promoted it to the right people.

That is what we are going to look at in this section of the book. Of course, you should be developing content that your visitors love and want to share with others via their social media channels, but social media links don't really help long-term search engine rankings.

Effective link bait and promotion strategies

As part of your content development strategy for your site, I am suggesting two different types of content for your site.

1. Great content for the average visitor. The stuff they'll want to share on social media, and comment upon.

2. **Link Bait** specifically for **influencers.** You'll then contact the influencers and ask for the link.

The Link Bait you create for your niche's influencers is not necessarily the type of content your average visitor will want to read. However, Link Bait can attract a lot of high-profile links, if done properly. Link Bait allows you develop pages on your site with high page authority, which in turn will increase your overall domain authority.

As you create more Link Bait and promote it to the influencers, your website will increase in domain authority with each new backlink. As domain authority increases, all pages on that domain will rank more easily. If there is a specific page you want to boost in the search engines, you can add a single keyword-rich anchor text link to that page, from the Link Bait post.

Remember, with increased domain authority, comes increased ability to rank all pages on the site.

What Makes Good Link Bait?

When developing ideas for Link Bait, you need to consider the influencers. What are they already linking to? What are their interests? What are they writing about on their blog? How can you get them to react emotionally to something?

Let's look at a quick example.

I find an influencer in my niche that has written a controversial article on something. Their post got a lot of feedback, both positive and negative. The influencer himself received a lot of personal criticism. I could write a Link Bait post on my site that agrees and supports his article (assuming I do of course). If I then send him the details of the post, do you think he would share it? Link to it? Probably. It would help vindicate his position and make him look good.

Any content you write that makes an influencer look good is more likely to get a link from that influencer.

But it's only one link, right?

Remember quality over quantity!

Of course, you can use the same principle to write content that makes a lot of influencers look good.

If I created a page that listed the top 50 websites that were helping to save the bees, do you think that any of those 50 websites might link back to my page?

Probably. Why wouldn't they?

If my site was of high quality, then my page is making them look good. They would want to share my page (social and/or link) with their audience. If I offered a "Top 50 #SaveTheBees" badge that they could post on their own site, some might even use that. Of course, the badge would link back to the site that awarded the badge (mine). Remember the process:

1. Create Link Bait that makes influencers look good.

2. Reach out the influencers to let them know the content exists.

Formats of Successful Link Bait

There are several different types of Link Bait you can create. With any type of Link Bait, the number one rule is:

Choose a topic that influencers care about, and if possible, make the influencer look good! Of course, you can make an influencer look good in different ways:

1. Stroke their ego.

2. Give them something that they will want to share with their readers because it makes them look good. It could just be awesome content that tells the influencer's tribe that he/she has a finger on the pulse. Or maybe an exclusive, "you heard it

here first" type of post.

IMPORTANT: If you can create content that makes an influencer look awesome in front of his/her audience, then you have already won the battle. They will more than likely link to you. This whole strategy for backlinking relies on it.

With that in mind, let's review some of the best formats for Link Bait.

Comprehensive List Posts

List posts are very popular on some of the most authoritative sites on the web:

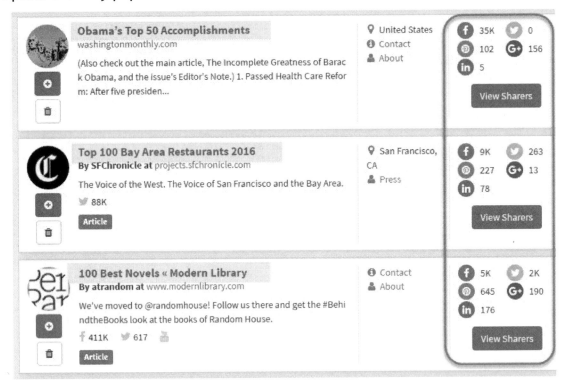

You can see the title on the left, and the number of social shares on the right.

That top article has been shared more than 35,000 times on Facebook!

The third article is simply a list of books but has been shared over 5,000 times on Facebook.

When you create a list post, it needs to be comprehensive. You want people to arrive on your post and just think "Wow". List posts are one of the most shareable types of post.

You can get ideas for this type of post by using a special type of search in Google. Here is an example:

In this Google search, I am asking Google to return all pages that include the phrase diet, but also have the phrase 10 tips, 11 tips, 12 tips, etc., all the way up to 500 tips. That ".." between the numbers specifies a range.

By being creative, you can find a lot of great content ideas using number ranges together with words like tips & top. You can also force Google to only show those pages where the search term is in the title, using the **intitle** tag, like this:

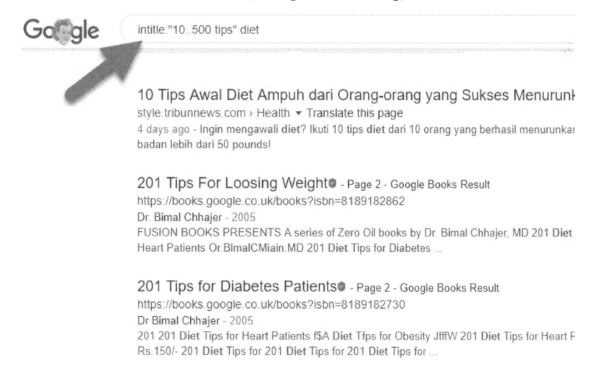

Guides

Create in-depth guides on topics that are of interest to your influencers, and you could be onto a winner. These guides should be comprehensive. I've seen some that are several thousand words long. Again, you want influencers to arrive at your guide and think "Wow". Think in terms of creating the ultimate or definitive guide to a topic your influencers care about.

You may even want to call it "The ultimate guide to …". Here are a few I found. Check out the share data:

To get ideas for guides in your niche, try a Google search for something like
"ultimate guide" KEYWORD

Here is an example:

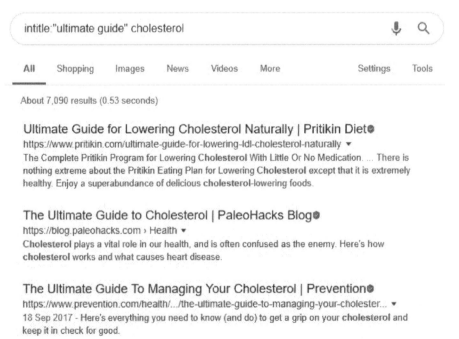

It's worth checking out a few "ultimate guides" in your own niches. They'll give you ideas but remember to create yours around topics that interest your niche influencers.

Experts Posts

I am sure you have seen this type of post.

> ### The Top 100 SEO Experts of 2018, Back by Data (110 Free SEO ...
> https://www.thestorytellermarketer.com/seo/experts/ ▾
> 24 Feb 2018 - Click to read a data-backed list of the top 100 SEO experts to follow to help you start and grow your business, with 110 SEO resources from the ...

> ### 10 Forward-Thinking SEO Experts You Need to Follow | Marketing ...
> https://marketinginsidergroup.com/.../10-forward-thinking-seo-experts-need-follow/ ▾
> 14 Aug 2017 - If you want to survive digital marketing and put your content in front of a bigger audience, follow these top SEO experts on social media.

> ### 47 Experts on the Top SEO Trends That Will Matter in 2018
> https://www.searchenginejournal.com › SEO ▾
> 14 Dec 2017 - Want to up your SEO game and be more successful in 2018? Here are the key ... Here's what you need to know, according to 47 SEO experts.

> ### 140 of Today's Top SEO Experts to Follow - SEO 101
> https://www.searchenginejournal.com › Beginner's Guide to SEO ▾
> 27 Dec 2017 - Want to learn more about search engine optimization? Then you should learn from the top SEO experts. Here are 140 brilliant ones to follow.

This type of post leverages other people's expertise and time, to create fantastic Link Bait for your site. There are two different types of expert post I want to suggest you think about.

Top Expert Posts

This type of post is a roundup of all the experts you think are worth talking about in your post,

e.g.

> "Top 25 Alternative Health Experts You Should Be Following".

For this type of post, you simply need to write a paragraph or two about each expert. Include information like who they are, what they did to get your recommendation, their website, and a photo if you can get one. Also, consider including their Twitter and Facebook contact details.

Repeat for all influencers.

This type of article is one where you would notify the influencers after it is published, letting them know that they made your list. Also, ask them if it is OK to include their photo and social channel links. The fact that they made a list is confirmation of their status, something they may want to link to or share with their audience.

I don't find this type of post as successful as it used to be. For a higher success rate, consider the next option.

Top Expert Opinion Posts

For this type of post, you'll send an email out to the experts, asking them for their opinion on something.

e.g.

"Top 50 Alternative Health Experts Give You Their Thoughts on Cholesterol"

Your first task is to identify the influencers in your niche and decide what it is that interests them. What do they write about, what do they share, what do they link to. Ultimately you are going to want them to do just that to your post. Do you think they would be happy to give you their opinion about your chosen topic? What is in it for them?

Note that the more interest or controversy there is in a topic, the more exposure participating experts could have after your article is published. That is an incentive for those experts to be included, and that is an incentive for them to share your content with their audience.

When you have the topic, do a little due diligence. Has the topic been done before? How many influencers were in those other articles? Can you include more? Or better influencers? If not, then maybe you need to change your topic a little to give you a unique angle. Find a topic and enough influencers to approach so that your expert opinion post is the best out there.

Send out an email to as many influencers in your niche that you can find, asking them if they'd like to be involved in your study. If they agree, send them the question.

Compile answers into a post. Include a biography of each influencer surveyed together with their answer.

At the end of the post, summarize the results and publish the study.

You can now reach out to the influencers involved in the study and send them the link. You don't even need to ask them to link to it, as most will anyway. It makes them look good to have been involved in the study.

I'd recommend you search Google for some opinion posts like this. See how other websites have structured their posts, and what kind of information they include about the contributors.

Search Google for "experts roundup" to get some ideas.

Interviews

In the expert roundup suggestion, the idea was to get the opinion from lots of influencers and hopefully get links from most of them. An expert interview is different because you'll only be talking with one influencer. One influencer will usually only provide one link, so why bother?

True, it's a lot of work. However, the benefits of this type of post are a little different. You hopefully:

1. Will get a link from a top influencer in your niche.
2. Will have increased credibility because you talked with the top influencer.
3. Will have started to build a long-term relationship with the influencer, and they will appreciate that you chose them above all others for the interview.
4. Will have multiple marketing opportunities (see below).

The first thing you'll need to do is get on the influencer's radar. The easiest way to do this is to sign up for their newsletter and follow them on social media. Once you've done that, comment on their blog. Really add to the discussion on the post you are commenting on so that your comment gets approved. When an opportunity arises, add a comment that tries to bring the influencer back into the conversation. Maybe a "how did you find out...", or "do you think that maybe..".

If they reply to your comment, then answer their comment. Depending on how you think it is going, you may now want to use their contact form to introduce yourself. Tell them how interested you are in an aspect of their work/expertise.

If they reply, ask them if they would be interested in a short interview about your chosen topic (and one that they are an expert in). Let them know that you chose them above all others because... Tell them that you will send the questions ahead of time and that the interview can be email based, or Skype (audio or video), at their convenience. Tell them where and when you intend to publish the interview.

Before you do an interview, make sure you do your research. That is all part of the work in preparing the questions to send to the influencer. Make sure the questions are of interest to the influencer, and that they have expressed their opinions online about the topics of conversation. You want them to be passionate about the interview and getting their ideas across.

With everything agreed, you'll then conduct your interview.

If it is an audio interview, post the audio on your site with a transcript of the interview below it. The transcript will act as search engine bait, but apart from that, a lot of visitors prefer to read this type of thing rather than listen to it.

You can also upload audio interviews to audio sharing sites. Search Google for **audio**

upload and look for opportunities where you can create a backlink to your site. You can create a very natural backlink on this type of audio sharing site by saying something like "Prefer a transcript? Read the full interview on…" and then link directly to your transcript page using the title of that page as the anchor text. Alternatively, you could upload the first few minutes of the interview on these audio sharing sites, and link to the full interview on your site.

If the interview is a video, upload the video to YouTube, and other video upload sites. Create a post on your own site and embed the YouTube video. Include the transcript of the video (for the same reasons as above) on your site. In the YouTube description of the video, add the URL where people can "read the transcript".

Finally, remember to give the interviewed influencer the page URL so that they can find the interview on your site. They will more than likely link to it, and possibly tell their own visitors/mailing list about the interview too. It's a great way of attracting a powerful backlink from an authority site in your niche. Attracted links are links you have no control over, and remember, these are the most powerful and natural links a website can get. These are the links that will increase domain authority and allow the other pages on your site to rank more easily.

Infographics

Infographics are graphical representations of complex topics and data. They are favorites for sharing on social channels, e.g. Pinterest, but often get re-posted on other sites, so you can get a backlink.

If you can create a great looking infographic that is of interest to your influencers, you may be able to get them to link to it or post it on their own website. Infographics often contain a list of resource websites underneath, and these links can point to influencers. Contact them and tell them about it. They may feel their ego sufficiently stroked to offer you a link, or post your infographic on their site ;)

A great tip from Brian Dean of Backlinko is to offer to write a unique introduction to the infographic for each influencer. If they agree, then send them the introduction and infographic. Something they can copy and paste would be ideal. Then there are no real barriers for them posting your introduction, infographic, and link back to your site, on theirs.

When you post the infographic on your own site, you can include the HTML code for other webmasters to copy and paste onto their own sites. This will display the infographic on their site, with a small link back to your own page:

Copy/paste the code below to share this image on your site or blog!

```
<div align="center"><a href="http://www.getnp.com"><img
src="http://www.transparentcorp.com/research/images/beta-brain-wave-infographic.jpg"
width="800" height="3837" /></a><br>Source: <a
href="http://www.transparentcorp.com/research/beta-brain-waves.php">Beta Brain Waves - An
Infographic</a></div>
```

Create Controversy

Controversial posts are always popular. When people are controversial, they usually evoke a strong response. I cannot tell you how to be controversial in your own niche, but I would just say, make your controversy factual. Making something up just to be controversial won't work, and it will annoy your visitors too.

A while ago, there was lots of information coming out about how good intermittent fasting was for losing weight and improving health in general. Everyone was jumping on the bandwagon. One website went against the grain with a headline along the lines of "Intermittent Fasting Is Bad for Women". It caused quite a stir. The important point about this controversy was that it was factual.

The article went on to explain that certain types of women developed problems during intermittent fasting (typically those with low body fat). This controversy resulted in a lot of natural backlinks as people debated it on blogs and forums. Of course, it also brought in a lot of extra traffic for the webmaster.

Scripts & Tools

Scripts & tools that people will bookmark and share with others make great link bait.

Webmasters will always link to useful tools, especially if they are free. The screenshot shows one example of a tool that searches for the nutritional information of food.

Another good example is a currency converter script, where you can convert one currency to another.

A time zone converter could prove popular too.

What about a cholesterol conversion tool, converting between the two popular units for cholesterol - mg/dl and mmol/L.

Any tool you can create, or have created for you, and that people find useful, will inevitably attract links from other websites as well as through social sharing.

Outreach – The Best Way to Get Links

If your content is targeting links from multiple influencers in your niche, the best way to get those influencers to link to your content will be with email outreach.

You need to reach out to the influencers. You need to send them an email and try to get them interested in your Link Bait. If you have chosen your topic well, this should be relatively easy to do because it is a topic that they are interested in, and maybe even makes them look amazing. Let's look at email outreach.

Email Outreach

Although time-consuming, email outreach is the very best way to get high quality, white hat links that will help your site rank higher in the SERPs. The entire process can be carried out manually, but you need to track everything. Who you sent an email to and when. Did they reply? When? What did they say? Do you need to follow up with them? When? One advantage of using outreach tools is that this is all done for you. I'll mention the outreach tool I use in a minute, but first, I want you to understand the process.

The Process

The first step in any outreach program is to define your goals. What is it you want to achieve? Since you are probably using outreach to get links to your content, then that question is largely answered, as is the second step. Identify targets.

If you've created a piece of content that targets specific influencers, then you have your goal and targets mapped out already. The next step is to email the influencers with your pitch. This can be daunting, to begin with, but the rewards far outweigh any embarrassment you may feel.

What you say to these influencers will depend on what you want from them, or the content you are promoting. However, here are some tips:

1. In the subject line of the email, try to summarize your pitch in a short sentence. E.g. A question about your malt whiskey roundup.
2. Write the subject in normal case to appear more informal, and not "pushy" (a tip by Neil Patel).
3. Start the email by using their full name.
4. Explain who you are, and why you are important to the influencer. Show your credibility. E.g. My name is Jack Daniels, and I own a whiskey company.
5. The first email should be a short initial pitch to gauge interest.
6. Show proof that you have been reading their articles.
7. Explain how this pitch is mutually beneficial to you both.
8. Provide different options for the influencer to contact you. E.g. email, phone, Skype, etc.

If you are really stuck for what you need to say, search Google for **outreach templates**.

Google   outreach templates

All   Images   Shopping   News   Videos   More   Settings   Tools

About 17,000,000 results (0.56 seconds)

9 Link Building Email Outreach Templates That Actually Work
https://blog.hubspot.com/marketing/link-building-email-templates ▾
28 Apr 2017 - I've created nine different templates for killer outreach emails that you can borrow and adapt for your own link building strategy.

16 Email Outreach Templates for Every Situation - Mailshake Blog
https://blog.mailshake.com/outreach-templates/ ▾
25 Sep 2017 - 16 Email Outreach Templates for Every Situation. Land any guest post with this email template. Claim easy backlinks by fixing broken links. The perfect outreach template for resource page link building. More easy links: The "Guestographic" method. Promote your blog before you even publish it. Post-publish promotion ...

28 Awesome Email Outreach Templates That Are Yours To Steal
fuzeseo.co/28-awesome-email-outreach-templates/ ▾
11 Oct 2017 - Email outreach can build backlinks, generate leads and more but getting a response can be tough. These email templates will get you ...
COLD AND WARM EMAIL ... · CUSTOMER ... · GENERATING ...

The Ultimate List of 34 Guest Post Outreach & Email Marketing Scripts ...
https://ninjaoutreach.com/the-ultimate-guide-to-outreach-scripts/ ▾
Blog post promotion template by Groove What Makes It GreatOne thing I love about Alex's messages is that they always include an easy click to tweet. I don'

11 Outstanding Influencer Outreach Email Templates - NinjaOutreach
https://ninjaoutreach.com/influencer-outreach-email-templates/ ▾
9 Oct 2017 - Having the right outreach email can make or break your influencer campaign. Here are 11 outstanding influencer outreach email templates.

Link Building Outreach: 6 Email Templates to Build Solid Backlinks
https://blog.monitorbacklinks.com/seo/link-building-outreach/ ▾
17 May 2018 - Use these proven link building outreach strategies and email templates to fire off irresistible emails that land high-quality backlinks!

Email Outreach Tips: +22 Link Building Email Templates - Kaiserthesage
https://kaiserthesage.com/outreach-templates/ ▾
26 Jun 2017 - Below are some of the easy-to-personalize outreach email templates we've used in the past. Feel free to test and improve them. Pro Tip: ...

You will find a lot of free outreach templates that you can use and modify for just about any use, including:

- Guest posting
- Broken links
- Resource page links
- Interviews
- podcast guest
- Infographics (Guestographics)
- Cold calling email

- Product review
- Brand mentions

To track your emails and responses, (if you are tracking manually) I recommend you use a spreadsheet that has columns for:

1. Influencer
2. Email
3. URL
4. Date Contacted
5. Email template used
6. Date Reply Received.
7. Follow Up #1
8. Follow Up #2
9. Follow Up #3

There may be other bits of data you want to record as well.

If you don't get a reply after about a week, I'd recommend sending a follow-up email asking if they received it and including the short pitch again.

You may want to follow this up a third time before giving up on that influencer.

You can find some templates for follow up email by searching Google:

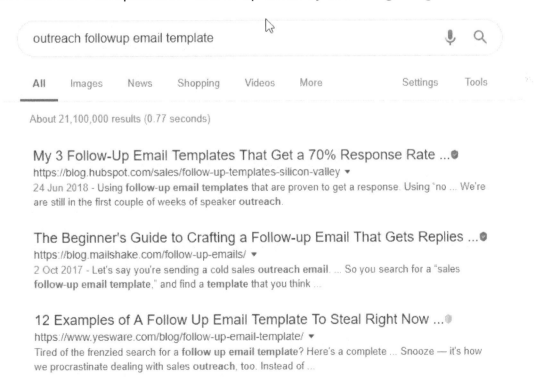

As you can see, email outreach can be time-consuming. Especially all the tracking of who you sent an email to, when, and what that email was. To make things easier, there are some tools available that can do all of the tracking for you and remind you when and what you need to send. The tool I use is called Ninja Outreach.

Automation with Ninja Outreach

Ninja Outreach gives you the tools to:

- Find Influencers and their contact information.
- Find the social channels of those influencers.
- Choose topics for your Link Bait.
- Carry out your email outreach to secure the backlinks or promote products. The template driven system makes it easy to send personalized emails to influencers. Ninja Outreach keeps track of who you've written to, replies you've received, etc.
- The whole process can be largely automated

As an all in one solution, I find it's a great tool. There's plenty of information on their website, plus, at the time of writing, an option to try it for free. You can find out more information here:

https://ezseonews.com/ninjaoutreach

Other White Hat Link Building Techniques that Work

Broken Link Building

Broken link building is actually one of the least effort backlinking strategies that actually works. Essentially you look for broken links (related to your own site) on other websites. You then contact the owner to tell them about it, offering your own link as a replacement.

As an example, let's consider a website on health and nutrition. If I owned that site, I'd go out looking for websites that had broken links to any articles on health or nutrition.

Let's say I find a page about the importance of vitamin A for good eye health, and one of the links on that page goes to a 404 Error - Page Not Found. I would contact the webmaster of the nutrition site, informing them that the link went to a 404 error, and tell them I have a page on the same topic if they need a good replacement source to link out to. Obviously, I would include my URL for consideration.

The advantage of this type of link is that it's often on an aged page, possibly on an authority site. A backlink from this type of site would be a good one. It's added by the other webmaster and gives you no control over the link text.

Let's see how you would go about finding broken links on related pages.

There are a number of tricks we can use.

The first is to search Google for resource/links pages in your niche using a "footprint". Here are a few that work well. Just swap out KEYWORD for a phrase that relates to your niche/web page:

"KEYWORD links"
"KEYWORD resources"
"KEYWORD web links"
inurl:links "KEYWORD"

That last one is an interesting search phrase as it looks for web pages that include the word "links" in the URL and are about your keyword. Here is an example search for that "footprint":

Google   inurl:links "juicing for health" 🎤 🔍

All   Images   Videos   News   Shopping   More   Settings   Tools

About 59 results (0.46 seconds)

Links – Juicing with Jeremy
https://jgjuice.wordpress.com/links/ ▾
Juicing Vegetables Facebook Page Juicing Recipes Juicer Buyers' Guide PBS Juicing | Need to Know
Daily Juice - Austin **Juicing for Health** - Facebook Thug ...

Juicer Recipes Now » Healthy Links
juicerrecipesnow.com/healthy-links/ ▾
Juicing for Health– This is one of my favorite juicing websites created by Sara, from Kuala Lumpur,
Malaysia. Contains a lot of information about fruits and ...

Related Links to Healthy Living Ideas - Juicer Reviews and Recipes
https://www.juicer-reviews-and-recipes.com/related-links.html ▾
See how **Juicing for Health** can prevent chronic diseases and promote good health. The Superfood-
Guru puts the facts about superfoods and nutrition on the ...

home remedies: home remedies links
gharremedy.blogspot.com/2015/10/home-remedies-links.html ▾
4 Oct 2015 - http://**juicing-for-health**.com/prevent-varicose-veins.html http://geethaachalrecipe.
blogspot.ca/2015/10/how-to-clean-silver-vessels-pooja-items.

See how the top results are clearly links pages about "juicing for health"?

TIP: You could also email a webmaster and ask if they'd include your site on their "resource" page, even if there were no broken links.

Using footprints like this offers the quickest way of finding broken link opportunities. You first find the links pages and then check them out to see if any links are broken.

Now, before you think you need to go through every link on a page and manually check if it's broken, relax. There is a free Google Chrome extension called **Check My Links**. Search the Google Chrome store for the plugin and install it.

Once installed, you'll have a button in the toolbar for the extension. Now all you need to do is visit the page you want to check for broken links and click the extension button. You'll get a badge in the top right of the screen, giving you a breakdown of the links on the page:

I can see from this badge that there are five invalid links. Scrolling down the page, the links are color coded for easy identification:

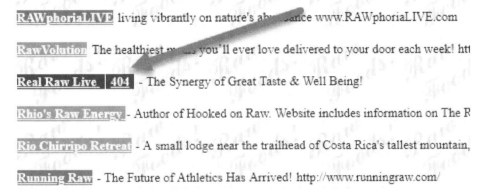

You can see how easy it is to spot the broken links. If I had a good page on raw food, I'd be writing to this webmaster about swapping out that link with my own.

But what if my health site did not have a page on raw food?

The answer is simple. I'd create one, providing it was viable of course.

My first step would be to head off to the Way Back Machine:

http://archive.org/web/

The Way Back Machine might allow you to check out the expired page if it was archived.

In this case, although that raw food page no longer exists, the Way Back Machine has cached copies of most pages, of most websites. Here is what that page looked like when it was live:

This archived page will give me some ideas for my own page before I contact the webmaster about the broken link. Can I spot anything that originally drew the linker to this page?

At the end of the day, if that webmaster ignores me, or just deletes the broken link without using mine, I still have a great new piece of content on my own site which I can then use for outreach from other influencers.

The easiest broken backlinks to find are on this type of resource page. I know a lot of SEOs will tell you that links on link resource pages are a waste of time, but that simply is not true. Start judging ALL backlink opportunities by the quality of the page (and site) your link will appear on, rather than the type of page.

To find out if the page is of value to you, ask the following five questions:

1. Is the page good quality?
2. Does the page only link to sites within a very narrow niche topic?
3. Does the page only link to quality sites?
4. Is the page genuinely useful to visitors of that site?
5. Is the page part of a quality website that has some domain authority?

If these guidelines apply, then the page is a good one for your backlink(s).

Broken backlink building is a good way to get quality backlinks on aged, authority pages in your niche.

The only other recommended way of getting backlinks with SEO benefits is guest posting (also called guest blogging).

Guest Posting

Guest posting works like this:

There are sites out there that are willing to publish articles from authority bloggers in the niche. You write a piece of content and submit it to these sites. If they like your article, they will post it on their website.

When you submit your guest article, you include a resource box with a link back to your website. You will need to check the terms and conditions of the sites you are writing for to see whether it's possible to include links within the body of the article. If you can do that, then make sure your links look authoritative, like we discussed earlier. Remember this?

> Curcumin has shown remarkable <u>anti-cancer properties</u> not only in stripping the cancer cells defenses to make them more visible to the body's natural immune system, but also in cell apoptosis.

That looks a lot spammier than this example:

> Curcumin has shown remarkable anti-cancer properties not only in stripping the cancer cells defenses to make them more visible to the body's natural immune system, but in an article "<u>Curcumin initiates cancer cells death</u>", the author describes experimental results showing cell apoptosis occurring.

The second one is also more Google-friendly as it is not using keyword anchor text. Instead, it uses the title of the article it links to, like a real reference. This link looks natural.

If you can use a contextual link in the article, don't link to the same site in your author bio box. Instead, use that to link to your social media profile. Remember that Google expects author bio boxes to use the nofollow tag, and that is especially important if you are linking to your own website from the bio box. If you are linking to your social profile, that can be left as dofollow.

Finding Guest Blogs

The way most people find guest blogging opportunities is to use a search string in Google:

"write for us" + KEYWORD

KEYWORD is obviously your main niche word or phrase.

e.g. "write for us" + health

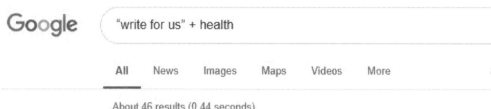

This will return all the websites that have the phrase "Write for Us" and are related to the health industry.

However, this type of site is not usually very high quality, and everyone looking for guest posting opportunities will find the same sites.

A better method is to identify high profile guest bloggers in your industry and see where they are posting their content. Try contacting some of the sites that are accepting their content and see if they'd like to review some of yours.

If you find some high-quality sites that do accept your content, bookmark them. Not only can you get backlinks, but you'll also get to post your photo and site URL, which further boosts your personal authority in the niche.

OK, we've looked at the very best way to get high-quality backlinks. The number one method is the link bait and outreach, and that is the method I recommend you use for most of your backlinking campaigns. Identify topics that influencers care about and write link bait posts followed by email outreach. This is how all the top authority sites generate backlinks.

To supplement your backlinks, broken link building is also good. To a lesser extent, guest blogging.

A discussion about backlinking would not be complete without mentioning some of the older ways we built links. Many are still taught today, even though they don't work very well. Some can still be used today, with care.

Gray & Black-Hat "Traditional" Back-linking

A lot of the backlinking methods we used a few years ago are no longer effective. We'll go over the more popular methods here, and I'll tell you my thoughts on their use today.

If you simply want to get a few links to kick-start a new site and cannot be bothered with link bait and outreach, this is what I recommend you try.

Create a high-quality, text-based article and repurpose it:

1. Try to get the article accepted as a guest post on an authority site in your niche.
2. Re-write it a little (so it is not identical to the guest post), add images, and create a PDF version for submission to one or two of the more popular PDF sharing sites.
3. Create a slideshow presentation of the main points of the article to upload to sites like Slideshare.net.
4. Create an infographic of the main 6 or 7 points.
5. Create a video using the contents of the article. In its most basic form, this can be the slideshow presentation with a voice-over.

From doing one piece of research, you now have several different media types to use for backlinks. Let's look at the types of places you can submit these documents to.

NOTE: What follows are the typical backlink resources recommended by most SEO courses and books. I'll give you my thoughts on each of them, and how to use them if they are useful. If you do go ahead with any of these, I really do suggest you ignore the popular advice to use keyword rich anchor text in your backlinks. Stick with page titles, site name or bare URLs, and try to insert the link so that it looks natural.

Article Directories

In 2019, Article directories are not worth considering for backlinks. I recommend you avoid them altogether. Instead, search out sites that accept guest posts and offer them exclusive rights to publish your articles.

Forum Participation

In the past, forums have been heavily spammed by webmasters looking for easy link opportunities.

There are two obvious ways to get links from a forum. The first way is by adding your site URL to your forum profile. This backlink is called a forum profile link. Nothing good can come from this type of backlink, so avoid them at all costs.

If you do get legitimately involved in a forum, fill out your profile, but fill it out completely so your forum profile page has a lot more information on it than just a website link.

If you have 1 or 2 forum profile links in your backlink profile, Google won't mind, especially if these pages are filled out with great information. If, however, you use an automated software tool to create 500, 5000 or even 50,000 forum profile links, get your flak jacket on. You're going down!

The second link opportunity on forums is within the forum posts themselves.

Get involved in the forum discussions and help people. Pop in and contribute every now and again. As you get well known on the forum, you will be allowed to post the odd link to your site, if it helps people. However, this type of link is a huge amount of work, often for 1 or 2 links (possibly nofollow). In my opinion, it's more work than Link Bait and outreach.

YouTube & Other Video Sites

Be aware that links in YouTube descriptions are nofollow, so they won't help with search engine ranking. Videos are more a way to brand yourself and build an audience on the YouTube platform.

Creating videos that offer valuable information in your niche is a great way to increase authority and "social proof" (especially when your photo or brand image appears in the video).

Videos that you create do not need to be 10 or 15 minutes long. You can easily create short two- or three-minute videos that discuss issues briefly in your niche. Video descriptions can be quite long, and they can include a (nofollow) link back to your site. Popular videos can bring you traffic.

YouTube allows you to create a video channel, which lists all your videos in one place. Your YouTube profile can even have a link back to your site (where you can post the video and provide a transcript underneath). If someone likes one of your videos, they can check out your channel to see what other videos you've created. They may even follow you on social media, post your videos to their own social networks, and/or visit your website.

Twitter

You can use Twitter to include a brand photo and link back to your main site. As you add tweets, your photo goes through the Twitter system and ends up again in front of people that have subscribed to your twitter feed. Even if you don't have many followers, your twitter page will have links back to your main site, which adds further authority to your persona. Twitter links won't help you rank in the search engines, though.

Facebook Page

Another way that you can increase your authority is by setting up a Facebook page for your site or your business.

Facebook only allows you to have a single Facebook account. One of the biggest concerns I hear from my students is that they don't always want their friends and/or family to be aware of their business posts on Facebook. Don't worry. If you set up a Facebook page for your website, it is totally separate from your personal profile account. You need a personal Facebook account to set up a Facebook page, but that's as far as the association goes. You can post specifically to your website Facebook page, and none of your friends or followers will even know it exists unless you tell them about it.

You can have multiple Facebook pages if you like, promoting different websites or products. When you log into Facebook, you will see direct links to your pages in the side column of your personal Facebook account, but these are not visible to your followers.

Web 2.0 "Blogs"

Several SEO "experts" still recommend setting up Web 2.0 blogs and then using them to link to your money site. I recommend you don't. Google doesn't like it, and believe it or not, you are leaving footprints that Google can follow. If you try to use Web 2.0 blogs for backlinks, you will get found out, and penalized.

Of course, it is also worth considering the huge amount of work involved in setting up a blog for backlinks. To make the blog truly useful it needs high quality, unique content. That's a lot of work. Most SEOs that use blog networks use spun articles to generate content. This is something that Google can easily spot, so my advice is to stay clear of this technique.

RSS Feeds

If you use WordPress to build your site, then you already have an RSS feed for it. An RSS feed contains all the most recent posts in a single file. You also get to define how many posts show in the feed from within the WordPress Dashboard.

You can find the feed by adding "/feed" to the end of your URL (without the quotes obviously).

For example:

https://ezseonews.com/feed/

Once you have your feed URL, you can then submit that feed to several different RSS Feed websites.

Every time you add new content to your site, the feed updates on these sites automatically, and you get a link back to the posts listed in the feed.

This type of link does not help improve search engine rankings for the pages that are linked to. On the contrary, if you submit to a lot of these sites, Google will probably just see you as a link spammer.

I would recommend submitting your feed to only one or two of the highest authority RSS directories that you can find. The reason for submitting the feed is not for the backlinks (or ranking). It's to help new content get indexed quicker.

I'd also recommend that you set up your feed to only display excerpts (and a maximum of 10 posts). This should keep you safe from the spammers who try to scrape content by stripping entire posts out of RSS feeds.

Site Directories

Getting your site listed in directories is one of the oldest forms of back-linking. However, directory listings don't give much (if any) of a ranking boost.

There are software programs that can submit your site to multiple directories, but I recommend you stay clear. Site directories will not help your rankings in the search engine. Only submit to a site directory if there is another reason for doing so. i.e. you would even if search engines did not exist. The only type of site directory I would consider is if I found one specifically about my niche.

PDF Distribution

You can distribute PDF files, which contain links to your website, to several PDF distribution sites. Again, each site you distribute the PDF file to can include your profile picture and link back to your own site. To create PDFs, you can use existing content or simply write new content for the file.

Microsoft Word or the free OpenOffice suite, both have built-in features to convert text documents into PDF format.

One of the best-known examples of a site that you can upload PDF documents to is:

https://www.scribd.com/

You can find a lot of websites that accept PDF submissions by searching Google for "submit eBooks" or "submit PDF".

Again, like everything else, look for quality sites and think less about quantity.

Blog Commenting

Blog commenting is easy. Go to a blog post related to your own niche and leave a comment with a link back to your own site (most comment forms have a URL field).

Blog commenting has been heavily abused by spammers over the years and gets a lot of bad press because of that. It's not something that will help your search rankings, so only leave comments if you would anyway, even if search engines did not exist. I personally would only leave a comment on a heavily trafficked page, as that can bring traffic from that page's visitors.

To leave useful comments:

1. Read the article you are commenting on and read other people's comments.
2. Add a comment that interacts with the original author, or another commenter. The comment should add to the conversation on that page. Add something that the webmaster will want to approve.
3. When adding a comment, you'll have fields for "your name" and "website URL". If there is no website field, don't waste time leaving a comment unless you

really want to. In the name field, add your real name (or the pen name you use on your site), either first or full name is fine. Never add a keyword phrase in the name field. In the URL field, enter your website homepage URL.

4. Note that many webmasters will delete comments with URLs in the body. Never add links to the body of your comment, unless there is a good reason for doing so, i.e. answering someone's question.

Backlinks to Backlinks

Whenever you build a site you should be tracking a lot of information so that you can fine tune things when necessary. One of the most important things to track is the backlinks pointing to your website. I would suggest you login to the Google Search Console at least once every couple of months to check what links Google is reporting there. If there are any spammy links, on poor quality pages, consider disavowing those links. See later for detail on how to do this.

But what about those links that are good?

One thing that is very common in SEO is the process of backlinking backlinks. This is also called "link reinforcement" and can give more power to the pages linking to your site. It's the process of building links to the pages that link to your pages.

Many webmasters make a critical mistake with this strategy. They don't worry about the quality of the backlinks they create. I mean it's not their site, right? Instead, they blast thousands of profile links, social bookmarks, spun articles, etc. at these backlinks to boost them. It doesn't work.

Most webmasters who use this strategy assume that their site is safe since these spammy links DO NOT point directly at their own site. They think the site they are linking to acts as a buffer, protecting their own sites from a penalty. That may have been the case before negative SEO (and the Disavow tool) became a reality, it's not anymore.

Google hates linking schemes, and pyramid systems like this are no exception. Is it too far-fetched to think that the negative SEO we saw earlier could render this type of link pyramid not only useless but also harmful to your site?

I don't recommend you engage in backlinking backlinks. Instead, concentrate on building new high-quality links to your own pages, through Link Bait and broken links (and guest posting). It's no more work, and you'll end up with better links and authority naturally.

So how do we deal with bad links pointing at our own pages?

The Disavow Tool - How to Fix Bad Links to Your Site

Several years ago, webmasters were not held responsible for the links pointing at their pages. Negative SEO just did not work, and Google themselves told us that bad links could not hurt a site's rankings.

But things have changed.

Poor quality links pointing at your web pages *can* now hurt your rankings. However, because of the whole negative SEO angle, Google needed to provide a system to make webmasters truly accountable for the links to their sites, whether they had created them or not. In other words, if a website became the target of a negative SEO campaign, Google wanted the webmaster to fix it, and so the Disavow tool was born.

The Disavow tool allows webmasters to report bad links pointing to their sites, in the hope that Google will not count them as part of that site's backlink profile.

Therefore, if a competitor points a lot of spammy links at your site to try to get it penalized, you have a way to combat them. Google gave you this tool so that you could tell it about those links, and hopefully get them devalued to the point where they no longer contribute to your rankings.

Is it too far-fetched to think that Google had another motive for releasing this tool? If a web page or site is disavowed by lots of different webmasters, doesn't that help Google identify bad neighborhoods?

Before we look at the Disavow tool in more detail, let me just state something.

Just because we can report "bad" links to Google, it does not mean Google will listen to us or take action.

Google has said that webmasters should use the Disavow tool as a last resort. The first step should always be to contact webmasters who are linking to you and ask them to remove the offending link(s). If those webmasters refuse to remove the links, or simply ignore your requests, then that is what the Disavow tool is for.

I should also mention that if Google does disavow links, it could take some time. One of my sites was the victim of negative SEO, and after disavowing those bad links, it took around six months for the site to recover. I recommend you constantly monitor the backlinks to your site (Google Search Console will show you the recent backlinks it has found) and disavow spammy links as you find them. Google wants you to try to get the link removed by contacting the webmasters first, but this is not practical. In many cases, there can be thousands of spammy links to a site.

Checking Your Link Profile & Creating a Disavow File

The first step in using the Disavow tool is to find the links that point to your site and evaluate them. You need to identify the links that may be causing your site harm. These links include:

1. Links on pages with scraped content.
2. Links on pages with spun content.
3. Links on pages with very poor/limited content (in terms of language, spelling, grammar, etc.).
4. Links to sites that have been penalized in Google.
5. Links to irrelevant sites, or sites with dubious content.
6. Site-wide links that appear on all the pages of a linking website.
7. Any link that you would not want Google to manually inspect.

Fortunately, Google Search Console provides us with an easy way to do a link audit. You need a free Search Console account for this, with your site linked to that account.

Assuming you have linked your website to your Search Console account, Google will list the backlinks to your project. It can take a while for these backlinks to start showing, so link up your site as soon as possible

To see the links, log into Search Console and click on the site you want to inspect. At the time of writing, the new Google Search Console is available as well as the old one. The old one is currently better, but I'll briefly cover both here.

Old Search Console Interface

If you are using the old search console user interface (and I suggest you do if it is available for reasons you'll see in a moment), then in the menu on the left side, select **Links to Your Site** from the **Search Traffic** menu.

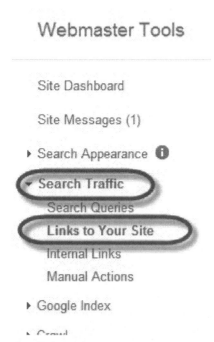

On the right, you'll see a list of links to your site:

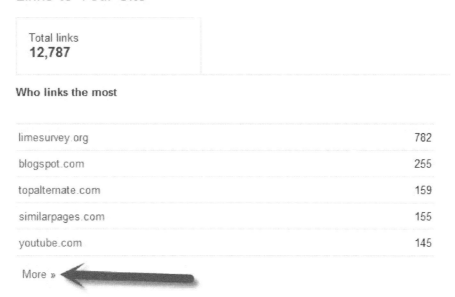

Google only shows you a few links by default, but if you look at the bottom of the list, you'll see a link to "**More**". Click it.

You now have a button to "**Download latest links**". Clicking this button will allow you to choose the format of the download.

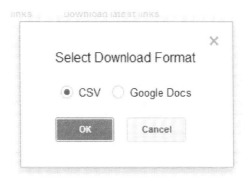

The CSV format will download a spreadsheet that you can view in Excel or similar spreadsheet programs. Alternatively, you can download the file in Google Docs format.

If you don't use Google Docs, I recommend you give it a try. Just go to **docs.google.com**

You simply login to Google Docs with your Gmail account.

Now if you select Google Docs from Search Console, and then click the OK button, the spreadsheet opens directly in Google Docs:

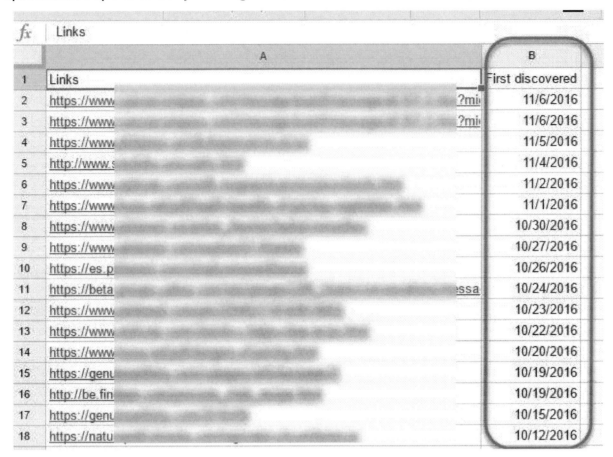

This spreadsheet will list the links Google is counting towards your rankings.

Not only do you get the URL, but you also get the date that the link was first discovered. This means you can check all links the very first time you do a link audit. Then, in a month or two, you only need to check the new links that Google is reporting since your last check.

You need to work your way through the list of links and pull out any that you suspect are harming your website.

New Search Console Interface

If you are using the new search console interface, select **Links** from the left sidebar menu. You will then get a list of internal, external, and top linking sites:

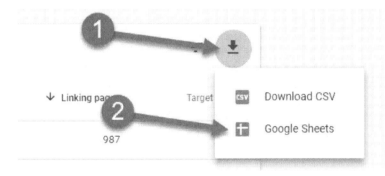

Click the **More** link in the **Top Linking Sites** section.

You can then download the list of links:

The table of data you get is not actually as useful since it trims the URLs of the linking pages to the root:

Site	Linking pages	Target pages	
amazon.com	987	13	
blogspot.com	185	31	
scoop.it	104	1	
webcontentstudio.com	85	2	
sett.com	60	1	
eitci.cloud	29	1	
edlc.online	20	1	
youtube.com	14	1	
eitca.org	13	1	
hdvidzpros.com	12	2	
neilshearing.com	11	1	
activegrowth.com	11	1	

That means you don't know the actual URL of the page linking to you. However, when it comes time to disavow links, I will usually disavow a whole domain (based on it being spam) rather than an individual URL. Therefore, while I preferred the older table of data, this new one may do me a favor by simplifying my process.

Dealing with Bad Links

Google gives you two ways to deal with bad links. You can either report them on a link-by-link basis, or you can report a whole domain. If you report the domain, then all links from that domain are disavowed. You can create a plain text file to use as your disavow list.

To disavow a single URL, just list the URLs, one on each line.

The format for reporting an entire domain is as follows:

Domain:somebaddomain.com

Google also encourages you to use comments in your disavow file. These comments can be for you, or for Google, outlining the steps you have carried out to get the links removed.

For example, if you have tried contacting a webmaster to get links removed, and they have ignored your requests, you can include that information in a comment. Comments start with the # symbol, so a valid comment would look something like this:

 # Webmaster has ignored my request to remove these links.

Google provides the following example as a valid disavow file:

```
# example.com removed most links, but missed these
http://spam.example.com/stuff/comments.html
http://spam.example.com/stuff/paid-links.html
# Contacted owner of shadyseo.com on 7/1/2012 to
# ask for link removal but got no response
domain:shadyseo.com
```

In the example, the webmaster wants two URLs disavowed, plus all links on the shadyseo.com domain.

Once you have built up your disavow file, you need to upload it to Google. One thing I recommend you do is to add the following comment to the beginning of the disavow file:

 # Last updated 10/10/2018

Save the file to your computer when you're done. The next time you want to do a link audit, you will know the date of your previous audit and can just look at the new links since that date (remember that Google gives us the date a link was found).

Uploading the disavow file to Google is simple.

Go to this URL:

https://www.google.com/webmasters/tools/disavow-links-main

You will need to log in using your Search Console details.

Select the website from the drop-down list, and then click the Disavow button:

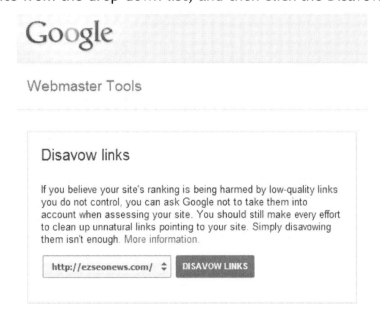

You will get a warning before you can upload the disavow file:

Disavow Links

This is an advanced feature and should only be used with caution. If used incorrectly, this feature can potentially harm your site's performance in Google's search results. We recommend that you only disavow backlinks if you believe that there are a considerable number of spammy, artificial, or low-quality links pointing to your site, and if you are confident that the links are causing issues for you.

Disavow Links

If you want to proceed, click the **Disavow Links** button.

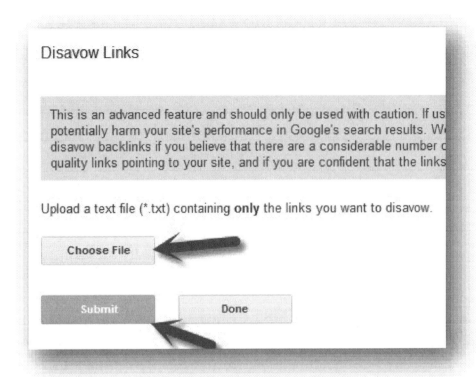

Now you have a button to **Choose File**. Click that and select the disavow text file that you saved earlier.

Finally, click the **Submit** button to upload the file to Google.

Updating the Disavow File

When you need to update the disavow file, e.g. to include more URLs or domains, simply add the new URLs and domains to the file. Make sure you change the comment at the top to the current date, so you can keep track. Once done, go back to the disavow tool and re-upload your updated file. Google only keep one file per site, so the last one you upload will be the file it uses for "disavowing".

I'd recommend you do a complete link audit on your site, and then recheck new links every month or two after that. Now that you are responsible for all links pointing to your site, you need to know who is linking to it and whether those links are potentially harmful to your rankings. If they are, contact the webmaster and ask for removal. Failing that, disavow them without hesitation.

I also want you to think about something else.

If there is a spammy web page linking to you, and you know that it can only be harmful to your rankings, it is possible that the site in question has more than one link to your site, even though you are not aware of them all. In cases like this, I always disavow the entire site rather than just the URLs. If the page on that site is so bad that you want to disavow it, the chances are the whole site is pretty bad as well.

Future Alternatives to Link Building

Google is pretty good at detecting backlinks created for ranking purposes. It is also happy to slap any site that runs aggressive back-linking campaigns. So, what does the future hold?

For the foreseeable future, backlinks will continue to be a major ranking factor, but there are other things you should start doing now.

Build Your Brand with Mentions

A "brand mention" is simply your "brand" mentioned in an article on another site. There is no physical backlink, just a mention of your brand.

Google can recognize (and reward) brand mentions, associating the mention with the correct website. Quite often, your brand will be your domain name, so the more brandable your domain name, the more chance you have of Google correctly associating your brand mention with your site.

For example, if your site is buycontactlensesonline.com, your domain is essentially a commercial keyword phrase that you have turned into an exact match domain (EMD). Any mention of "buy contact lenses online" on another site will not help your site since your site is not a recognized brand.

However, if you named your site BetterVisionContacts.com, and your site had some authority, then another site mentioning "Better Vision Contacts" would probably work out as a brand mention in the eyes of Google.

Brand mentions are likely to form part of the ranking algorithm. They certainly help build your authority, and authority, in the eyes of Google, is King.

The beauty of brand mentions is that this is a very safe way to get a ranking boost. Google won't be penalizing unlinked text anytime soon. If you write guest posts for other websites, try inserting your brand into your article instead of a backlink.

Build Backlinks for Traffic Instead of Rankings, Using Nofollow

I mentioned previously that if you would build a backlink, even if Google did not exist, then it is natural in the eyes of Google. The reason is that you are not building it to improve your rankings; you are building it because it can benefit you in other ways.

A good example of why you might build a link, even if search engines did not exist, would be for click-through traffic. If you can get a link to your site on a high traffic web page, then the chances are that link would bring you some decent traffic since it's visible to a lot of eyeballs.

The only danger here is whether Google accepts the reason for the link. Google might consider it a link to improve rankings, rather than a link for natural reasons. Don't worry. In cases like this, where your intent is to drive extra traffic from the web page, just nofollow the link. Google will then understand that the link is natural and not there to give you a ranking boost. It's always nice to get a boost in the rankings, but in this case, that's not why you placed the link on the page.

The temptation is there to never use nofollow tags on links, but it is becoming increasingly important to prevent penalties. It might all sound a bit too much right now, but I can promise you that once you get these things into your mind, you will intuitively know what to do in any given situation.

Summary of Backlinks

Just remember these simple guidelines when getting links:

1. Try to get links from as many different places as possible (we want IP diversity).
2. Look for quality rather than quantity. A handful of quality links will do more for your rankings than hundreds or thousands of spammy links (which could get your site penalized).
3. Focus on Link Bait and email outreach methods for most of your backlinks.
4. Don't use keyword-rich anchor text in links you obtain on other websites. Always use your website title, URL, page URL or title of the page you are linking to as the anchor text.
5. Use internal linking (links that go from one page on your site to a different page on the same site) to introduce keyword rich links to a page.
6. Carry out a link audit periodically on your site, and ask webmasters to remove any low-quality, spammy links that may be affecting your rankings. Failing that, use Google's disavow tool.

4. What's in It for the Visitor?

You never get a second chance to make a first impression.

When a visitor arrives on your website, you have a very short time to make a good first impression. That first impression will decide whether they stay or go. The first thing you need to do is make sure your site looks good. If you're using WordPress, then that's quite easy. There are lots of attractive, responsive WordPress themes to choose from. Changing is as simple as installing and activating a new theme in your Dashboard.

Another important consideration is how fast your pages load. This needs to be as fast as possible to avoid having visitors waiting for stuff. In fact, most visitors won't bother to stay if the page is still loading after just a few seconds.

Install Google Analytics and Get a Google Search Console Account

These two free tools can give you a huge amount of information about your site and visitors. They are also Google's way to communicate with YOU. If there is anything Google is concerned about, you'll get a message inside your Search Console account. Google will also notify you when your site is down, or there are other important situations you should know about.

A lot of webmasters will tell you to avoid these tools. They'll argue that it gives Google too much information about you. I disagree. Google already has all the data it needs on your site, and anyone who thinks otherwise is just deluding themselves. These two tools are a great way for Google to share that data with you.

Google Analytics will tell you how fast your pages are loading, bounce rates, time on site, navigation path through the site, and a lot more.

Another great free tool I use regularly to check page load times is GTMetrix. You can find it here:

http://gtmetrix.com/

Enter your page URL and GTMetrix will measure the load time while you wait:

Report generated: Fri, Feb 22, 2013, 2:06 AM -0800
Test Server Region: Vancouver, Canada
Using: Firefox 14.0.1, Page Speed 1.12.9.1, YSlow 3.1.4

Looks like you're running WordPress
Have a look at our WP optimization tips »

Summary

Page Speed Grade:		YSlow Grade:		Page load time: 2.63s
(81%)	**B**	(76%)	**C**	Total page size: 916KB
				Total number of requests: 81

Not only do they give you the time in seconds for the page load, but they will also tell you which parts of your site are slowing things down, and what you can do to fix the problems.

Website Stickiness

In Google Analytics, Google will tell you the average time a visitor stays on your site, as well as the bounce rate (how quickly someone bounces back to Google search after visiting just a single page on your site).

Bounce rate and time on site are measures of how "Sticky" your site is.

Here is the bounce rate for one of my sites, taken at the time of writing:

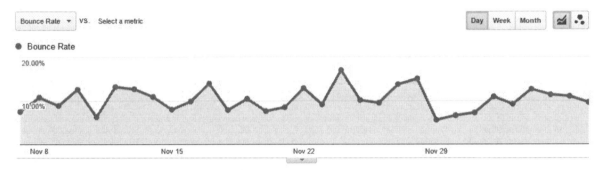

This is the average for the whole site.

You'll notice that the maximum bounce rate over the last month was less than 20%, with the average being around 10%. This means that only about 10% of people visiting my site go straight back to Google after reaching the landing page. Here are the averages for this site over the last month:

The average bounce rate of 10.32% and an average time on site of around 20 minutes. I'd say that this site was quite sticky, wouldn't you?

While that data is for the site as a whole, you can examine these metrics for individual pages too. This is good because it helps you find the weakest links, so you can fix them.

The next screenshot shows the data for several URLs on my site.

Avg. Time on Page	En.	Bounce Rate
00:20:04 Site Avg: 00:20:04 (0.00%)	18	10.32% Site Avg: 10.32% (0.00%)
00:54:04		6.98%
00:05:23	19	31.90%
01:08:36	18	4.85%
01:20:36		4.93%
00:06:14		10.27%
00:17:28		8.18%
01:20:31		5.31%
01:10:07		16.00%
01:09:19		7.45%
00:02:48		0.00%

Just look for the pages with the lowest "Avg. Time on Page" (left column) and the highest "Bounce Rate" (right column) and see if there is something you can do about those pages to improve their content and make them stickier. Any page with a high bounce rate is clearly not giving the visitor the "experience" they were looking for.

This book has already covered some of the information in this chapter. Even so, it is nice to have all of these ideas in one place, for easier reference as you work on your site. Let's look at the key ideas to bear in mind as you work on your website.

Important Aspects of a Web Page

You need to capture your visitor's attention and let them know what you have in store for them.

In terms of articles on your website, this can mean an eye-catching headline that makes them want to read more. If your visitor reads the headline and finds it interesting, they'll more than likely go on to read the opening paragraph. The first paragraph is almost as vital as the headline itself. You might like to create an opening paragraph that summarizes what your visitor will find further down the page. Tell them what goodies lie in wait for them if they keep reading.

As you write content, try to keep sentences short (20-25 words). For paragraphs, look at four or five sentences each wherever possible. People hate large blocks of text. They also hate long sentences because they can become confusing and difficult to read.

When you have finished writing your content, read it aloud to yourself. If you find any part(s) that need re-reading to fully understand them, then something needs fixing. Similarly, if you find yourself hesitating over a word or sentence, something is interrupting the flow, so fix that too.

To make your articles easier to read, use sub-headings and bullet points.

Pictures and diagrams can also help break up blocks of text, making the piece easier on the eyes for your visitor. Like that old adage goes: "A picture is worth a thousand words." It's true too, providing the image catches the reader's attention of course.

NOTE: Use ALT tags on images, but do not stuff them with keywords. Simply use an ALT tag that describes the image clearly.

Use colors and fonts wisely. Don't put white fonts on a black background or any other combination that causes eyestrain. Black font on a white background is the best. A lot of designers go for design over practicality and use a dark gray font. This can cause eyestrain. Black is best!

Use fonts which work well online, like Verdana, Trebuchet, and Georgia.

If you want to see some truly shocking usage of colors on the web, search Google images for the term **bad website design**.

While we're on the subject of content, be aware that people are a lot less patient than they used to be:

http://news.bbc.co.uk/2/hi/technology/7417496.stm.

Be concise and to the point. Don't waffle just to get a higher word count. Waffle just bores your visitors and will negatively affect your rankings.

To make your site sticky, you need to give your visitors what they want. That's it, in a nutshell! In order to do this, you need to know your visitor. Ask yourself the following questions:

- Who is it?
- What do they want?
- What answers do they need?
- What do they want to ask me?

Your homepage should guide the visitor quickly and easily to the section of your website that is of interest to them. Your visitor should be able to find what they need swiftly and effortlessly. Needless to say, a search box is essential for this purpose. Fortunately, adding a search facility is easy with WordPress ;)

Ways to Build Trust

1. **The First Impression**: Remember the "Above the Fold" algorithm? Check out your web pages and see what a visitor will see when they first land on your site. Is it just adverts? Or is there something that will catch their attention and encourage them to explore your website? Build trust by thinking about the visitor experience when they first land on your pages.
2. **The Mugshot**: Include a photo of yourself in a prominent position on your website. The sidebars or in an author bio are great places for this. A photo helps build trust because the visitor can see who they are interacting with. Putting a face to the name is always a good thing when it comes to building an online reputation.
3. **Create a Gravatar**: If you use your photo as a Gravatar http://en.gravatar.com/), then every time you post comments on other

websites (or guest post on other sites), your photo will appear automatically next to your thoughts. This goes back to what we were saying in the section on building authority. How much better is it for a visitor to arrive on your site and recognize your face? This can really help towards building a high level of trust.

4. **Fresh content rules**: Contrary to what some SEOs will tell you, fresh content is not a ranking factor. Google DO NOT reward websites that are constantly updated. However, there is another consideration here. Your visitor... If people arrive at your site and see that the content is several years old, this may be enough for them to click the back button. Keep stuff like reviews up to date. If you update a review, change the timestamp of the post in WordPress to reflect the new date. If the content is "ageless", consider removing the date/time stamp from the post.

5. **Visible links to**: A Privacy Policy, Terms of Use, and a Contact Us page are great ways to help build trust. On your contact page, you should ideally have a real address as this helps further with the trust building. Again, it's a good idea to have your photo on the Contact Us page as well.

6. **Create an About Us page**: Here you can mention who you are and what your goals are for the site. On many websites, this is often one of the highest traffic pages, so don't be afraid to insert a signup box if you have a newsletter or short course to offer.

Types of Content Your Visitors Want:

There are different, specific types of content you can create for your visitors. Here are a few ideas:

1. Answer "real" questions on your pages: You can find the questions that people want answers to by looking at sites like AnswerThePublic.com or Quora.com. Find real questions and create a Q&A section on your site using those questions. You can use the **site:** operator at Google to search for information on specific sites. Here is an example where I am searching Google for questions about juicing Vs blending at Quora.com:

blender v juicing site:quora.com

Web   Shopping   Videos   Images   News   More ▾   Search tools

About 525 results (0.51 seconds)

Showing results for blender *or* juicing site:quora.com
Search instead for blender v juicing site:quora.com

⊘ Should I get a blender or juicer to make raw fruit/veg juice ...
www.quora.com › ... › Kitchens › Kitchen Appliances › Blenders   Quora ▾
Oct 14, 2011 - Answer 1 of 4: I've used both a Champion **juicer** and a Vitamix.
Champion is great ... Thinking a **blender** has less waste and easier to clean up.

⊘ Juicing: When juice is made from whole fruits in a blender o...
www.quora.com › ... › Health › Medicine and Healthcare   Quora ▾
Dec 11, 2012 - Answer 1 of 1: According to the Department of Agriculture, **juice** is
enzymatically identical to whole fruits. Also, the soluble fiber from fruit is ...

⊘ Is there a way to make a fresh juice that retains the raw frui...
www.quora.com › Food › Beverages   Quora ▾
A **blender**, on the other hand, will break down your fruit or vegetable into a mix of **juice**
and pulp. If you are into making smoothies, you will probably want to ...

I am sure you can see how easy it is to find relevant, on-topic questions to use as the basis for some website content.

2. Buyer Guides: For example, if your site is about Android Tablets, give your visitors a free PDF that tells them what they need to know when it comes to buying one of these devices. You can use that free guide to build a list if you want to, by making visitors opt-in to your list before they get the free download URL.

3. Tutorials: Provide helpful tutorials for your visitors if you can think of some that are relevant to your niche.

4. Videos: Create informative, relevant videos and embed them in your web pages. Put a great title above the video to entice your visitors to watch it. Never have videos start automatically. Always give the visitors that option. Make sure the video content lives up to the title. Upload videos to Youtube.com and develop your own YouTube channel in your chosen niche. This will not only bring you extra traffic, but it will also build credibility and trust. You can link to this YouTube channel from your website.

5. Terminology Page: One type of page I usually include on my niche sites is a Terminology Page. A niche has its own vocabulary as we have seen, and often people want to know what certain words or phrases mean. A Terminology Page serves this purpose.

6. **What is popular in your niche**? Find stories in your niche that have gone viral. If something is hot, write about it and then share it with the same people that shared those original stories.

Make Your Site Interactive

1. Allow Comments from visitors at the end of your articles. Invite or encourage your visitors to use the comments box. It's amazing how simple it is to say something along the lines of: "Hey if you've got a question or an opinion on this, leave a comment at the bottom of this post". A lot of people don't bother, but it's an effective **call to action**.

Full-time blogger Darren Rowse wrote a nice article on getting your visitors to comment:

https://problogger.com/10-techniques-to-get-more-comments-on-your-blog/

It's over 12 years old now but still offers some great advice.

A lot of webmasters turn comments off on their site because of the huge amounts of spam they receive. However, by using a good spam blocker like Akismet (commercial) or the free WordPress "Stop Spammers" plugin (an aggressive anti-spam plugin that eliminates comment spam) you can eliminate 99% of all spam:

https://wordpress.org/plugins/stop-spammer-registrations-plugin/,

Comments allow your visitor to interact with YOU, as well as with other commenters. If a visitor asks a question, make sure you always answer it. This starts a dialogue with your target audience and builds trust and authority. Visitors like to see that you're answering questions personally. Answering questions bring visitors back to your site, especially if you have a plug-in installed that allows visitors to track responses to their own comments (recommended).

2. By using a rating and review plug-in (search the WordPress plugin directory), you can give your visitors the chance to award products their own star rating when they leave a comment. Some plugins will also provide the review ratings to Google in a format it can use in the search results. See the chapter on structured data.

Best Link Building Services - Warrior Forum
www.warriorforum.com/internet...reviews.../49342-best-link-building-services.html ▾
Jan 25, 2009 - Hi folks, We all know that **link building** is alfa and omega, no links - no rankings. I would like you to post here all the best link buil.

SEO Tool Review: BuzzStream for Link Building - Online Marketing Blog
www.toprankblog.com/2009/05/seo-tool-**review**-buzzstream-for-**link-building**/ ▾
★★★★★ Rating: 5 - 1 vote
As I work with our clients on their **link building** projects, I am often testing out new tools to make the process more efficient. After meeting with Lee at.

Link Building and Link Earning Services - Brick Marketing
www.brickmarketing.com/white-hat-**link-building** ▾
You will have a scheduled meeting with one of your Dedicated SEO Specialis each month to **review** the monthly **link building** activities and to **review** the reports ...

See how that middle result stands out? I bet it has a better CTR because of that rating system.

3. Polls are a great way to get your visitors involved. They allow visitors to express their opinion by casting a quick vote. There are a few free polling scripts around to choose from.

4. Provide Social Media Icons after each post so that people can spread the word on your great content. There are lots of free plugins available. I recommend you try a few of these out to see which one works best with your site and its theme.

5. Add a forum. Forums can be time intensive, so only consider one if you have the time to monitor one. Several WordPress plugins are available that will add a fully functional forum on your site. If you are interested, search the Wordpress plugins repository for SimplePress, or wpForo.

Using Google Search Console to Improve CTR

A few years back, Google started to hide the search terms people were using to find your website. Gone are the days when you knew exactly what search term someone used to find your site. Now, in Google Analytics, the majority of your incoming traffic search keywords will appear as follows:

	1. (not provided)	**5,266** (93.15%)

That's 93% of search engine traffic where Google is hiding the keywords from me. We still do get some keyword data, but not much. It looks like this:

	5.	e452i	6	(0.11%)	83.33%
	6.	e221 e224	3	(0.05%)	66.67%
	7.	how mach % of sodium benzoate use in orange juice	3	(0.05%)	33.33%
	8.	how to measure sodium benzoate for drinks	3	(0.05%)	33.33%
	9.	potassium magnesium citrate for kidney stones	3	(0.05%)	100.00%
	10.	antivitamins	2	(0.04%)	100.00%

I can see that in this period, 6 people found my site for e452i. However, what did those 5,266 people type in at the search engines to find my site? No idea.

Although this keyword data was taken away, Google Search Console does partly make up for this.

Login to the Search Console. We'll use the new version of the console interface since we'll have to make the switch at some point. Select the site you are working on and click on the **Performance** link in the left menu.

This is a page that is full of powerful information for any SEO. With it, you can identify under-performing pages on your site, and try to fix them.

Let me walk you through a quick example.

At the top of the page, you'll have some general data about the site including:

- Total Clicks
- Total Impressions
- Average CTR
- Average Position

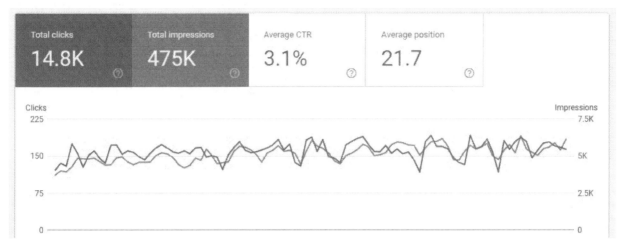

Underneath you'll see a table of data with several tabs along the top. **Queries** is selected.

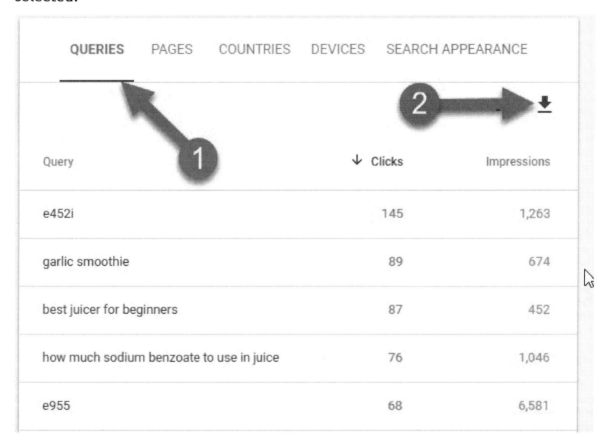

That table shows you keywords used to find your site, clicks, and impressions. You can get more data if you click the download button. Here is the downloaded Google spreadsheet:

	A	B	C	D	E
1	Query	Clicks	Impressions	CTR	Position
2	e452i	145	1263	11.48%	2.87
3	garlic smoothie	89	674	13.20%	3.92
4	best juicer for be	87	452	19.25%	2.07
5	how much sodiur	76	1046	7.27%	3.54
6	e955	68	6581	1.03%	6.56
7	juicing for rosace	62	131	47.33%	1.43
8	juice for gout	61	1295	4.71%	6.94
9	best juice for gou	49	729	6.72%	5.7
10	decolorized aloe	49	574	8.54%	4.87
11	juicing the rainbo	39	50	78%	1
12	serrapeptase acr	36	153	23.53%	1.23
13	juicing for kidney	35	226	15.49%	4.21

You can see:

- The number of impressions my page received (in other words, how many times my page appeared when this term was searched for).
- The average position my page ranked for that term.
- The number of clicks my listing received (i.e. people clicking through to my web page).
- The CTR, or Click Through Rate.

So, if a page is shown to searchers 100 times, and only one searcher clicks on my listing, the CTR would be 1%. If 10 people clicked on my listing, the CTR would be 10%.

Obviously the higher the CTR, the more traffic you will get.

If you have a CTR of 1% and manage to increase that to 5%, you end up with 5 times more traffic.

Since you have the data as a spreadsheet, you can filter the results to find those entries with low CTR and high impressions.

73	decolorized aloe vera juice	3	12	25%	3.7
74	cryptoxanthin	3	542	0.55%	8.9
75	juicing for bladder health	3	24	12.50%	5.5

If you can find these, you can find pages on your site that are being shown to and ignored by searchers at Google.

The one above has a CTR of just 0.55%, even though it ranks in the top 10. With 542 impressions, this is a reasonable one to tackle, since the low CTR is more likely to be statistically relevant.

The search term is **cryptoxanthin**. People don't find my title and description very enticing. Here is my listing in Google:

We can use Cryptoxanthin to make vitamin A, but it also gives...
juicingtherainbow.com › Nutrients ▾
Cryptoxanthin in a nutshell: **Cryptoxanthin** is a plant chemical that acts as an antioxidant (as well as a precursor to vitamin A). It's thought to be active in ...

Notice that the title and description are both truncated. This does not help.

Also, what is the searcher's intent for this keyword? If I knew what they were looking for, then I could tailor my title and meta description to be more attractive to them.

In this case, looking at the listings in the top 10 of Google, I'd imagine that the people searching for this are probably more likely to be researchers, biologists or chemists. My page is about the health benefits of this compound, but most people trying to find out how it can help with health would probably have used a "health" word or synonym in their search.

Interestingly, if I check my list of search terms, I do find one that is specifically looking for the health supplement:

| 52 | non-decolorized liquid aloe vera | 3 | 15 | 33.33% | 2.4 |
| 53 | beta cryptoxanthin supplements | 4 | 80 | 5% | 4.6 |

This one has a CTR of 5%, which is 10 times higher. The listing in Google for this search term is a little different:

We can use Cryptoxanthin to make vitamin A, but it also gives egg ...
juicingtherainbow.com › Nutrients ▾
Alternative names: Cryptoxanthin; **beta-cryptoxanthin**. .... Unlike some other **supplements**, the ester form of cryptoxanthin is equally well absorbed as the normal ...

Google has changed my description. I mentioned earlier in the book how this works. If the search term is in the page Meta Description, chances are the Meta Description will be used for the listing. If the search term is not in the Meta Description, Google will choose some other text on the page that does include the term. It is Google's way of trying to auto-optimize your listing. Anyone searching for **beta-cryptoxanthin supplements** will see those words in the listing description. This encourages the click.

We can use this information to try to improve CTR. Using the Yoast SEO plugin (Wordpress users), you can change the SEO Title and SEO Description for any post.

Go into the Dashboard and edit the post. With Yoast SEO installed, you should see the Yoast SEO settings. This is where you can edit the title and description:

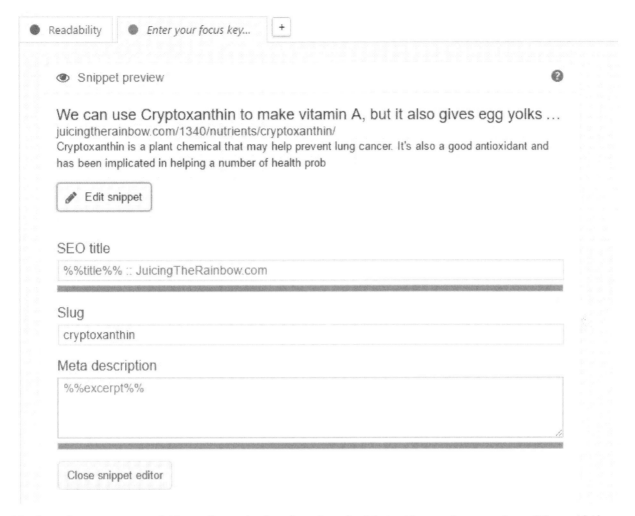

Notice that my actual Meta Description hard coded into the web page is neither of the ones that Google used for those two listings. Google didn't think they were good enough, or relevant enough for those search terms.

For this article, one thing I definitely want to do is reduce the number of characters in the title (and description). I should also try to get the important search terms into an enticing description so that my description is used in the listings.

To find the best titles and descriptions, look to see if there are adverts listed in the search results for the terms you are working on. In my case, there isn't. If there is, use those for ideas because advertisers pay a lot of money, tweaking titles and descriptions for maximum CTR. Borrow their ideas for your pages!

OK, I've edited my SEO Title and Meta Description as follows:

Cryptoxanthin, Vitamin A & your Health

juicingtherainbow.com/1340/nutrients/cryptoxanthin/

▶ Cryptoxanthin is an important antioxidant and vitamin A precursor. Do you need to take beta-cryptoxanthin Supplements? How can you get it in your diet?

> ✏ Edit snippet

SEO title

> Cryptoxanthin, Vitamin A & your Health

Slug

> cryptoxanthin

Meta description

> ▶ Cryptoxanthin is an important antioxidant and vitamin A precursor. Do you need to take beta-cryptoxanthin Supplements? How can you get it in your diet?

> Close snippet editor

I have made both a lot shorter. I've also included the words beta-cryptoxanthin and supplements in the description, so my description should now be shown by Google for those search terms. Will it perform better than the previous listing? Time will tell.

Once you make changes like this, you need to wait for pages to be re-spidered and updated in the SERPs. Check periodically, and then once the listing is using your new title and description, leave everything as it is for 30 days before checking on CTR again.

Has it improved?

My CTR increased to 6.25% for this page. Clearly, I've still got a way to go, but you get the idea.

Testing and experimenting with CTR is a great way to increase traffic.

As I mentioned above, if there are Google adverts in the listings for keywords you are ranking for, use those to help you craft shorter, more enticing titles and descriptions. After all, many of these advertisers will have spent hundreds or thousands on testing titles and descriptions. You can piggyback off their hard work and expertise.

Is CTR a Google Ranking Factor?

This is difficult to answer. I would suggest it is unlikely to be an actual Google signal on its own, as it would be too easy to game the system. You can imagine software bots being created with the sole purpose of clicking a specific link in the SERPs. Google would not allow that.

Google probably uses CTR as a measure of quality, though, so a page with a low CTR could quite rightly be demoted in the rankings. Using the same argument, a page with a high CTR could also rise in the rankings, as it would be deemed higher quality. However, many other factors will determine whether that improved ranking is justified. If a listing has a high CTR, but high bounce rate and low time on site, what would you do if you were Google?

There are a couple of studies that have shown CTR can affect your organic search ranking. Perhaps the most famous was Rand Fishkin's experiment:

https://sparktoro.com/blog/queries-clicks-influence-googles-results/

Rand discusses CTR in this Whiteboard Friday video:

https://moz.com/blog/impact-of-queries-and-clicks-on-googles-rankings-whiteboard-friday

I would suggest you also read this post on SearchEngineLand, as it also discusses CTR as a ranking factor (or not):

http://searchengineland.com/ctr-ranking-factor-227162

Even if CTR is not a real Google ranking factor, the fact remains – increase CTR and you will increase traffic. That is enough of a benefit to persuade any webmaster that they should be trying to improve CTR for their pages in the SERPs.

Part 2 – SEO Site Audit

Why Part 2?

The first part of this book is an overall White Hat strategy for SEO. However, for many of my students and clients, the biggest problem is where to start on an existing site that has lost rankings and seen a drop in traffic. This section answers the question "What the heck do I do now?"

We'll go through a checklist of things you should objectively critique/fix on your website. Before I go on, I need to point out that a lot of people are not very objective about their own work. It's often hard to take criticism from other people and even harder to admit that you made a mistake somewhere along the way. However, for this process to work, you need to step outside of yourself. It's time to view your website differently, as a complete stranger might view it after arriving on your site for the first time.

I'd also like to say that although you do need to be constructively critical, I don't want you to be too hard on yourself. Nearly everyone I know lost a site or two in the Google updates over the years, myself included. When Google first moved the goalposts, it caught a lot of people out, and I do mean a lot of people.

Pre-Panda and pre-Penguin, Google tolerated certain activities. Post-Panda and post-Penguin, it doesn't. As a result, Google is enforcing the Webmaster Guidelines, something that SEOs never really believed they would. It's Google's change in tolerance that got so many of us into trouble.

Let me give you a "moving of the goal posts" example.

We have known for some time that Google doesn't like us building backlinks to our sites, especially with automated tools. How did we know? Google told us. So why did so many people engage in link-building campaigns using automated tools that created hundreds or thousands of low-quality links in a short space of time? The answer is simple. At that time, Google tolerated this behavior; in fact, Google rewarded it. When you see your competitor building all these links and jumping ahead of you in the search engine, it's only natural that you want to do the same to get your rankings back, so that's what many of us did.

As long as Google tolerated (and rewarded) aggressive link-building, people continued to do it. Google knew that.

Google Panda, and probably more specifically, Google Penguin, changed all of this. Google went from being a very tolerant search engine to one of zero tolerance, overnight!

For as long as I can remember, Google has published Webmaster Guidelines to tell us what is considered acceptable or not. Before Panda and Penguin, these guidelines were simply that – **guidelines**. Most of us chose to ignore them because we had no choice. If we followed the guidelines, then we could not rank above our competitors who also ignored them. However, with the arrival of Panda and Penguin, these guidelines became **strict rules**, and rules that had to be followed. It was Google's way or the highway!

All the previously tolerated techniques like link building were suddenly a big problem for the websites that used them. Webmasters who held the number one spot for years, suddenly found their site gone from page one. Many sites were gone from the Google SERPs altogether.

The reason why so many websites lost their rankings overnight was simply that those sites had not followed the guidelines in the past.

I wrote this section of the book to help you more easily identify and fix the problems you may have with your website. I use the same checklist on my own websites, and those of my students and clients, so I know it works when followed closely.

A Reminder of What Google Wants

Before we start the checklist, I thought it would be a good idea to have a quick reminder of what it is that Google wants. You can read its guidelines for yourself, here:

http://support.google.com/webmasters/bin/answer.py?hl=en&answer=35769

Near the top of that page, it says:

> We strongly encourage you to pay very close attention to the **Quality Guidelines** below, which outline some of the illicit practices that may lead to a site being removed entirely from the Google index or otherwise affected by an algorithmic or manual spam action. If a site has been affected by a spam action, it may no longer show up in results on Google.com or on any of Google's partner sites.

It is important that you take this statement seriously. Google will remove or penalize your site if it catches you carrying out any activities it doesn't approve of. Unlike the rhetoric of the past, Google means what it says these days.

There are a lot of webmasters out there who resent Google's attempts to stifle their SEO "creativity", and I often hear people say things like, "Who cares what Google wants..." usually followed by "I'll do whatever I want with my own site. Stuff Google!" This is all fine if you know the risks and can accept the consequences. At the end of the day, this is Google's search engine and it can do what it wants. The bottom line is this: if you want free traffic from Google, then you need to follow its guidelines.

Please understand that you can no longer walk the black or gray hat path and stay under Google's spam radar. Google encourages webmasters to report those sites that abuse its guidelines. Look:

> If you believe that another site is abusing Google's quality guidelines, please let us know by filing a spam report.

So now, if a competitor is cheating their way to the top, you can report them. Similarly, if you are cheating your way to the top, those competitors you leapfrog in the SERPs will also be able to report you.

Black and gray hat SEOs not only have to keep under Google's radar, but they also have to keep under the radar of their competitors who will be quick to report them. With so much profit in ranking on page one of the Google SERPs, any new web page that pushes out established sites from the top 10 slots will most certainly come under heavy scrutiny.

What to Avoid

According to the Webmaster Guidelines, here are some things you need to avoid.

- **Pages designed for the search engines, not the visitor.** We've all seen these in the search engine results pages (SERPs). They are the pages designed with the sole purpose of ranking well in Google, without any thought given to what the visitor might think when they arrive at the site. Google wants engaging, unique content (and I'm talking unique in terms of "voice", discussion or ideas, not just the words and their order on the page).

- Any **trick** or **"loophole"** designed to help a web page rank higher in the search engine. That pretty much covers most of the SEO before 2012.

- **Content that is auto-created using a software tool.** Most content-generating software produces gibberish, so this is an obvious point. Even if it's not gibberish, it won't be the valuable, coherent, unique content that Google wants to see. One type of tool that deserves special attention is the article spinner. Spinners can produce hundreds of near perfect "unique" articles in just a few minutes in the hands of an expert. Many people have used these spun articles extensively in back-linking campaigns. Well, Google won't tolerate spun content anymore, whether it's on your site or used in backlinks to your site.

  Other examples of auto-generated content include articles translated by software (badly) without a human review, scraped content from RSS feeds, and "stitching or combining content from different web pages without adding sufficient value." This last point should be of interest to content curators who don't **add sufficient value** to the content they curate.

- **"Linking schemes" that are designed to manipulate rankings in the search engine.** Wow! That's a big one. Google has told us that it doesn't want us building links to our site for the sole purpose of better rankings. Back-linking is one of the most effective ways to improve your rank in Google, so obviously, we all still do it. Just by linking two or more of your own sites together can be considered a "linking scheme" if the sole point is to help those sites rank better. Other things Google doesn't like are sites which buy or sell links to pass on PageRank (PR). It also doesn't like reciprocal linking between sites or websites that have used automated tools to build backlinks. Google doesn't even like text links inserted into the body of articles (yes, "guest posts") if those links are simply there to manipulate your web page rankings.

- **Websites that serve up one version of a page to the search engines, yet a different page to the visitors.** This is what we call "cloaking". Webmasters use this to try and trick the search engines into ranking the "sales" page higher. The page the search engines see is keyword rich (helping it to rank), whereas the version the visitor sees is completely different.

"Sneaky redirects" are similar to cloaking and often achieved with JavaScript (computer programming language commonly used to create interactive effects within web browsers) or a Meta refresh (a method of instructing a web browser to automatically refresh the current web page). The result is that the page the visitor sees is not the same page that the search engine spider crawled and ultimately ranked for in Google.

- **Pages that have "hidden" text.** In other words, text that is invisible to the visitor. This is achieved using CSS to make the text the same color as the background. Visitors don't see the text but the search engines do since they crawl and read the text-based document.

- **Websites that use "doorway pages".** These are poor quality pages, designed to rank for a single keyword or key phrase. Sites that use doorway pages often have hundreds or thousands of them. Their sole purpose is to rank high for a single search term and deliver visitors from the search engine.

  As an example, think of a double-glazing company that wants to rank in every state of the United States for the term "double-glazing Utah" (or whatever state a person is searching from). One way this has been done in the past is to create a generic web page optimized for "double-glazing Utah" and then duplicate it, swapping out the word "Utah" for "Texas" and then repeating the process for every state. That's 50 pages of "duplicate content", in Google's eyes. That same site might identify 99 other keyword phrases they want to rank for besides the obvious "double-glazing". If they create doorway pages for each state, with all of the phrases they want to rank for, the site would end up with 5,000 pages of duplicate spam.

- **Affiliate websites that don't add enough value.** These include the typical Amazon affiliate website where each page is a single review of a product that links back to the Amazon store via an affiliate link. In many of the poorer sites, the review content contains nothing that isn't already on Amazon or the manufacturer's own website. Affiliate sites MUST add significant value.

Google Suggestions

- **Use clear, intuitive navigation on your site with text links.** Every page on your site needs to be reachable from a link somewhere on the site. A sitemap helps here (Google recommends you have one), but it is also a good idea to interlink your content, providing that is, it helps the visitor navigate your site. We discussed navigation in the first section of this book.

- **Don't have too many links on any given page.** Sites like Wikipedia: http://www.wikipedia.org/, seem to ignore this rule, yet it still ranks well for a huge number of searches. However, Google trusts and accepts Wikipedia as an authority website, so what's good for Wikipedia may not necessarily be good for you and your site.

- **Websites that have useful, information-rich content**. Think here in terms of content written for the visitor, not for the search engine.
- **ALT tags that actually describe the image**. Be aware that ALT tags are often read to the visually impaired by text-to-speech software. That makes the ALT tag an important source of information for people who cannot actually see the image, so use this tag to describe the image in a brief but accurate way.
- **Sites should not have broken links**. Screaming Frog SEO Spider can check these for you, so there is no excuse.

OK, I'm sure by now you get the idea.

We'll look at some of the other likes and dislikes of Google as we work our way through the checklist.

The SEO Audit

I have divided this audit into two parts. The first part offers you a 10 Point checklist, and mainly covers what we know Google wants in terms of site design, visitor experience, and quality. At the end of this checklist, I'll show you some of my favorite examples of bad SEO that illustrate some of the points we talked about in the checklist.

The second part of the audit is more technical in nature (think site architecture) and looks at a range of issues that can affect a site, from pages not being found, to poorly constructed headers. Technical issues can be time-consuming to find and fix, so for this section of the audit, we'll use the Screaming Frog SEO Spider tool. There is a free version of this tool which will cover a lot of things you'll want to check if you have a relatively small website. For larger sites, and a complete audit, the paid version of the tool is necessary. I will be using the paid version in this book.

You can read more about the Screaming Frog SEO Spider on their website:

https://www.screamingfrog.co.uk/seo-spider/

I am in no way affiliated with this company. It is just the best, most comprehensive tool out there for carrying out a technical SEO audit on a website.

Manual 10 Point Checklist

Manual Check #1 – Evaluate the Domain Name

Exact Match Domains

In the past, keywords in your domain name helped your website to rank for those keywords. The ultimate ranking boost was from something called an **Exact Match Domain**, or **EMD** for short. An EMD took keyword "stuffing" to the extreme, by making the domain name identical to the main keyword phrase you were trying to target.

For example, if you wanted to rank well for "buy prescription drugs online", then the exact match domain would be buyprescriptiondrugsonline.XXX where XXX is any one of the top-level domains (TLD), i.e .com, .net, .org, etc. By merely having that exact key phrase in the domain name gave you an unfair ranking advantage for that phrase. SEOs soon spotted this and EMDs became hot favorites for anyone trying to make quick money online.

On September 28, 2012, Matt Cutts (head of Google's webspam team) tweeted the following:

Google had finally decided to take action on "low-quality" EMDs and prevent them from ranking, simply because of the phrase in the domain name.

Now, if you have an EMD, don't panic. Google's algorithm targets **low-quality EMDs** from the search results, not good sites that happen to be on an EMD. Having said that, there is often some collateral damage with big changes to the algorithm updates, so it's inevitable that a few good sites get hit at times. You need to decide if your site is a quality EMD or a low-quality one, before deciding to keep it or not.

The first thing I recommend you look at when evaluating the quality of an EMD is whether it is a commercial phrase. If it is, then there may be no hope for your site unless the phrase is your actual brand.

As an example, here are the estimated costs per click for some contact lens related phrases as reported by Google's keyword tool.

☐	contact lenses online order ▼	€5.96
☐	contacts lenses online ▼	€5.65
☐	buy contact lenses on line ▼	€5.60
☐	ordering contact lenses online ▼	€5.56
☐	order contacts lenses online ▼	€5.55
☐	order contacts online ▼	€5.52
☐	online contacts lenses ▼	€5.52

Any of those phrases turned into an EMD would be suspect. It would be hard to convince Google that your site was quality if you used any of those commercial terms as your domain name.

Google's update eliminated the power of EMDs, meaning webmasters stopped using them, or at least webmasters who understood SEO did. Take that first phrase as an example. The EMD would be:

contactlensesonlineorder.com

Surely someone would have registered that in the past to take advantage of the EMD ranking power. If they could rank for that phrase and stick AdSense ads on the site, then they'd be making a good chunk of change every time someone clicked on an advert.

When typing that domain into my web browser, this is what I get:

However, if I search using the Way Back Machine: http://web.archive.org, which looks for archived versions of websites, this is what I see:

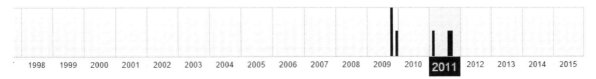
That site existed in 2009, and then again in 2011.

Using Way Back Machine, I can even look at that site as it appeared back in 2009 or 2011. Here it is in 2009:

INTERNET ARCHIVE

http://www.contactlensesonlineorder.com/

6 captures
2 Oct 09 - 19 Sep 11

Contact Lenses Online Order

Save up to 70% off retail contact lens prices. Fast, Simple and Cheap.

- Acuvue
- Biomedics
- Freshlook
- Soflens
- Proclear

We carry all popular brands of contact lenses including Acuvue, Biomedics, Focus, Freshlook, Soflens, Purevision prices.

Best Seller Contact Lenses

Focus Dailies Toric - 90 Pack Contact Lenses (90 lenses) $64.95   Biofinity Toric C

Notice the main header on the page uses the exact same phrase. This is a typical example of a low-quality EMD.

So, why is that EMD no longer an active site?

The truth is that no-one wants it now because of the problems associated with this type of EMD, and the fact that the domain may have picked up a penalty; something which isn't always removed when a domain changes hands either.

You can try a search for other EMDs from that contact lens list. If there is still a live

EMD site for a phrase, then the chances are it was a better site and more than likely de-optimized for that phrase. Either that or it's an abandoned site that the owner has left up for some other purpose.

Using the Way Back Machine to Check Domains

If your domain has never ranked properly, I'd recommend you check it at the Way Back Machine. You'll be able to see if your domain was used before you got your hands on it, and how. It is possible that the domain might have a penalty from before and that it carried over to you. If this is the case, you could file a reconsideration request at Google.

https://support.google.com/webmasters/answer/35843

While it's not guaranteed to work, it might if Google can see that the domain has changed hands.

Keyword Stuffed Domains

Another potential problem with a domain name is keyword stuffing.

Let's suppose your website is selling cosmetic contact lenses. If your domain was **cosmetic-halloween-colored-contact-lenses.com,** then it's clearly stuffed with relevant keywords. This would get you into trouble, but even if it didn't, what would visitors think of a domain name like that? This type of domain is not one that I would be anxious to hold on to.

Back in March 2011, Matt Cutts (at the time, a Google engineer) discussed the use of keywords in the domain name in a YouTube video:

http://www.youtube.com/watch?v=rAWFv43qubl

He suggested that a brandable domain is probably better than a keyword rich domain, and I agree. Despite being old, that video hints about the changes to come in the way keyword rich domains ranked at that time.

Of course, these are just general guidelines on domain names. Once you have your domain, there really isn't anything you can do about its name. Your choice is to either stick with it or move your site to a different domain. In this video, Matt Cutts offers some advice on moving a domain:

http://www.youtube.com/watch?v=wATxftE8ooE

Here are some other things to look out for which might indicate a low-quality EMD site:

- Is the site specifically targeting that EMD phrase or does your site have a lot of quality content within the overall niche?
- Do you have a lot of backlinks with anchor text that matches the EMD phrase?

- Are there very few pages on your site?
- Reading your content, does there appear to be a bias towards using that EMD phrase to try and help it rank better?
- Is that EMD phrase repeated numerous times on the homepage? What about other pages on the site?
- Is that phrase used in internal links pointing back to the homepage from other pages on the site?
- Is your on-site SEO specifically targeting that EMD phrase?

The Domain Name Checklist

- EMD? If yes, then be aware that this will work against you and you'll need to de-optimize the site for the phrase in the domain name.
- Is the EMD highly commercial in nature and not your brand name? If yes, then this might be a clear signal to Google that you are a spammer. The only option may be to move your site to a new domain.
- Is the domain name stuffed with keywords? If yes, there isn't much you can do with this other than to move the site to a better domain. Keyword stuffed domains look spammy and don't instill much confidence in visitors. Unless there is a good reason to keep the domain, like it still makes good income or ranks well, then I'd seriously consider moving the site to a better, more brandable domain.
- Has your domain ever ranked properly? If not, then check its history at the Way Back Machine. Consider submitting a reconsideration request to Google if the site looks like a poor quality, spammy project from the past.

Manual Check #2 - Web Page Real Estate

You should focus on two main areas when checking your web page real estate. These are "above the fold" and "sneaky links".

In January 2012, Google released a document that outlined a new "page layout algorithm improvement". You can read it here:

https://search.googleblog.com/2012/01/page-layout-algorithm-improvement.html

In releasing this change, Google was hoping to improve the user experience. No one likes to arrive at a website if all they see in their browser are Google ads, banners or email subscription forms. The general idea of this update was to penalize sites that didn't have much useful content above the fold. "Above the fold" simply means the viewable area in your browser before you scroll further down the page.

In the past, a lot of people made good money by throwing up quick, cheap "AdSense sites". These were designed to rank well in the SERPs, and many of them did just that. However, these sites showed visitors very little content, just money-generating adverts. On arrival, a visitor could click on an advert (and make the webmaster money), click the back button on their browser to return to the search page they came from, or they could scroll down the page to find the content. Because of the poor user experience on these sites, most people probably chose for one of the first two options as they figured the content would not be up to much. If something caught their eye in the adverts, they would click the ad as a way to get away from the page.

NOTE: If you are a member of Google AdSense yourself, you will have experienced the Google AdSense team advising you to put MORE adverts on your pages. The Google AdSense team seem to be at odds with what Google the Search Engine actually wants. Be aware that the two parts work separately and each has its own objectives and goals.

Look at your page above the fold.

I'd recommend resizing your browser to 1024x768 (most people use this resolution or something higher these days, according to W3Schools.com):

https://www.w3schools.com/browsers/browsers_display.asp

Once you've set your browser resolution, see what shows above the fold on your site.

You then need to ask yourself if there is any meaningful content visible. If you removed the adverts from that area, what are you left with? Does it now offer value to visitors in terms of the remaining content above the fold? This is also an interesting test for your page as a whole. Is the remaining content of high quality if you remove the adverts from a page? The answer should be a resounding YES.

NOTE: If you have some adverts above the fold, you may be OK. On the page layout algorithm announcement, Google says this:

> *"This algorithmic change does not affect sites that place ads above-the-fold to a normal degree, but affects sites that go much further to load the top of the page with ads to an excessive degree, or that make it hard to find the actual original content on the page."*

Sneaky Links in Footers, Headers or Elsewhere

Does your site have links in the footer? Links *per se* are not a problem, but if they are links with keyword rich anchor text, then they could be. If the links in your footer are there simply to make another web page rank better for a keyword term, then there is a problem.

Look at your footer links, and if you see any that use keyword rich anchor text, remove them.

If you have other footer links to things like Twitter, Facebook, Contact, Privacy etc, then these are fine.

If the links are site-wide (appearing on every page on the site), you might like to add a "nofollow" attribute to those links.

Web Page Real Estate Checklist

- Resize your browser to 1024x768 and see what loads above the fold. Is the content useful? Are there too many adverts? If there are too many adverts, especially above the fold, consider removing (or moving) them.
- If you removed all of the adverts from the pages on your site, would those pages still offer the visitor what they are looking for?   If not, then the content is not good enough.
- Does your site have sneaky links in the footer, especially keyword rich anchor text links, either to other pages on your own site or to external sites? If yes, then get rid of them.

Manual Check #3 – Site Structure

Is your site navigation helping your visitors find what they want quickly?

If you think in terms of needing every page on your site to be just one or two clicks away from the homepage at most, then you're on the right track.

Good website navigation should be intuitive to the visitor. They should immediately be able to see where they are at, and where they need to go for the information they require.

A good test here is to use a volunteer who has never been to your website before. Ask them to find a particular piece of information. Once they find it (if they find it), check to see how long it took them.

Include a Search Box

I'd highly recommend you have a search box on your website to help people find information quickly and effortlessly. If you are using WordPress, just know that the default search box that comes with the program is very poor. People won't be able to find what they want on a large site because WordPress doesn't rank its results by any kind of relevance, at least not any that I can detect.

An Example

On one of my websites, I had written an article on "vitamin A". I had also referenced vitamin A in 120+ other articles on the same site. The WordPress search box placed my main "vitamin A" article around position 125. That's not very good, and certainly not what I wanted to see.

WordPress or not, check out the search script your site is using. Do some searches. Does it return the most relevant pages in the results for search queries? If the results are not very good, then you need to look for a new search box script. There happens to be a very good one that I can recommend.

What if you could use Google's search engine to power the search box on your own site?

The good news is that you can. Google is king of search and relevance, so using a search box powered by the search engine giant itself ensures people find the most relevant pages on your site quickly and easily. After installing the Google search box on my own site, I then searched again for "vitamin A". This time my main article came up as #1, just as it should do.

You can find out more about Google Custom Search here:

https://cse.google.com/cse/

If you have an AdSense account, you can create the search box within that account to use on your site. Note that this will display AdSense ads in the search results. Even so, you do make money if people click on any of those ads. If you want to opt-out of the adverts in your custom search engine, visit the link above as Google does have a paid option for this too.

Site-wide Links

Site-wide links are links that appear on all pages of your site. You do have to be careful and not overdo these. If you do have site-wide links, they should not use any keyword phrases that you are trying to rank for.

NOTE: Site-wide links can either be to pages on your own website or link out to different websites.

In the past, swapping site-wide links with webmasters of other websites was a common SEO practice, with the emphasis on "was". Today, I am saying don't do it. Google's quality guidelines clearly state that IF these links are there as an attempt to manipulate search rankings, they should not be used.

If you are a WordPress site owner, the typical site-wide links that come pre-installed with the program include the blogroll (a list of links that appears in your sidebar). I recommend you remove this from your site, even if you have edited the blogroll with more relevant websites.

Site-wide links are typically found in the header, footer or sidebars of a site. One of the most common forms of site-wide links is the main menu of the site. This menu links to the main areas of the website and serves a useful purpose. I would recommend that your main navigation menu is not keyword-focused. Instead, create this menu with the visitor in mind, as a useful way to help them find what they are looking for.

On smaller sites (10 or so pages), the main navigation menu usually links to all of the pages on the site. Again, avoid keyword-rich anchor text in these menus, and always think about what is most helpful to your visitors.

As your site grows, it becomes unnatural and impractical to link to all the pages from the main site-wide menu. A far better strategy is to create individual menus for each section of your site and then put these menus on the pages in those sections. Let's consider "context-sensitive navigation".

Context-sensitive Navigation

The navigation system on your site can include menus in:

- The header
- The footer
- The sidebar
- Within the content area, usually at the end of a piece of content.

On larger websites, the navigation system you use should not be the same on every single page of the site. The navigation should change, depending on the page and its location on the site. I'm not suggesting every page on your website has a different navigation menu, but certainly, sections of your site could use their own custom menus.

The easiest way to think about this is with an example. Let's say you have a health site and the visitor is on a page about osteoporosis. A menu that could help the visitor would contain links to other articles about osteoporosis or conditions that cause the disease. You could still include a navigation "block" linking to the main areas within the site, but you'd also include more specific options for your visitor, related to the current article they are reading.

Let's consider another example. If you had a travel site and a visitor was on a page talking about restaurants in Bali, it would make perfect sense to have navigation options that show other articles on Bali, maybe hotels, attractions, and surfing, etc.

For a third and final example, let's say you have an e-commerce website that sells baby products. You might have a main site-wide menu that includes links to all of the main sections/categories on your site. This might include things such as strollers, cots, car seats and so on. Now, if your visitor is browsing the section on strollers, a menu with links to 2-seat strollers, jogging strollers, double and triple strollers, etc., would be very helpful. Always think in terms of how your navigation can best serve your visitors as that will help to keep you focussed when putting your site together.

This type of dynamic navigation is clearly easier and more practical to implement on larger sites. However, if you have a small site with a site-wide menu, do look at your navigation and make sure your links are not keyword-focused, and that the navigation helps, and not hinders the visitor experience.

A Tip for WordPress Users

Three plugins I recommend for helping you create a dynamic navigation system are:

Dynamic Widgets:
http://wordpress.org/extend/plugins/dynamic-widgets/.
This allows you to set up different sidebar menus (created as widgets) in different areas of your site.

Contextual Related Posts:

https://wordpress.org/plugins/contextual-related-posts/

This allows you to set up a related posts section after each piece of content. When a visitor gets to the end of an article, they'll see a list of related posts and be tempted to click through to one. This type of internal linking is also beneficial from a search engine perspective as it links related content together.

C.I. Backlinks:

https://ezseonews.com/cibacklinks

This is the plugin I use to automatically link internal pages on my site. It works the way I do because I helped design it and consulted at every step of its development.

Content Organization on Your Server (Non-WordPress Sites)

Organization of your content on the server and your site's navigation system go hand-in-hand. One mirrors the other. Well organized content is stored in a logical, intuitive manner, which should reflect in the navigation system.

The physical organization on your server is only important if you are building your website using something like HTML, which stores web pages as separate files. This doesn't apply to WordPress because it does not save content as individual files.

Let's use a theoretical example of a pet website. It might have content written about:

- Fish
- Birds
- Dogs
- Reptiles
- Amphibians
- Cats

There should be a folder/directory on your server for each of these content areas, and all files need saving into their corresponding folders. You see how this physical organization would mirror the navigation system of your site.

The first thing for you to check is whether your content is properly organized. In other words, are the right files placed in the right folders on your server, that is, are all dog-related articles physically located inside the dog folder (aka a directory), cats in the cat folder, and so on?

If the dog section on the site grows, we'll need to add to the structure of the folders/directories on our server. When the site gets bigger it's time to re-organize our content, in the exact same way we did with the navigation system earlier.

For example, if your pet project was an informational site, you could add the following sub-folders under your "dog" folder on the server:

- Training
- Toys
- Beds
- Food & treats

Each of these sub-folders would then store the content related to those files. So for example, all articles on dog training would be located in the "/dogs/training/" subfolder on your server.

If your site sold pets, perhaps a more logical way to organize the content would be to have sub-folders like:

- Alsatians
- Terriers
- Dalmatians
- Huskies

...And so on.

By efficiently organizing your content into logical folders on your server, the URLs of these pages would now look something like this:

mypetsite.com/dogs/training/clickers.html
mypetsite.com/dogs/training/choke-chain.html
mypetsite.com/dogs/training/walking-to-heel.html
mypetsite.com/dogs/food/mixers.html
mypetsite.com/dogs/food/tinned-dog-food.html
mypetsite.com/dogs/food/snacks.html

These URLs give the search engines big clues about the content. For example, the search engines would know that all six of those web pages were about dogs. They would also know that three of them were related to training dogs, and three others to dog food.

This type of physical organization helps the search engines categorize and rank your content. This is because your pages end up in "silos" of related material, with links between related content, thus joining them all together.

This folder organization on your server should match the menu navigation on your site.

NOTE: If you are using WordPress, you can get the same types of URLs by using categories. While categories are not physical locations like directories/folders on the server, they still serve the same purpose in categorizing your content into logical groups.

WordPress actually takes things a stage further and includes a feature called tags. You can think of tags as an additional way to classify your content, the main way being with categories. I won't go into how to use WordPress categories and tags in this book, other than to give you a couple of quick tips:

1. Never use a word or phrase as both a category and a tag. If it's a really important part of your site structure, it's a category. If it's less important, use a tag.
2. Never use a tag for just one post. If a tag is important, it will be used on several posts on your site. If it's not, then it's not important, so delete it.

Internal Linking of Content

When one of your pieces of content references information that is elsewhere on the site, it makes perfect sense to link to that other page within the body of your content. If we look at this Wikipedia page you can see a lot of links:

Glutathione

From Wikipedia, the free encyclopedia

Glutathione (GSH) is an important antioxidant in plants, animals, fungi, and some bacteria and archaea, preventing damage to important cellular components caused by reactive oxygen species such as free radicals, peroxides, lipid peroxides and heavy metals.[2] It is a tripeptide with a gamma peptide linkage between the carboxyl group of the glutamate side-chain and the amine group of cysteine (which is attached by normal peptide linkage to a glycine).

Thiol groups are reducing agents, existing at a concentration around 5 mM in animal cells. Glutathione reduces disulfide bonds formed within cytoplasmic proteins to cysteines by serving as an electron donor. In the process, glutathione is converted to its oxidized form, glutathione disulfide (GSSG), also called L-(–)-glutathione.

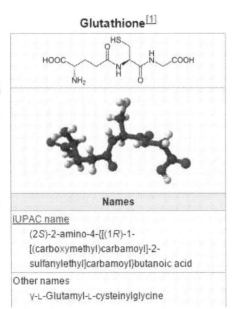

Glutathione[1]

Names	
IUPAC name	(2S)-2-amino-4-{[(1R)-1-[(carboxymethyl)carbamoyl]-2-sulfanylethyl]carbamoyl}butanoic acid
Other names	γ-L-Glutamyl-L-cysteinylglycine

NOTE: The actual links on Wikipedia pages are not underlined. I changed this to make the links easier to see in this book.

Each of these links goes to another web page on the Wikipedia website. Not only does this internal linking help the search engine spiders (programs that visit websites and read their pages and other information) to index the pages on the site, but it also helps the visitor to navigate more easily. If someone reading this article wants to learn more about something mentioned in the piece, they can easily click the relevant link and read about it in more detail before returning to the original page to continue reading.

Internal linking helps both visitors and search engines. Links with anchor text tell the search engine what the page is about. The only recommendation I'd make with internal linking is that you vary the anchor text in those links, much like you do with external links pointing into your website.

I did an experiment on internal linking and published the results on my site:

https://ezseonews.com/backlinks/internal-linking-seo/

The article gives you tips on using internal linking to best effect, and the results of an experiment I ran.

Essentially, I took one of my web pages that ranked at #190 for a particular phrase I was targeting. Using nothing but internal links, I managed to move that page up to position #14 in the Google SERPs. That indicates to me that Google like internal linking when it helps the visitor and it clearly helps pages rank better too.

The things I'd recommend you look at on your own site are as follows:

1. Do you make use of internal linking in the body of the content, much like Wikipedia?
2. Do you vary internal link anchor texts that point to a specific page?
3. For any particular anchor text, make sure you only ever link to one URL with it. Using the same anchor text to point to two or more different URLs is confusing, especially for the search engines.

Site Structure Checklist

- Is your navigation intuitive?
- Are all the pages on your site just one or two clicks away from the homepage? They should be.
- Do you have site-wide links in the sidebar?
- Do you have site-wide links in the header?
- Do you have site-wide links in the footer?

NOTE: Site-wide links with keyword-rich anchor text are potentially the most damaging.

- If you have a large site, do you use dynamic menus, which change depending on the section of the site the visitor is viewing?
- Do you have a search box? If it is a WordPress default search box, I highly recommend you switch to a more efficient script like Google's custom search.
- Do you internally link the pages of your website from within the body of your content, and not just via the navigation menus or a related posts menu?
- Is your content logically organized into "silos" where all related content is in

the same category or folder? If necessary (e.g. on a large site), do you use sub-folders to help make the navigation even more intuitive?

- If you are using WordPress, do you have any tags that are only used once or twice? If so, remove them.
- If you are using WordPress, do you have any tags that are identical to some of your category names? If so, remove them. Never use a phrase for a tag if it is being used (or will be used) as a category.

Manual Check #4 - Comments

A visitor-friendly site is one which offers your visitors the chance to interact with you. How you implement visitor interaction will depend on the type of site you run. For example, a business site may simply have a contact form (all sites should have one), and not want visitors commenting on individual pieces of content. Other sites may prefer full interaction by allowing visitors to leave comments on some or all web pages.

There are contact form scripts and comment form scripts available for HTML websites. Content management systems, like WordPress, have the comments built in, and contact forms are readily available as plugins.

I recommend you implement both on your site if it makes sense to do so.

If you already have a comment form on your site, check the comment settings. If you have your comments set to "auto-approve", then set it to "administrator approval" so that ALL comments must go by you first. If you set up comments for auto-approval, you will more than likely get a lot of spam comments published, and they could bring the quality of your site down. Get too many of these spam comments on your pages, and they might cost you a penalty, especially if they link out to "bad neighborhoods".

Bad neighborhoods? OK, for anyone not familiar with the terminology, let me explain what a "bad neighborhood" is.

Most spammers leave comments with the sole intention of getting a backlink and potential new traffic to their own website. Many of these will be low-quality sites, porn sites, gambling, or other types of sites that you would not want to associate with your project. Google refers to these types of sites as "bad neighborhoods". In addition, there is nothing to stop someone who has left a comment on your site (and had it approved some time ago), from redirecting their link to a bad neighborhood at a later date. To be safe, make all comments on your site **nofollow**.

Once everything is set up properly, go through **every single comment** on your site and delete any that are either fake or blatant spam.

Fake Comments

Fake comments are those that you (or someone you hired) wrote to make your page look more active than it actually is. I'd advise you not to do it.

Most of the time, fake comments are easy to spot and don't exactly instill trust once you've been rumbled.

Typical ways that fake comments stand out are:

1. Several comments posted within a very short space of time of each another, and then nothing; at least for a good while afterward.

2. Groups of fake comments rarely have author images (Gravatars) associated with the comment, which makes them stand out even more.
3. Comments are "bland" and don't really add anything to the content/conversation.
4. Comments are copied and pasted from another website like Amazon.

Spam Comments

Spam comments are not always easy to spot. They are written with the sole intention of getting a valuable backlink, so spammers have become creative in the way they do their spamming. There are even software tools available that help spammers to carry out mass-scale spamming of comment-enabled websites.

As a rule, don't approve any comment that is "stroking your ego", or "patting you on the back for a job well done".

> Submitted on 2013/03/05 at 08:42
>
> You blog post is just completely quality and informative. Many new facts and information which I have not heard about before. Keep sharing more blog posts.

While I have no doubt that this comment is true ;), sadly it is also blatant spam.

This flattery is supposed to stroke the ego of the webmaster so that it gets through the approval process. Don't approve these types of comments UNLESS you know the comment is legitimate, i.e. you recognize the commenter. Note too that comments like these make absolutely no reference to the article. In other words, they could just as easily be on a page about how to make cupcakes as one which looks deeply into astrophysics.

However, other comment spam is not always so obvious and disguised much better than the example above.

For example, a spammer might find a page they want a backlink from on the "health benefits of zinc". They'll then go and find an article on the web about this topic and grab a quote from it to use as their own comment. The quote will look like a real comment about your article, but will, in fact, be content copied from another website. This type of comment spam is often difficult to catch, except to say that in most cases it won't look quite right in the context of your article, not least because it will probably be overly formal and make no "specific" reference to your post or any of the other commenters' remarks. If in doubt, grab the content of the comments, put it in quotes, and then search Google for it.

Another type of comment spam is where the commenter is just trying to drive your traffic to their website. Here is an example of that:

> Submitted on 2013/03/08 at 13:34
>
> I would certainly not recommend 1&1. My recent experiences are detailed on my blog, here:
>
> I have always found Bluehost easy to use, Hostgator I find a little "clunky" but my favourite has to be Dreamhost. They had a few issues in the past but everything works like a dream for me and I find their unique control panel interface so easy to use.

You can see that I've blurred out the URL linking to his web page.

His page is a basic review of his favorite web hosting company (which does include his experiences with 1&1), and an affiliate link to that host. He left a comment that I would have otherwise approved, but not with that link to his web page. He is probably targeting any "high traffic" website that has reviewed the 1&1 web host, or even Hostgator and leaving similar reviews in the hope that he can piggy-back off their traffic as well as benefit from the relevant backlink.

General Rule for Approving Comments

Only approve comments if:

1. It is clear from the comment that the person has read the article.
2. The comment adds to the article, like another point of view on something specific to the post.
3. If you know that the person is real because you recognize their name (but only if the comment is also not spammy).

Obviously, these are just guidelines. In the field of battle, you'll have to make some tough decisions, but I recommend only keeping the best comments that you're sure are genuine. Delete EVERYTHING else. As you become familiar with comment spam, in all its forms, you will intuitively know what is genuine and what is not.

Comments Checklist

- Does your website have a comments section where visitors can leave comments, thoughts, and questions? Should it?
- Does your website have a Contact Us form? It should!
- If you have comments enabled, are you manually approving all comments? You should be.
- Check through all comments on your site and remove any fake or spam

comments. In fact, remove any comment where the sole purpose is to get a backlink to a website.

- Make comment links nofollow by default. Wordpress does this by default for comments.
- Going forward, only approve legitimate comments where it is clear the visitor has read your content and added to the conversation with their insight.

Manual Check #5 - Social Presence

Under the umbrella of social presence, I include two things:

1. The website and its author have a social presence on social media sites.
2. The website has social sharing "buttons" on its pages to allow visitors to easily share the content with their own social media followers.

Check your website. Do you have both present?

Let's look to see exactly what I mean here, as well as give you some ideas for a "bare minimum" social approach.

The Website and Website Author Has a Social Presence

The two main social channels I'd recommend you look at are:

1. Facebook
2. Twitter

If you have a lot of images you want to share, then extend that list to include Instagram. Depending on the type of site you run, LinkedIn is also a good one to include.

I recommend you consider these in that order of priority as well. If you have a Facebook account, you can easily set up a Facebook Page for your website. You can then link to the Facebook page from a prominent position on your pages.

You can see how I have this set up on one of my sites. Visitors can follow me on Twitter and Facebook or get my RSS feed.

Your Facebook page offers your visitors an additional channel for starting a "conversation" with you and your audience. From your point of view, you can post updates to that page which include things like:

- Tips and tricks for your industry/niche.
- Current news in your niche.
- Interesting articles you find around the web.
- New posts on your site (this can be automated).
- Videos, images, etc.
- Current special offers from your website.
- Anything else that is relevant to your site and niche.

Think of your Facebook page as an extension of your website. A Facebook page that has a good following will give your "brand" a huge amount of social proof. It's so easy to set up that I recommend all websites have a Facebook page.

As far as Twitter is concerned, it's also very easy to set up an account for your website. You can even set up your website to send a tweet to your Twitter account automatically, every time you publish new content on your site. You can, of course, send tweets with information related to your niche too (the same kind of stuff that you can post on Facebook). Services like Hootsuite: http://hootsuite.com allow you to schedule tweets (as well as Facebook and other social networks) in advance, which can prove useful.

As your Twitter following increases, you'll automatically be increasing your "authority" in the eyes of your visitors. Let's face it, if you have a Twitter account with 10,000+ followers, a lot of people will think: "Wow, this site must be good if it has that many followers. I must follow too". To help increase your Twitter follower number, learn how to effectively use hashtags, as these will help you reach a much larger audience when you send your tweets.

As your site grows in authority, you will find your Twitter following increases naturally, with more targeted individuals. It then becomes more than just a social proof thing. It becomes a useful tool for business.

When you have a Twitter account, make sure you link to it from your website so that people can follow you on that platform.

I don't recommend wasting any time with Google Plus. In October 2018, Google announced it would be shutting down Google+ for consumers.

Let's now look at how you can give your visitors the opportunity to share your content with their own followers, using social sharing buttons.

Social Media Share "Buttons"

If I show you an example, I am sure you'll recognize what I am talking about:

Typically, social media sharing buttons appear in a "panel", either above, below (or above AND below) the content on the page. This panel can be horizontal or even floating vertically (as in the screenshot above) over the web page on the right or left, or in a sidebar.

In my screenshot, the top social button is Facebook, the second Twitter, and again, I'd recommend concentrating on these two above all others.

Other social media sites you might like to have buttons for include Pinterest (if your site has a lot of images that you want to be shared) and StumbleUpon (a discovery engine that finds and recommends web content to its 25 million+ users).

For WordPress users, there are loads of plugins to add this sharing functionality to your site.

For HTML sites, you'll need to find a script that has these features, or manually go to each social media site and grab the button code to include in your own social media "panel".

What Do These Buttons Do Exactly?

These buttons give visitors to your site the opportunity to share your web page with their own social media followers.

For example, if I clicked on the Tweet button in the panel above, a short Tweet is constructed automatically, with the URL and title of that page included in the tweet.

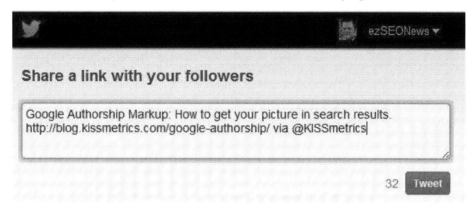

You can see at the end of the Tweet how Twitter has added **via @KISSmetrics**. This sends "KISSmetrics" (the author of the content) an auto-notification that someone has re-tweeted their content. This is one way how you can connect with the leaders in your niche.

When you have these social share buttons on your website, your visitors become your army of promoters, if your content is good enough, of course.

So, check your site. Do you have social sharing buttons? If not, I highly recommend that you add them (at least for the main three, namely Facebook, Twitter, and Google+).

NOTE: Google does index tweets and probably use them as a social signal in ranking (although probably only for a limited time). Google also knows how many Facebook likes your content gets and may use that as a social signal too.

Social Presence Checklist

- Does your website have a presence on Facebook?
- Does your website have a presence on Twitter?
- Does your website need a presence on LinkedIn or Instagram?
- Does your website have social sharing buttons that allow your visitors to share your content with their own social media followers? Remember, you should include Twitter and Facebook as a bare minimum.

Manual Check #6 – Would You Trust the Site?

This section looks at the trust levels for your site. We've already discussed some of the things that can help people trust you and your site, but let's now look at a more comprehensive list.

People like to deal with real people. When someone arrives at your site, do they know who they are dealing with?

The All-important Photo

A lot of split testing has shown that a photo of a real person increases conversions. From my own experience, the photos that work the best are NOT the ones that look like "stock photos", but those which look like a real person, or the person next door, so to speak. There's a reason for this. Websites that show real people help to build trust. When someone trusts your site they are more likely to follow through with your calls-to-action (CTA).

Where are the best places to put a photo on your site? Well, it really depends on the type of site you have, but a photo in the header or the sidebar usually works well.

Your photo needs to look natural, and not something that has obviously been grabbed from a stock photo website:

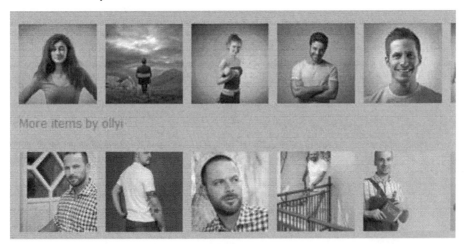

Whichever photo you use, make sure you look like a real person and not a photographic model. You want people to trust the image and anything that looks too glitzy may not appear genuine in the eyes of your visitors.

My favorite place to include a photo is in an author's resource box, at the end of each piece of content. Here is an example:

There's a separate case in progress that may lead to the Microsoft patent being ruled invalid, but that doesn't appear to have any bearing on this case at the moment.

A final decision is expected in May.

Related Entries

- Google In Privacy Flap With Germans Over New iOS Maps
- Google, Microsoft Cooperate To Invalidate Broad Online Mapping Patent

Related Topics: Google: Legal | Google: Maps & Local | Google: Outside US | Legal: Patents | Top News

 About The Author: Matt McGee is Editor-In-Chief of Search Engine Land. His news career includes time spent in TV, radio, and print journalism. His web career continues to include a small number of SEO and social media consulting clients, as well as regular speaking engagements at marketing events around the U.S. He blogs at Small Business Search Marketing and can be found on Twitter at @MattMcGee and/or on Google Plus. You can read Matt's disclosures on his personal blog. See more articles by Matt McGee

Connect with the author via: Email | Twitter | Google+ | LinkedIn

This author's bio box is at the end of the article. Notice how Matt includes links to his social channels underneath the bio.

If you don't have a photograph of the author or owner on your site, I recommend you add one ASAP.

The "About Us" Page

Every website should have an About Us page. Those that do, often find it's one of the most visited pages on the site. The About Us page is something that many webmasters skip over, but it really does help to build trust when people can find out more about you and your site. It also gives your visitors an opportunity to learn more about you on a human level. They like to find out what drives you and your site. This can be very important on dry, technical types of sites. If you want more advice on how to create a great "About Us" page, I recommend you read this article:

https://www.quicksprout.com/2018/03/05/how-to-create-an-about-us-page-that-generates-leads/

Comments Enabled

We've already talked about comments earlier in this book. Make sure you have a comment system installed on your site so that visitors can leave feedback. Good feedback can only help build trust and social proof for you and your brand.

Does the Site Pretend to Be a Merchant?

This specifically refers to affiliate sites who send traffic to a merchant site in return for making commissions on any sale.

Some affiliate marketers don't make it clear that they are just an intermediary in the sales process. They let visitors believe they are the actual merchant.

A typical case of this is when marketers use links that say, "Buy here" or "Buy now", without letting customers know they'll be visiting a different site to complete the transaction. Look at it from a visitor point of view. Don't you think it's a bit of a shock to be on one site, click the "buy" button, and then end up on say Amazon, for example? Sure it is.

Is the Site/Webmaster a Recognized Authority?

Being an authority means you are recognized as someone to trust within your niche. It's something you can achieve relatively easily if you do one thing:

BE EVERYWHERE!

Part of the reason I look for a social presence on the websites I critique is that it helps build authority. If someone finds your Facebook page (where they see your photo) in Google and likes it, then when they go to your website (and see your photo) and think, "Hmmm, I've seen this person before and they know what they're talking about." The same goes for any social media channel. The important thing here is to only ever share quality information to those channels, and never, whatever you do, get into heated debates with anyone who happens to disagree with you.

One method I use to extend my reach into a niche is to use the same photograph (either me, or my persona for a project), on my website, my Facebook page, Twitter & Google+ pages, and as a Gravatar: http://en.gravatar.com/, which is set up on the main email address for the site. A Gravatar is just an image associated with an email address. Whenever you post on forums or comment on Gravatar-enabled blogs, your photo shows next to your post. People will start to recognize you everywhere they go within that niche because you are "Everywhere". If the information you share through these channels is good, then you can quickly build a reputation as someone to trust and become a real authority figure within your niche.

NOTE: Being a recognized authority is particularly important on health sites. You need to know what you are talking about first and foremost, but secondly, people need to trust you. If you are a doctor or have specific training related to your site, let your visitors know this.

If your site relates to health or finance, are you a recognized authority? If not, then that is something you might like to work on.

Other Reasons People Don't Trust Your Website?

There are a few other reasons why people won't trust a website. I won't go into details on each of these reasons; I'll just list them. If any of these things are missing from your own website, then you might want to consider making some adjustments.

The Distrust Checklist

- No Contact page.
- No privacy page.
- No business address or phone number, or nothing that is clearly displayed.
- The site doesn't seem to have been updated in years.
- No testimonials.
- Copyright notice on the website is out of date.
- Lack of "trust symbols", e.g. Better Business Bureau, VeriSign, McAfee, etc.
- Web pages with typos, spelling mistakes or grammatical errors.
- Lack of response when visitors have posted comments/questions.
- Bad reviews.
- Poorly targeted emails, and difficulty unsubscribing from your newsletter.

The Trust Checklist

- Does the site have a photo of the webmaster/author of the content?
- Does your site have an About Us page?
- Are comments enabled?
- Does your site pretend to be a merchant?
- Is the author of your site a recognized authority in the niche/industry?
- Are you using a Gravatar set up on the email address that you use for your site?
- Does your site display your business address, preferably with a phone number?
- When was your site last updated?
- If appropriate, are there any testimonials and if yes, are they up to date?
- Does the copyright notice on your website display the correct year?
- Do you display any trust symbols (if appropriate)?
- Check all content for spellings and grammatical errors. Check your navigation systems for these errors as well.

Are there any unanswered comments on your site?

Manual Check #7 – Bounce Rates & Time on Site

There are two metrics that Google monitors as a way of determining visitor satisfaction.

The first is the bounce rate and the second is the time they spend on your site.

According to Google:

"Bounce rate is the percentage of visits that go only one page before exiting a site."

In other words, someone only views one page on your site before exiting. Typically, high bounce rates are bad for your site's reputation. It usually means people are not finding what they want on your site and therefore feel the need to leave and look elsewhere.

Time spent on site is the length of time a visitor stays on your site overall. Low time on site may indicate a problem with your content since people aren't sticking around to read it.

If you haven't set up Google Analytics on your website, I recommend you do so. Once it's set up, leave your site to collect new data for a month or so before trying to analyze these metrics. Then, go through your analytics to find pages that have high bounce rates AND low time spent on the page(s).

A page with a high bounce rate but with high time on the page is not a problem. Look at these examples:

Avg. Time on Page	Entrances	Bounce Rate ↓
00:52:18	3	66.67%
00:00:00	2	50.00%
00:17:41	2	50.00%
00:00:00	4	50.00%

The top page in the list has a bounce rate of 66.67% (the site average is around 10% so 66.67% is high). Despite the high bounce rate, I am happy with this page because there were three visitors, with an average time on that page of 52 minutes, 18 seconds. This tells me that the visitor must have found the information useful and engaging, even though they didn't visit any other pages on the site.

Similarly, the second page I highlighted above has a bounce rate of 50%, this time with two visits. However, the average time on that page was 17 minutes 41 seconds, so again, those two visitors must have found what they were looking for (or at least found it interesting) before they hit the back button and returned to Google.

The two pages that would concern me are the examples that I haven't circled. Both pages had an average time on site of 0 minutes. I would go and look at these pages in more depth, and over a longer period, to see whether there may have been a glitch in the reporting during the above screenshot, or, whether these pages historically have high bounce rates and low time spent on the page.

What you need to do is identify pages with high bounce rates AND low time spent on the page. Once you find them, you need to work out why visitors are not satisfied with what they see. If the content is good, maybe it's just not a good match for the search phrase they found you with on Google. Or maybe something else is pushing them away from the page(s). You need to look for ways to increase the visitor time on these pages (and hopefully decrease the bounce rates).

Bounce Rate & Time on Site Checklist

Install Google Analytics and allow it to run for a few weeks so that you have sufficient data to work with. Once you're ready, check your bounce rate and time spent on the site.

- Are your average bounce rates high?
- Are visitors spending a long or short time on your site?
- Look for specific pages where bounce rate is high AND time on site is low. Try to work out why these pages are suffering and fix them accordingly. Perhaps your page title does not accurately match the page content? This would mean that your listing in Google is misleading people to click through to your page, so when they do arrive there, they are disappointed and click the back button. Always consider tweaking page title and Meta description tags on any page with a high bounce rate, and then monitor the situation to see if your changes improve things.

Manual Check #8 – Legal Pages

There are certain pages on a website that I call "legal" pages. These are things like:

- Privacy Policy
- Disclaimers (including any medical or earnings disclaimers).
- Contact Us
- Terms
- About Us (we talked about this earlier in terms of visitor trust).
- Any other documents that should be displayed on your site. These might include things like cookie policy, anti-spam policy, outbound link disclaimer, and so on.

Does your website include all the necessary documents? Privacy Policy? Disclaimer? Terms? I cannot tell you what legal documents you need, but there is plenty of advice on the internet. Depending on where you live in the world, you may need different documents.

Legal Pages Checklist

Not all of these pages are necessary for all types of website, so check which pages your site needs and add them if they are missing.

- Do you have a privacy page?
- Do you have a disclaimer page?
- Do you have a "terms of use" and conditions page (TOS)?
- Do you have a contact page?
- Do you have an about us page?
- Do you have a medical disclaimer page?
- Do you have an email policy page?
- Do you have an outbound link policy page?

Manual Check #9 – Content Quality

This is a huge component of modern SEO.

If Content Is Bad, Getting Everything Else Right Won't Fix the Site

You need to have a website that you are proud of. More than that, you need to have a website that you would be proud to show anyone at Google. Content is what separates an average site from a great one, and the best way to understand what Google is looking for is to ask yourself one simple question:

"Could the content appear in a magazine?"

I took this question from the Google blog, in a piece about quality content. This is what you should be aiming for; this is what Google wants.

Obviously, e-commerce sites have a lot of pages that wouldn't satisfy this question, but it's certainly a great question to ask on any article-based content.

Here is another question that can apply to most types of content:

"Is your content the type of content that people will want to bookmark, or share socially?"

NOTE: Google can certainly detect bookmarks and social shares, so can use them as indicators if it chooses. However, forget Google for a moment. Having content that people want to bookmark is a good indication that it is of value to visitors. This means they will want to share and link to your pages naturally, without being coerced or tricked. Remember Link Bait? It's important to create some link bait specifically for the influencers in your niche, just for great backlinks and an authority boost. But, it is also important to create high-quality Link Bait content for your regular visitors too. Their social shares and occasional backlink will help build your authority on many levels.

Who Is a Good Judge of Your Content?

The biggest problem I have found concerning content quality is that webmasters themselves are not very impartial when it comes to judging their own material. If you can, it's always better to get someone else to honestly evaluate your content for you.

Besides the quality of your writing, there are a number of other things to look out for as you assess the content on your website. Here is a checklist (in no particular order):

- Have other websites copied and published the content?

This is a common problem, though these scraper sites are usually very low-quality and recognized for what they are by Google. In the past, these types of sites could hurt your rankings, but as Google developed its algorithms, this method of copying other people's content has become less of an issue.

To check whether your content has been stolen you could use a site like Copyscape: http://www.copyscape.com. Alternatively, grab a sentence or two from your web page and search for it on Google between quotes. If that block of text is on any other website(s), Google search will let you know. Here is an example of what it looks like when you do this type of search and other sites have copied (stolen) your content:

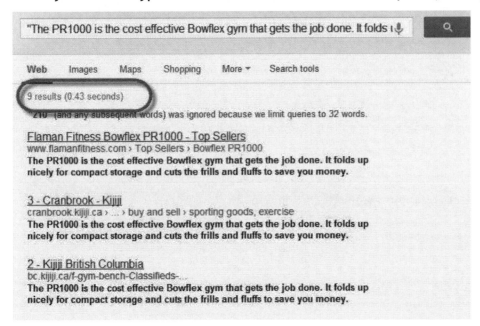

See how there are nine results in Google, each with the identical text.

If other sites have stolen your content and used it on their own sites, I'd recommend you contact those other sites and ask them to take the content down right away, informing them that they're breaching your copyright. Usually, the threat of getting their hosting company involved is enough for most people to remove your stuff.

Do a Google search for **dealing with copyright infringement** and you'll find lots of great advice.

If you prefer, you can hire services to deal with content thieves.

DMCA: http://www.dmca.com is one; although I've never used them, so cannot personally vouch for their service.

OK, let's now look at some other "quality" guidelines to consider:

- **Product reviews unbiased?**

If you have product reviews on your site, are they unbiased, or positive, positive and more hyped up positives? See, the thing is you need to share both sides of the story. Consumers know that ALL products have some things that are not perfect, so you need to highlight all sides.

- **More than just a rehash of the merchant site content?**

On the topic of reviews, is the content just a rehash of what you can find on the merchant site or perhaps Amazon? Your reviews need to be PERSONAL. Readers must know that you have personally tried the product and therefore your review must contain insights not seen on ANY other website. Write your review from personal, first-hand experience.

- **Affiliate link disclaimer?**

If your site is an affiliate site, do you have an affiliate link disclaimer? Do people on your site know that you are not the actual merchant?

This all comes back to the issue of trust. I realize that an affiliate link disclaimer can hurt conversion rates, so try to tell your visitors in such a way that they don't mind you being an affiliate. After all, you are helping them with their buying decision, aren't you?

In my experience, if someone reads an impartial review by someone who has actually used the product, then they don't mind clicking a link knowing it's an affiliate link. If they read a hyped-up sales pitch, on the other hand, and then find out your link is an affiliate link, then you're going to lose both trust and respect.

- **Keyword stuffing**

Keyword stuffing is really bad SEO. In the past, webmasters knew that adding keywords to their content would make it rank better for those keywords. Consequently, articles often became stuffed with keyword phrases. Today, that kind of thing will get your site penalized or even booted out of Google SERPs altogether.

As you read your content, ask yourself if it looks like it's written for a human or a search engine. If the latter, then re-write it or scrap it altogether.

A quick test for keyword stuffing is to read your content carefully (or get a friend to read it). Can you pick out phrases you think the article was designed to rank for by the way it repeats a phrase? Or maybe it's written with slight grammatical errors just so a particular phrase could be inserted?

You MUST take out any keyword stuffed content. Whether that means re-writing it or deleting it, that's your choice.

My advice when you are writing content is to WRITE NATURALLY!

If you hear anyone talking about keyword densities, ignore them. The correct density for any word or phrase on a page is the density that it ends up with when written naturally. It might be 2%, it might be 1%, and it might even be 0.1% or 0%. Bear that in mind. As you read your content, try to see if any word or phrase seems overused more than is natural.

- **Fluff rating**

Fluff rating is a term I use with my students.

Looking at the free dictionary: http://www.thefreedictionary.com/fluff, one of the definitions of fluff is:

> **3.** Something of little substance or consequence, especially:
>   **a.** Light or superficial entertainment: *The movie was just another bit of fluff from Hollywood.*
>   **b.** Inflated or padded material: *The report was mostly fluff, with little new information.*

Part (b) is exactly what I am referring to - an article that goes on and on but doesn't really say anything.

Webmasters have typically tried to increase the length of their content because they think that more words rank better. This means that an article that could be covered in just 400 words in a quality piece, is now stretched out to say 600 words - 200 of which are fluff - and only included to raise the word count. What effectively happens in cases like this is that an otherwise good article is watered down and becomes less valuable and/or readable.

An article that says very little, despite its word count, has a high fluff rating and should be deleted or re-written to provide quality information on a given topic.

- **Information duplicated on multiple articles**

Does information on one page of your site appear on other pages as well? In other words, is there a big overlap between the content on the various pages of your site? If so, you need to remove it. If two or more articles are so closely related that they share the same information, consider merging those pieces into one big article.

The pages on a website should all contain different information and there should be a bare minimum of content overlap.

- **Check the sitemap**

A sitemap is a great way to check your content. As you look through the sitemap, are there instances where two pages have very similar filenames or titles? If so, are those two pages covering the same information? If yes, then you might want to combine them into a single quality article.

In the past, a common strategy for building a website was to carry out keyword research and then write content around the keyword(s) that have high demand and low competition. Many keywords were very similar to others, meaning lots of articles overlapped in the information they delivered.

e.g. In the past, it was common to find sites that had separate articles based on each of these phrases:

- Best vacuum
- Best vacuum cleaner
- Which is the best vacuum?

Can you see how those three phrases are saying the same thing? So how can there be three separate articles for these phrases?

Here is an example I found on one website:

The mood of the party is set right at the beginning.

Baby Shower Invitation Idea
Here is a fun baby shower invitation idea to help cr
occasion.

Baby Shower Invitation
A great baby shower invitation for the internet age.

Baby Shower Invite
Since the baby shower invite is the grand introduct
with it.

Do those three articles on baby shower invitations really have useful, unique content without the fluff? If I was critiquing this site, this would be the kind of thing I would look out for in the sitemap, as clues of content problems.

What about these two pages found on the same site:

Many companies now offer beautiful satin baby shower invitations.

Baby Shower Invitations For Twins
Double the blessing and a baby shower invitations for twins should convey the excitement.

Twin Baby Shower Invitation
A twin baby shower invitation has the added feat of acknowledging more than one gender.

The reason webmasters do this is not for the benefit of the visitor. It's for the benefit of the search engine. They hope that each page will rank well for its variation of the phrase, and therefore bring a lot more traffic to the site than just one article optimized for one of the phrases.

While this once worked, it doesn't today. Google will count **baby shower invitations for twins**, and **twin baby shower invitation** as the same phrase. That means a single article is all you need. You'll also avoid the duplicate content issues that come with two separate articles saying roughly the same thing.

Check through your sitemap to identify possible problems. You can combine similar articles into one piece, but make sure you cut out the fluff and make these articles the best that they can be.

1. Titles & headlines

The <title> tag is an important part of a web page. It tells the visitor what the page is about (the title is often used in Google as the anchor text to the page). The headline on the page is also important for similar reasons. Google has traditionally used keywords in the title and headlines to help rank a page. And in case you're wondering, yes, webmasters have abused these areas – a lot!

Let's look now at the white-hat approach to titles and headlines.

1. You should write your titles for HUMANS, not for search engines.
2. You should write your headlines for HUMANS, not for search engines (are you seeing a pattern here?).
3. Your **headline** should be unique to the page it's on (not duplicated on other pages).
4. Your **title** should be unique to the page it's on (not duplicated on other pages).

In the past, one of the best ways to rank a page for a phrase was to use the exact phrase for the title and the opening headline. Of course, the same phrase would be sprinkled down the page as well, but the title and headline were the strong ranking factors. Today, this won't work (at least for the long-term), so don't use a single keyword phrase as either the title or the headline, or both. Titles and headlines should be crafted to draw the reader in. They can include topic-related phrases but don't stuff, and above all else, **write them for humans.**

While we are on the topic of page titles, make sure that no two pages on your site share the same title. This also goes for Meta descriptions if you use them, and that includes a "template" description that just substitutes a word or phrase each time it's used (as is typical on doorway pages).

- **Written for the search engine or the visitor?**

We've touched on this several times already, but it is so important that I am including it as a separate bullet point. Was the content written for human viewers or for the search engines? If the latter or you are just not sure, then that piece of content needs some work.

- **Hidden text on the page?**

One way that webmasters have tried to fool the search engines is with hidden text that contains keyword phrases. Hidden text can be achieved a few different ways, though the simplest is to use white text on a white background.

Fortunately, checking for hidden text is easy. Start by opening the web page in a browser and then click on it somewhere. Now press CTRL+A (command + A on a Mac computer) to select everything on the page. All the page contents should now highlight (select), including any hidden text. Check to make sure that all text on the page is visible. Any hidden text that you find needs removing immediately.

- **Visible blocks of text that are only there for the search engines.**

An example of this is when a web page lists "incoming search terms", like this one:

Incoming search terms:

- food presentation ideas
- food presentation
- fruit decoration images
- funny food presentation
- fruit art with kids
- fruits foods pictures
- garnishing with vegetables
- picture of joke flower
- food wallpaper
- funny food garnish

What is the point of that list? Does it in any way help the visitor?

Lists like this serve one purpose only, and that is to add keywords to the page to try to make it rank better in Google. Therefore, according to Google, it is spam.

Incoming search term lists are not the only type of block you'll find on web pages. On travel sites, I've frequently seen long lists of towns or cities. They are often not hyperlinked to relevant sections of the site, which suggests they only serve to add keywords to a page.

Any block of text on your page that is only there to increase keywords on that page really does need removing ASAP.

- **Over-optimization of the page.**

Google has gone out of its way to stop webmasters over-optimizing their sites. This is because SEO is spoiling the otherwise great search results by showing pages that don't deserve to be at the top.

While a lot of over-optimization relates to the backlinks of a website (and we'll cover that later), it also applies to what is on the website itself.

Look at the pages on your site to see whether a single phrase is used more than you might expect, thus making it obvious the phrase(s) was an intended target. If you find any of these, also check to see whether:

- Links to that page are using that phrase as anchor text?
- Is that phrase also in key areas of your web page, like title, meta description, H1 header, opening paragraph, ALT tag, image title tags, bolded, italic etc.

SEO Should Be "Invisible"

I don't mean that there is none, just that what is there should be discrete and not openly obvious or in-your-face.

There are WordPress plugins available, designed to help you check your on-page SEO. These are keyword driven checks and I think they are a bad idea. Content should NOT be keyword driven anymore, it should be theme driven with the focus being to please your visitors.

If you have been using an SEO plugin that checks for placement of keywords in an article, I'd recommend using it to de-optimize your articles (removing phrases from places they really don't need to be), and once you're done, delete the plugin.

- **Is your content driven by keywords or by what the visitors want?**

This is always a good check to make. Ask yourself whether the content you write on your site is driven by a specific keyword phrase, or by what your visitors actually want to see.

There will be keywords you want to rank for. That is natural. What I am saying is that instead of thinking you have to write an article about the phrase "tablet vs. laptop", just because it commands a high cost per click.

Keyword		Approximate CPC (Search)
☐ tablet vs laptop ▾		€4.84

.. consider writing an article on the "advantages and disadvantages of using a tablet instead of a laptop".

OK, it could be the same article, right? However, thinking about your content in terms of the visitor, instead of your keyword research, should ensure your content has a fighting chance of pleasing Google. Of course, you could include the phrase "tablet vs. laptop" in your article if you wanted too, and as long as it made sense to do. I'm just suggesting a different approach to choosing the topics you write about, that's all. Many of us got into bad habits in the past – we had to – but the only way forward now is to replace old habits with new. Think what article the visitor wants to see first, then go and see which keywords and theme words are relevant to the article before you write it.

To quote the wise words of Dr. Wayne Dyer:

"Change the way you look at things, and the things you look at change."

- **Does your content reflect search/visitor intent?**

Does your web page offer a good match for the search terms that found it?

Here's an example to illustrate:

Let's say you rank #1 in Google for the term "natural painkillers", but your web page only discusses pharmaceutical painkillers. Is the visitor going to be happy with your page? I doubt it. Their intent is for information on natural solutions, and you only offer drugs.

As we've seen, Google has ways of measuring how happy visitors are with your pages like bounce rate, time on site, social signals, visitor interaction and so on.

Therefore, it's important you don't try to rank for phrases that are a poor match for your content.

- **Does your page provide something not already in the top 10?**

Does your content provide something that is not already available in the top 10 of Google? If not, think about why it should replace one of those pages in the top 10 slots? What type of things can you add to your web page to make it stand out from the rest? What can you include that the other top 10 pages don't offer?

Consider things like:

- Personal stories.
- Your own opinions.
- Your own unique thoughts, ideas etc.
- Images or photographs that work with the topic of the page.
- Visitor interaction – maybe a poll asking for visitors' own opinions. A poll coupled with an active comments section creates a great resource, especially if the topic of your page was a little controversial.

Content Quality Checklist

Look at every page on your website. Use the following checklist to determine the quality of your content. Apply anything to your page that is missing.

- If the page is essentially an article, could it appear in a quality magazine?
- Is this the type of content that people would want to bookmark?

- Are people likely to share this content with their own friends and followers?
- Check a sentence or two in Google to see if your content is published (illegally or otherwise) on other websites. Contact any webmaster who is illegally displaying your content and ask them to remove it (see the article I linked to in this section of the book on copyright infringement). Take any reasonable measure you can to get the content removed from their site.
- Is it a product review? If yes, is it unbiased? Does it tell of the good, the bad and the neutral? Does your review add information that gives opinions and views which are not found on the manufacturer's website, or any other website for that matter?
- If you use affiliate links, do your visitors know they are affiliate links? They should do.
- Read each piece of content and look for keyword stuffing. Does it read naturally for a human, or was it written for a search engine? If any word or phrase appears more often than might be expected in a naturally written piece of content, then re-write it.
- How much "fluff" is in your article? Try to make sure your content does not contain fluff or watered-down filler text. Get rid of any sentences that are only there to increase word count. If you have to remove a lot of fluff, perhaps the article could benefit from a total re-write.
- Do any two (or more) articles overlap in terms of what they talk about? Do one or more other pages on your site repeat the same information? If yes, get rid of the duplication.
- Check your sitemap for possible problems. Are there any entries with similar filenames or titles that may indicate the articles cover the same/similar material? Are there any entries that suggest the content was written around keywords rather than around the interests of the visitor? If yes, get rid of (or re-write) all content that was not written specifically for visitors.
- Check all of your page titles and headlines to make sure you don't have the exact same title and headline on other pages. Headlines and titles should work together to entice the visitor. You should always write these for the visitor, and never for the search engines.
- Check Meta descriptions, if you use them. These should not be keyword stuffed. Once again, always write for the visitor, not the search engines, as a way to inform your visitors what the content is all about.
- Make sure you don't use the same Meta description (or "templated" description) on more than one page.
- Check each page for hidden text and remove any that you find.
- Are there any visible "blocks of text" on your pages that are only there for the search engines? If yes, get rid of them.

- SEO should be "invisible". Is it difficult to spot intentional SEO on your pages/site? It should be.
- Is your content driven by keywords or by what the visitor really wants to see? If the former, you need to clean up the content.
- Check to see what keywords visitors are finding your pages with. Does your page reflect the searcher's intent for these keywords?
- Does your page provide something not found on any other website's web pages?

If you are interested in learning more about writing and developing quality content for your site, I have both a book and a course on the subject. Check at the back of this book for links to these resources if you are interested.

Manual Check #10 – Inbound Link Profiles

Getting links pointing back to your website has always been one of the main jobs of any webmaster. Although Google doesn't like it, it did tolerate that behavior, at least until Penguin. Overnight, established websites dropped from the rankings. Pages that had been holding the top spot for years suddenly disappeared completely from Google's SERPs.

Google had done something that no-one believed it ever would. It started to enforce its guidelines relating to "link schemes".

Link schemes

Any links intended to manipulate PageRank or a site's ranking in Google search results may be considered part of a link scheme and a violation of Google's Webmaster Guidelines. This includes any behavior that manipulates links to your site or outgoing links from your site.

http://support.google.com/webmasters/bin/answer.py?hl=en&answer=66356

Any site that is seen to be participating in link schemes is in danger of a ranking loss. Even worse than that, any site that HAD participated in link schemes is also in danger. That means if you have a site that you are now running "by the book", but you had been involved in some dodgy link schemes in the past, your rankings could still be seriously affected if you never cleaned up those poor-quality backlinks.

Google is constantly looking for unnatural link patterns. That is, links which have clearly been built by the webmaster, usually, though not always, on a large scale, and often of low-quality.

To put it bluntly, **Google doesn't want you to build links to your own website**, at least not links whose sole purpose is to improve your rankings. As you look through your own backlink profile, it's important to be able to identify links that may be causing your site problems. If you do find any, deal with them accordingly. These include any links that Google would consider part of a "link scheme".

Before I go through the kinds of links that will hurt your site, let me be clear about one thing: If your site received a penalty because of its backlinks, cleaning up those backlinks WILL NOT return your site to the same "pre-penalty" rankings. The reason is that your pre-penalty rankings were achieved WITH the help of these spammy links because Google was still counting them back then. In other words, these spammy links were contributing to your success in the SERPs; the very reason why we used to build them. By removing them now means your pages won't have the same inbound links, and therefore won't rank as high. So, while cleaning up your links is vital to your long-term success, don't expect that cleaning them up will put your old rankings back to where they were because it won't. For that to happen, you'll need to build new, stronger, authority links to your site to replace the ones you've deleted/removed.

Ok, it's important to know first what constitutes a bad link. Before we look at that, though, it's probably better that I tell you how to find the links that point to your site.

Finding Backlinks to Your Website

There are several tools you can use, some free, others paid. However, the one you should be using as part of your backlink search is Google Search Console, which is totally free.

Google Search Console

If you don't have an account with Google Search Console, I recommend you create one right away. If Google wants to notify you of problems with your site (spiderability, spyware detected, links warnings, etc.), it'll do so through Google Search Console (GSC).

GSC also shows you the links that Google knows about.

See the section earlier in this book on the Disavow tool where I explain how to use GSC to find links.

What I love about GSC is that you get to see the link data that Google has for your website. I'm sure it doesn't show you everything, but it really is a great start to see the backlink data. GSC is always my first stop to find any problematic backlinks.

SEO Spyglass

SEO Spyglass is a commercial tool, though there is a free version to get you started. The free version won't let you save your data and there may be other limitations, but it can find any links that don't get reported in GSC.

SEO Spyglass:

https://www.link-assistant.com/seo-spyglass/

With SEO Spyglass you just type in the URL of your site and let the software do the rest. It goes off to numerous sources to find all the backlinks to your website.

SEO Spyglass gives you masses of information about the links to your site, things like:

- Which page it links to.
- The anchor text.
- Whether the link is dofollow or nofollow.
- IP address.

- Domain age.
- How many links per page.

And lots more besides.

SEO Spyglass really is a great tool for finding backlinks and specific link data for your site.

Ahrefs

https://ahrefs.com/

This site is the most popular site among SEO professionals. It does an excellent job of finding links to your website. Ahrefs provides a huge amount of data in the paid version.

The free version is very limited, so to get the best out of this tool you need a paid subscription.

Majestic SEO

https://majestic.com/

Majestic SEO is another very good tool, perhaps only second to Ahrefs. There is a limited free plan, and more comprehensive paid plans for those who want additional features.

Ok, so you now know how to find the links. The next step in the process is to understand how to evaluate them.

Link Schemes

"Any links intended to manipulate PageRank or a site's ranking in Google

search results may be considered part of a link scheme and a violation of Google's Webmaster Guidelines."

Link schemes include "any links intended to manipulate a site's ranking in Google search results".

Below are the schemes that can get you into trouble. You should check your site to make sure you are not engaging in any of these activities:

- **Buying or selling links that pass PageRank:** If your site has bought links or sells links, then Google will probably come after you. Please note that when I say "buy", I don't necessarily mean that money changes hands. You could pay for a backlink in any number of ways, e.g. goods, services, free products, etc. If a webmaster has taken any kind of "reward" to host your links, then they are considered part of a link scheme. This even includes links found in product reviews, where you have given the webmaster a free copy of your product in exchange for the review and backlink.
- **Partner pages:** These were all the rage 10 years ago. You put up a partner page on your site and linked back to other websites in return for a link. These were commonly known as resource pages. Get rid of any links on a resource/partner page that are reciprocated, that is, those sites which link back to yours.
- **Linking to undesirable neighborhoods:** If you link to any other site on the web, you are responsible for that link. Google sees links as votes for another website. If you link to spammy websites, or even websites unrelated to your content, then be warned. You could easily get penalized for it.

One of the places where webmasters unknowingly link to these bad neighborhoods is in the comments section of their website. When people leave comments, they often include their URL, which could end up as an active link in the comments section of your web page. Even if the link looks good now, there is nothing to stop the author of that comment redirecting it later on. They might redirect it to a porn site, or another undesirable website that you would not want to be associated with. Because of this, I recommend you make comment links nofollow. At least this way you are telling Google that you don't necessarily endorse that link.

- **Automated backlinks:** Backlinks built in an automated fashion, using software and/or spun content, will cause you a lot of problems. Not only are the backlinks generated by these tools of low-quality, but they are also fairly easy for search engines to identify. If you have backlinks built in this way, try your best to remove them, and sooner rather than later.
- **Links in articles that you publish on other websites:** Be careful here. If the anchor text is clearly trying to manipulate the rank of your web page, Google

will spot it. Google cites "large-scale article marketing or guest posting campaigns **with keyword-rich anchor text links**" as a problem, but then you should already know that by now, that's if you've read the preceding chapters.

Here is an example that Google uses within the guidelines:

> Links that are inserted into articles with little coherence, for example:
> most people sleep at night. you can buy <u>cheap blankets</u> at shops. a blanket keeps you warm at night. you can also buy a <u>wholesale heater</u>. It produces more warmth and you can just turn it off in summer when you are going on <u>france vacation</u>.

See how the anchor texts within the body of this piece are specific keyword phrases? These are clearly attempts to manipulate rankings, and Google will catch anyone who tries it.

If you write articles for other websites, say in the form of guest blogs, I recommend you use a resource box at the end of the article for pointing a link back to your homepage. Make sure you use either the site name or site URL as the anchor text. If you want to include a link within the body of the article, then I advise you to use either the URL of the page you are linking to or its title/headline as the anchor text. This approach is far more natural than keyword-focused anchor text.

- **Low-quality links in general:** Google specifically mentions low-quality directory and bookmark sites.

I know there are a lot of tempting back-linking gigs on places like fivver.com, but don't use them. Once you have been submitted to hundreds of low-quality directories or bookmark services, you won't be able to get those links taken down if you need to, meaning the damage is permanent.

Other types of low-quality links include any type of "profile link" that is clearly only being used for the backlink.

Forum signature links that use a keyword phrase are also bad for your rankings. If you are a member of a forum and you want to include a link to your site in your forum signature, then use your site name or URL as the anchor text. Using a specific keyword phrase is clearly an attempt at trying to get your page to rank better for that phrase. Google's web crawling bot can easily detect this old hat approach to link building.

- **Theme & widget backlinks:** In recent years, another link-building "loophole" was to create a template, or maybe a WordPress widget/plugin, that would be given away for free, but there was a slight catch. Anyone using the theme or plugin would have a link inserted into their homepage (usually in the footer), back to the author's website. It was a simple reciprocal arrangement. You got something for free and all you were required to do was accept a little link that pointed back to the developer's own website. Google clamped down on this during 2012 and penalized a lot of websites.

- **Site-wide links:** We looked at this earlier in the book. Any links that appear on all the pages of your site are site-wide links. An example would be a blogroll, on a WordPress site. Blogrolls typically list links to "favorite blogs" in the sidebar. However, people buying site-wide links on other sites in the past have abused them greatly. Google hit back hard on this arrangement and penalized anyone who took part, especially on a large scale.

I know we all have navigation on our sites. We also place some items on every page of the site. However, pay particular attention to any site-wide links that use a keyword phrase as the anchor text. These are the ones which are more likely to get you into trouble. You know the type, links that read like "make money online" or "buy cheap contact lenses", typically found in the footers of all pages on your site. All site-wide links with keyword rich anchor text need looking at carefully and changing/removing wherever necessary.

As you can see, link building has just become a lot more difficult. If you listen to Google, it'll just tell you to write great content and the links will come naturally. Unfortunately, the people at Google seem far removed from the reality of the situation. Getting others to link to your content, no matter how great it might be, is not as simple as Google suggests. This is because webmasters are not so generous about linking out to other websites. We, therefore, do need to find ways to get backlinks that at least appear to be more natural.

In terms of critiquing/cleaning up your backlink profile, your job is to try and identify your links and then clean up ALL the poor-quality ones that point to your site. The next job is to then build new, better quality links to replace the ones you've removed.

Make a List of All Bad Links to Your Site

The first step to cleaning the links you have identified as "bad" is to contact each webmaster, in turn, asking them to remove the offending link(s). Successful or not (and in most cases, it won't be), document every attempt you make. When you have the data to show you have tried to clean up your backlinks, you can then approach Google using the Disavow tool:

https://www.google.com/webmasters/tools/disavow-links-main?pli=1

The disavow tool tells Google that you want these links ignored AND that you have tried to clean them up. There are no guarantees with the disavow tool, but it is well worth a go when you consider your final option, which is to move the site to a brand new domain and begin the back-linking process from scratch.

There is a good article here that describes one person's positive results using the disavow tool:

https://moz.com/ugc/googles-disavow-tool-works-penalty-removal

Other Specific Things to Look Out for in Your Backlink Profile

1. **Diverse IPs:** Is there a good spread of IP addresses for the pages that link to your website? A lot of links from the same or very similar IP addresses may indicate a blog network or links from self-owned domains.
2. **Lots of links from the same domain:** These could indicate site-wide links that may need removing. If the site is an authority and you get traffic from that site, then you might want to leave those links intact. If they are site-wide, and on low-quality domains, then get them removed.
3. **Too many keyword phrase anchor texts:** Google Penguin is looking at the anchor text of inbound links. If you have a lot of links with the exact same anchor text, then that is unnatural, and Google knows it. If it is the name of your site, then that's okay. If it is commercial keyword phrases that you want your site to rank for, then that's not okay. In 2012, anchor text links became a lot less important. My advice is to water these down significantly and aim for links designed to increase your authority, i.e., using your domain name, brand name or domain URL as the anchor text.
4. **Too many backlinks on low-quality directories:** We mentioned this earlier so you know what to do here.
5. **Backlinks from spun content:** This is a huge problem if you have ever used automated backlink software to create backlinks using spun content. Spun content is one of the deadly sins of SEO. Google has been and will continue to be, on the warpath for this. It is getting better and better at detecting it too. If you find backlinks in spun content, do your best to get them taken down. Sometimes this type of backlink is easy to spot by looking at the titles of the pages containing the backlinks. Here is an example of backlinks I found in GSC for one site that clearly used spun content for its backlinks:

Links

- http://goarticles.com/article/Is-Serrapeptase-The-solution-to-Dupuytren-s-Disease/
- http://goarticles.com/article/Serrapeptase-A-Feasible-Therapy-For-Numerous-Sclerosis/
- http://goarticles.com/article/Serrapeptase-A-potential-Strategy-to-Multiple-Sclerosis/
- http://goarticles.com/article/Utilizing-Serrapeptase-to-alleviate-Bodily-Discomfort/

This type of backlink is VERY bad for your site. Fortunately, these links were on an article directory website. I contacted their support team about the spammy nature of these articles and they promptly took them down.

Inbound Link Profile Checklist

Check the links pointing to your site using the tools mentioned in this book. If you only use one, then I'd recommend GSC.

Have you knowingly participated in link schemes? This includes:

- Buying or selling links to pass PageRank? (Get rid of paid links).
- Do you have a partner/resources page on your site containing reciprocal links? If yes, remove all reciprocated links.
- Are you linking (knowingly or unknowingly, perhaps via the comments system) to bad neighborhoods? If yes, get all bad links removed from the comments.
- Do you have backlinks created by automated tools? If yes, try to get these taken down ASAP.
- Are backlinks pointing at your site from content that was spun? If yes, try to get the spun content taken down ASAP.
- Are there backlinks located in the body of articles which link to your site using keyword rich anchor text? If yes, I recommend you change these keyword links and use your domain name, brand name, domain URL or title/headline of the article, as the link text.
- Is there any low-quality directory or bookmarking links pointing at your site? These will cause trouble if you cannot remove them. Add them to your list of links to disavow, if you eventually have to go down that path.
- Are there any backlinks to your site from themes or widgets that you have created? If yes, you need to deactivate those links.
- Are there any links on your website that link out to other websites from themes or widgets you may be using? If yes, remove them.
- Are there site-wide links pointing to your site from low-quality websites? If yes, they need removing. Site-wide links from high-quality websites are

probably OK, and I wouldn't remove those except as a last resort.

- Are your links from a diverse range of IP addresses? If not, get more links from different IP addresses.
- Do you have links coming in from other websites that you own? If yes, are those links purely to help your pages rank better or is there a good reason to cross-link. If there is no good reason to cross-link the sites, remove those links.
- Are there lots of links from the same domain? If the domain is low-quality, get them removed.
- Is there a high percentage of inbound links using keywords phrases you are/were targeting as anchor text? If yes, I'd advise you to water these down. Include more links that use the domain/brand name, URL or title/headline of the content you are linking to.

Real-World Examples of Bad SEO

Modern SEO is not just about keeping the search engines happy, its primary role is to keep your visitors happy. Their time on the site, including bounce rate and social interaction with your pages, are increasingly important signals that the search engines use to help decide how good your content actually is.

In this section, I want to highlight some examples of bad SEO that I found while critiquing a number of websites.

An Example of Bad Navigation

This was the sidebar on one website.

There are four sections to the navigation bar of this WordPress site.

The first section is the search box, which is a good thing. However, this is the default WordPress search box, which isn't such a good thing because it's pretty ineffective.

Under the search box is a section labeled "**Pages**". Pages in WordPress are one of two forms of content, the other being "Posts". This site seems to be mixing pages and posts in a way that makes me think the webmaster had no clear plan for the structure of the site. Either that or the project was built initially with pages, and then the webmaster later wanted to add more content and so decided upon posts.

My own advice is to restrict the use of Pages in WordPress to the "legal pages", and use posts for all content written for the visitor. There are of course some exceptions, but this is a good general rule and one that allows you to make use of the excellent structural organization built into WordPress.

The next area of the navigation bar is an "Archives" section. What is the purpose of this? Does it help the visitor in any way?

If this site was news-based, where someone might like to check a news story from last week/month/year, then an archives section would be worth considering. However, this site isn't news-based. In fact, it's a fairly static site with little or no new content being added. Therefore, the archives section just clutters and distracts an already cluttered and distracted navigation system.

The final area of the navigation menu is the **"Categories"** section. This is actually a useful section for visitors because they'll be able to find relevant POSTS. Note I put "posts" in capital letters. This is because PAGES won't be included in the category system (which only shows posts). Likewise, the PAGES listed in the top section of the navigation menu won't be found using the category menu at the bottom.

You can see how the navigation system on this site is not very well organized and only serves to confuse visitors.

But that's not all. On the sitemap, I found 5 filenames that were quite similar:

> How-to-treat-depression
> Help-for-depression
> How-to-deal-with-depression
> Treatments-for-depression
> Depression-treatment-centers

How can those 5 articles all be unique and different in what information they cover?

The sitemap only had nine entries altogether, the other 4 being the homepage and three "legal pages". Only five content pages were included here, yet we can see from the sidebar navigation that this site had 40+ posts and a few content pages.

A sitemap should list ALL important URLs on the site, most notably the posts. Disclaimers and other "legal" pages can be left off the sitemap. The main role of the sitemap is to make sure the search engines can find the most important pages on your site. This one clearly misses the point.

Overall, the navigation system on this site (which I believe has now been taken down since my critique), is a good example of what NOT to do.

If you would like to test out your SEO sleuthing skills, have a look at the categories in the sidebar menu and see another major mistake that this site made.

An Example of Over-optimization

Have a look at this web page:

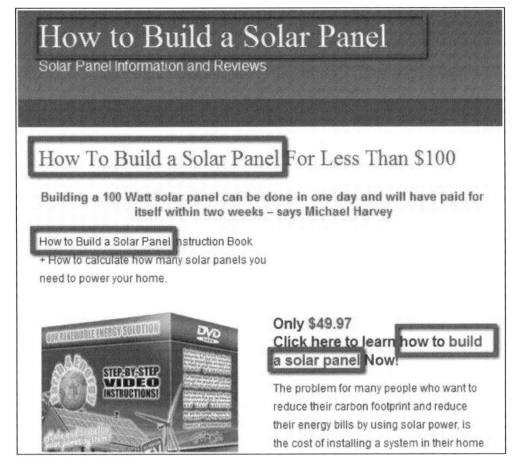

The webmaster was clearly trying to rank this page for "How to build a solar panel".

The top section of this page used the text "How to build a solar panel" in an H1 header. Then there is an opening H1 header which has the same phrase. That's two H1 headers on the same page, which is never a good thing. The exact same phrase then appears twice more, and this is all ABOVE THE FOLD. This phrase is also in the title tag of the page, and in the Meta description. It is also in the ALT text of an image on the page.

This is an extreme example of over-optimization.

Example of Fake Comments

Here are the comments on a website that I was critiquing:

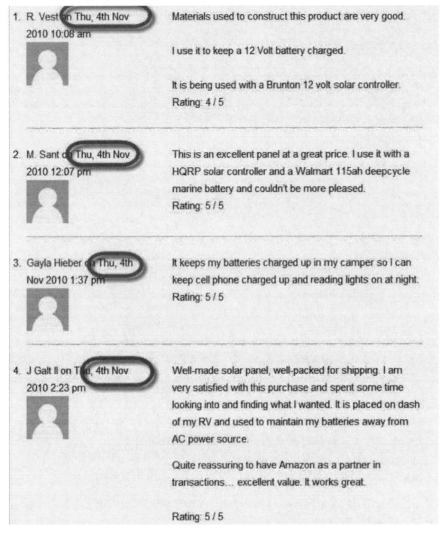

Notice that all of the comments were on the same day within just four hours of each other? That in itself is not unheard of, but the comments made me suspicious because they each included a high rating out of five (and none of them had Gravatar images).

To check the comments further, I took a sentence from one of them and searched Google for that sentence ("in quotes"):

"It keeps my batteries charged up in my camper so I can keep cell phone cl

Web   Images   Maps   Shopping   More ▾   Search tools

15 results (0.36 seconds)

Ad related to "It keeps my batteries charged up in my camper so I ... ⓘ
Ask an RV Tech Online - Technicians Will Answer in Minutes
rv.justanswer.com/Camper-RV
Questions Answered Every 9 Seconds.
Lawyer - Doctor - Nurse - Veterinarian

Amazon.com: Customer Reviews: HQRP 20W Mono-crystalline ...
www.amazon.com/HQRP-Mono-crystalline.../B002HT09TO
**It keeps my batteries charged up in my camper so I can keep cell phone
charged up and reading lights on at night**. Help other customers find the most
helpful ...

Amazon.com: HQRP 20W Mono-crystalline Solar Panel 20 Watt 12 ...
www.amazon.com › ... › Solar & Wind Power › Solar Panels
**It keeps my batteries charged up in my camper so I can keep cell phone
charged up and reading lights on at night**. Published on March 19, 2010 by Gayla ...

Amazon.com: Gayla Hieber's review of HQRP 20W Mono-crystalline ...
www.amazon.com/review/RW67BDW88G8WU
**It keeps my batteries charged up in my camper so I can keep cell phone
charged up and reading lights on at night**. Gayla Hieber March 19, 2010. Overall:
5.0 out ...

Looking for customer reviews for HQRP 20W Mono-crystalline Solar ...
askville.amazon.com › ... › Shopping › Lawn Garden
2 answers - 8 Jun 2011
**It keeps my batteries charged up in my camper so I can keep cell phone
charged up and reading lights on at night**. 4 of 4 found the following ...

Google found that exact same sentence/comment on 15 web pages, including Amazon.

Could the webmaster have found these comments on Amazon and added them to his website? Or maybe he paid someone else to add comments for him and they copied them from Amazon?

Whatever the answer is, this is bad.

I checked the other "fake" comments on the web page and every one of them was on numerous other websites, including Amazon.

Example of Sneaky Affiliate Links

There is nothing wrong with having affiliate links on your website. However, visitors should know that they are affiliate links. Having "hidden" affiliate links that are designed to set a cookie is never a good idea.

One site I critiqued a while ago used the whole of the background of his site (all the space to the left and right of the main content) as one big affiliate link. Each time you clicked on the background you were directed, via an affiliate link, to the merchant site. This clearly is not a good idea. As I was critiquing the site, I cannot remember how many times I ended up on the merchant site. I can only guess at how annoyed visitors got with this. That was an extreme case.

Here is yet another case of hidden affiliate links:

Divine Baby Shower Cakes

The centerpiece of any party is a ... whether to make o how much, can be difficult. Don't options available, you'll have a de

On this page, the webmaster had hyperlinked all of the images to Amazon with an affiliate link. The landing page was an Amazon search results page for the phrase **baby shower invitations**.

Why do this?

Does it in some way help the visitor?

Beautiful Baby Shower Decor

Decorations are a vital part of an ... important because the set the tone for a party from the choosing a color set that works

Or is it an attempt to set a cookie on Amazon?

Of course, it could have been a genuine mistake, but this type of thing is not adding to the visitor experience one bit. Usually, when a visitor clicks on a thumbnail image they are expecting to see a larger image of that thumb, and certainly not whisked off to some other website.

Baby Shower Theme Ideas

It can be hard to decide on a the pamper the new mom with a trip diapers, onesies, and baby acce some of ... below may ma

An Example of How NOT to Create a Contact Us Page

On the contact page of one affiliate site I critiqued, I found this:

Contact Information

If you have any questions about satellite TV systems or service, please call DISH Network or DIRECTV's toll-free telephone number, or click on the link listed below.

DISH Network

For questions about DISH Network satellite tv systems or service, contact U.S. Dish:

By phone: 1-888-228-0942

Online: Click here for <u>U.S. Dish online support</u>

DIRECTV

For questions about DIRECTV satellite TV systems or service, contact U.S. Direct:

By phone: 1-866-529-6828

Online: Click here for <u>U.S. Direct online support</u>

Instead of contact details for the site, it provided contact details of two merchants instead. That meant visitors had no way to contact the actual webmaster of this website.

It also looks like this webmaster is pretending to be the merchant or a website owned by the merchant.

Your contact page should give your visitors YOUR contact details so they can contact YOU. This not only builds trust but is also a basic requirement of doing business online.

Incidentally, the same website also had a link in their menu labeled "Affiliate Information". This is typically something only found on a merchant site. On the Affiliate Information page, this website linked to the affiliate programs of the two merchants.

Example of Bad Internal Linking

The purpose of internally linking pages on a website is to help the visitor. When done correctly, it helps guide visitors to more information about certain topics.

On one website I critiqued, something strange was going on with the internal linking. Here are two examples of the type of internal linking I found:

ccount while others will only apply
es actual dollars for the <u>consumer</u>.

Finding the best credit card deal for your spe
credit cards can often be a complicated, confu
have little or <u>no experience</u> managing cards.

The anchor text in the first example was "consumer", and the anchor text in the second example was "no experience".

When you internally link pages on your site using contextual links, the anchor texts MUST relate to the pages they are linking to. The anchor text must also be fairly self-serving, not leaving anything to the imagination as to what the destination is about. I mean, what would a visitor think the destination URL is about if the link text is "consumer"? What about "no experience"?

The "consumer" link went to an article on "mileage credit cards".

The "no experience" link went to a page on "credit card debt relief".

Do these help the visitor? Nope! The only point I can think of is that the webmaster was trying to make sure their pages were crawled and indexed (and PageRank passed around), and so they added more links to them in this way.

Here is another one:

reveal a **secret weapon** that you can use aga
cuss this strategy, let us just look briefly at th
d companies to recruit you as their customer.

What has "secret weapon" got to do with an article on credit cards?

Do you see the problem with these?

One final example on this site is this internal link:

6. Borrow against your 401k

When you **take a loan against your 401k** you are paying
your goal is a one time payoff of credit card debt it can
than to throw away 29% interest to a credit lending insti

The anchor text "take a loan against your 401k" linked to a page that did not include the word 401K!

I hope you have enjoyed looking at these real-life examples of bad SEO.

In the next section, we'll use Screaming Frog Spider software to perform a technical audit of a website structure.

The Technical Audit Using Screaming Frog SEO Spider

The Screaming Frog SEO Spider is a website crawler that collects a lot of useful data about your site as it crawls. This data can then be used to perform a detailed technical audit on the site. There are two versions of this software – free and paid. Obviously, the paid version will give you full access to all the analysis tools in the software and the free version will be limited. If you want to see a comparison of the free and paid versions, check out this webpage:

https://www.screamingfrog.co.uk/seo-spider/

In this book, I will obviously be using the full version of the software. If you find that something I am doing is not available in your free version, that is probably why. With that all said, let's begin.

Download and install the Screaming Frog Spider from that URL above and we can begin.

Connecting Screaming Frog to Analytics and Google Search Console

If you have the paid version of Screaming Frog, you can connect it to a few other tools so that it returns even more useful data about your website.

In the **Configuration** menu, move your mouse down to **API Access** and a menu opens showing what tools you can connect the spider to.

Connecting to Google Analytics and Search Console should be your first two connections, but feel free to connect to other tools if you use them.

Let me show you how to do this for Analytics, and you can then add your other accounts.

Clicking on **Google Analytics** opens the analytics account manager:

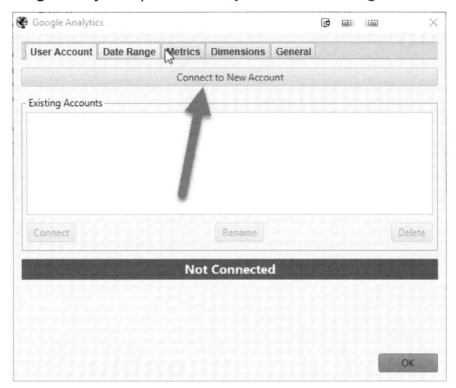

Click **Connect to New Account.**

A web browser will open asking you to login to your Analytics account.

When you successfully grant Screaming Frog Spider access to your account, your browser will display the message:

> Received verification code. You may now close this window.

When you close the browser window, you'll need to select the correct Analytics property to work with.

Repeat for Google Search Console, selecting your site from your GSC account.

Once these are added, Screaming Frog will collect data from Analytics and GSC when you run the spider.

Once you have added permission for the tools you want to use, you'll see that the spider adds new tabs to the interface to supply information from those sources:

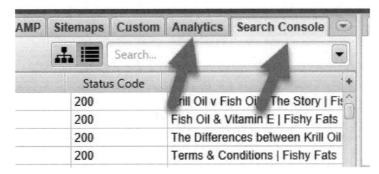

With that done, let's start the audit.

The first step in using the SEO Spider is to crawl your website. This will gather all of the information about your website, so we can analyze it later.

Let's do that now.

Crawling your Site

From the **Mode** menu at the top, make sure **Spider** is selected.

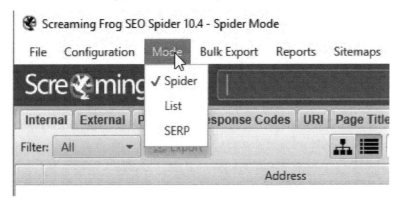

Spider mode does was it says. It spiders a website that you specify.

From the **Configuration** menu at the top, select **Spider**. This will open the spider options:

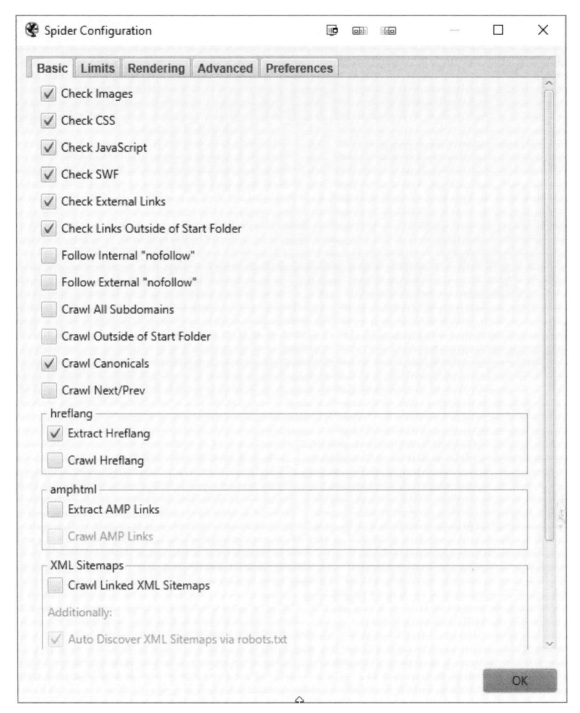

Screaming Frog SEO Spider has a lot of options and settings which makes it very powerful. For now, leave all the settings at their default values. Just realize that these are available as you become more experienced using this tool.

Enter the homepage URL of the site you want to analyze, and click the **Start** button:

The crawl can take a few minutes but will depend on the size of your site. The progress bar will show you the progress, so once it gets to 100%, we are ready to start looking at the data.

The spider will have the **Internal** tab selected, which are the URLs and resources that belong to your domain:

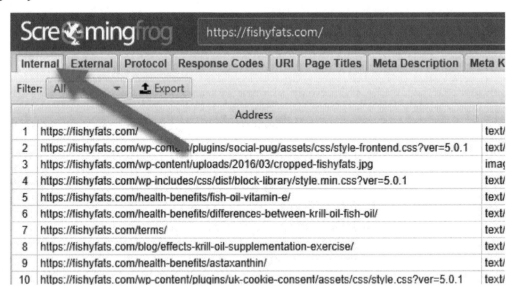

Right below that tab is a filter, which allows you to change what is shown in the results table. By default, **All** is selected, but you can choose to just show any of the following:

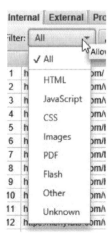

For example, Selecting **HTML** will just show the web pages in the list. If you were interested in checking the images on site, you could just show the **Images**.

Right next to the Filter box is an **Export** button that will allow you to export the data you are currently displaying. Data is exported in CSV format, so can be opened in Excel, Google Docs, or any other spreadsheet program you use.

Think of the **Internal** tab as a quick reference to all the available data. Scroll across the columns in the table and you'll find a huge amount of information listed. For quick reference, this tab is great. However, if you want to dig into one aspect of your site, the other tabs make this easier by organizing the data into logical groups.

For example, on the **Internal tab,** we can see columns for **Status Code** and **Indexability**. However, this data is duplicated over on the **Response Codes** tab which contains just the columns relevant to response codes.

The tabs in the spider give you a lot of flexibility over how you work. A lot of quick checks can be done on the **Internal** tab, and we will do some here. Alternatively, you might like the extra detail of the other tabs, looking at specific aspects of your site.

OK, let's start checking some of the data from our website.

The first check I make is to look at the **Response Codes** (also called Status codes).

Response Codes

The response code is simply the response a web browser gets when it tries to access a page or resource. The common responses are given a three digit number starting with the 1, 2, 3, 4, or 5. Here is a summary of what the response codes mean depending on the starting number:

1xx -The server is thinking about it.

2xx – Success!

3xx – URL was redirected.

4xx – Client Error! The URL was not valid or could not be found.

5xx – Server Error! There is a problem with your server.

The important codes you need to know as an SEO are as follows:

200 – Everything is OK.

301 & 302 are permanent and temporary redirects respectively.

404 – Not found.

500 – Internal Server Error. If a search engine spider came to visit and got a 500 error, it might be a while before it came back again.

503 – Service unavailable. This could be due to server maintenance or a temporary overload on the server. If a search engine spider came to visit and found a 503 error, it would know that it is likely to be a temporary problem, and therefore needs to come back later.

So, let's see what turned up on my test site. From the tabs across the top (or the **Overview** on the right), select **Response Codes**.

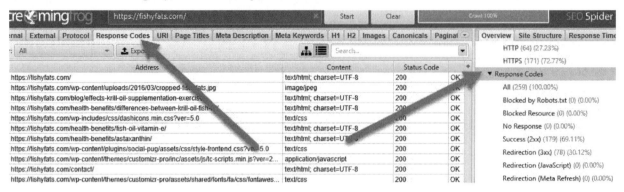

We can now filter our results using the filter drop down box:

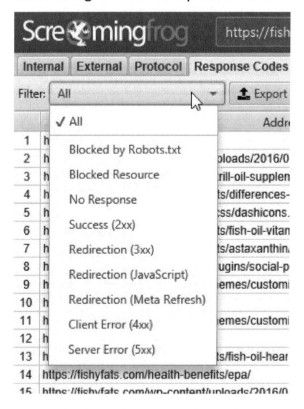

Each option will show you a different set of results. For example, the **Blocked by Robots.txt** report will show you any URLs that are blocked by your robots.txt file.

If you have any blocked URLs or resources, make sure they are supposed to be blocked, or edit your robots.txt file to make sure the search engine spiders can access them. You can view your robots.txt file by adding **/robots.txt** to the end of your homepage URL:

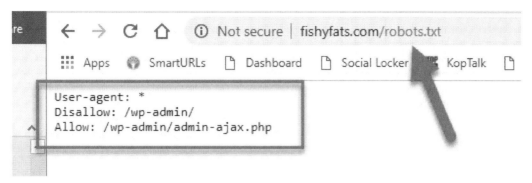

After checking your robots.txt file is OK, work your way down the list, checking **Blocked Resource** and then **No Response**.

On the **Success (2xx)** report you will see all the resources that are OK.

The next report shows **Redirection (3xx)**, so check this. My report shows several URLs:

Most of these URLs are links to other websites which is fine. What I am interested in are the pages on my own site that throw up a 3xx code. I can filter those by typing in part of my domain name into the search box:

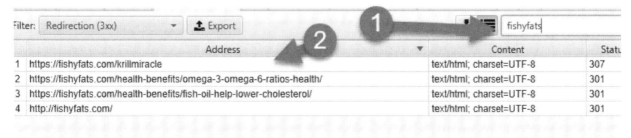

I can see three URLs showing a 301 (permanent redirect) and one showing a 307 (temporary redirect).

Clicking on an entry in the table will open some more details so I can explore the entry:

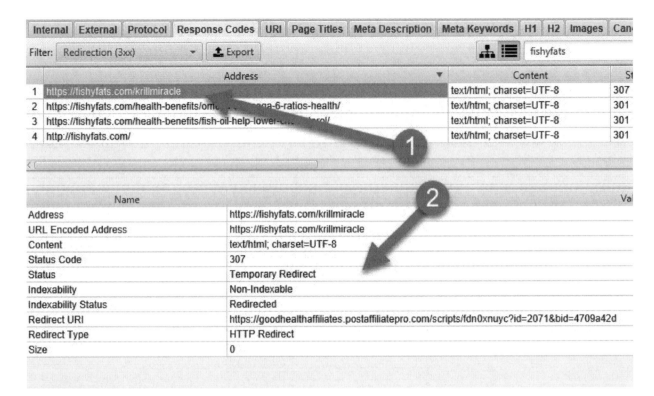

Address	https://fishyfats.com/krillmiracle
URL Encoded Address	https://fishyfats.com/krillmiracle
Content	text/html; charset=UTF-8
Status Code	307
Status	Temporary Redirect
Indexability	Non-Indexable
Indexability Status	Redirected
Redirect URI	https://goodhealthaffiliates.postaffiliatepro.com/scripts/fdn0xnuyc?id=2071&bid=4709a42d
Redirect Type	HTTP Redirect
Size	0

Looking down the information for that URL I can see the **Redirect URI** is to an affiliate product I am promoting. I know this link is a redirect I set up to automatically be redirected to that affiliate site. This 307 status code is fine.

The next two URLs in the report are also fine. On checking, I can see that I am redirecting the URL in the results table to another article on the site. I do this when I merge two or more articles into one. I can easily see the URL that this page is being redirected to:

Address	https://fishyfats.com/health-benefits/omega-3-omega-6-ratios-health/
URL Encoded Address	https://fishyfats.com/health-benefits/omega-3-omega-6-ratios-health/
Content	text/html; charset=UTF-8
Status Code	301
Status	Moved Permanently
Indexability	Non-Indexable
Indexability Status	Redirected
Redirect URI	https://fishyfats.com/health-benefits/healthy-omega-3-to-omega-6-ratios/
Redirect Type	HTTP Redirect
Size	0

The fact that the 301 is showing up means that some of the pages on my site are actually still linking to the old page and being redirected. As part of my SEO audit, I like to clear all of these up so that my own pages no longer reference the old URL, and instead, point directly to the new URL.

I can see which pages on my site link to the old page by selecting the URL in the results table and then clicking on the **Inlinks** tab at the bottom of the software:

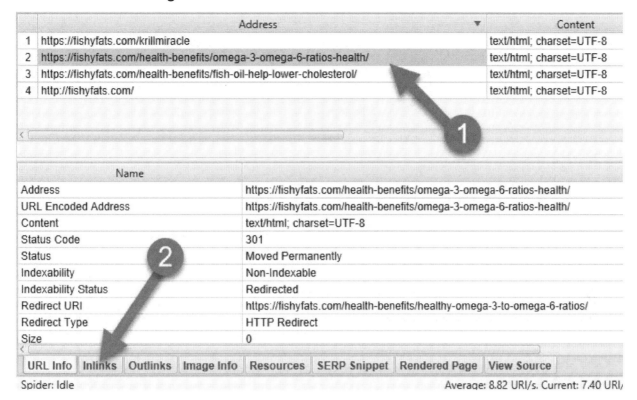

I can now see which URLs link to that old URL, and even the anchor text being used which might make it easier to spot on the web page:

You can right-click any entry in the table and open the page in a browser to spot the problem:

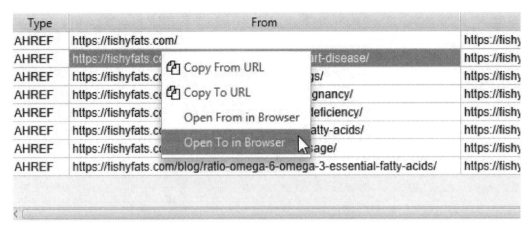

Here is the offending HTML code:

```
the balance of initiation and resolution phases in the body
is the "
<a href="https://fishyfats.com/health-benefits/omega-3-
omega-6-ratios-health/" class="ci-backlinks">Omega-6 to
Omega-3 ratio</a> == $0
". When a western diet is consumed, this ratio tends to be
very high, which is why cardiovascular disease is prevalent
in western societies. For there to be sufficient quantities
```

This is now easy to fix.

The last URL in my report is more worrying:

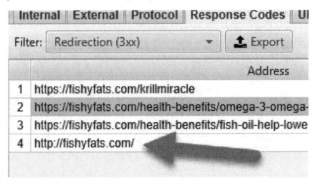

This is the homepage, and it is an HTTP version of the page. This site no longer has an HTTP version as I converted it over to the secure HTTPS, and all HTTP URLs should automatically redirect to https. Therefore, we need to fix this.

By selecting the URL and checking the **Inlinks**, I can see that all of the pages on the site are linking to the HTTP version of the webpage. A quick check of the source code shows me the offending links. It is in the footer, next to the copyright notice and date.

That is something that I can change in the theme settings to fix the issue.

Once you are done checking and fixing your 3xx status codes, look at the 4xx and 5xx codes. Fix anything that needs fixing.

What I tend to do after fixing the response codes is clear the results from the Screaming

Frog Spider:

Now clear any cache on the website, and re-spider with the Screaming Frog spider.

You can see I now have a clean bill of health for those 3xx fixes:

You'll remember that the one item that is still listed is the affiliate redirect link that I have set up deliberately.

So that is the first part of our technical audit complete. Not too hard, is it? Let's get on with some more auditing.

Indexability?

The next check we'll make is to see if the content that we want to be found in Google, can be. At the same time, we'll check that any web pages we don't want to be found in Google are marked appropriately with the noindex tag.

These checks can be done from the **Internal** tab or the **Directives** tab. We'll look at both methods, as the second option gives you more data. We'll start with the **Internal** tab first because I think it highlights just how useful this tab is for a wide range of quick checks.

The column we are interested in is the **Indexability** column, but we'll also look at the **Indexability Status** column, as that gives us more information. A great feature of the software is that you can drag and drop columns to re-order them. To help with the screenshots in this book, I will drag those two columns so that they are next to the **Address** column.

With my columns re-ordered, I now want to re-order the rows in the columns, so that I can easily identify those addresses that are "noindex". To do that, click the column header of the column you want to re-order. I use the **Indexability Status** column to sort for noindex. It requires a couple of clicks so that the "order arrow" is pointing down:

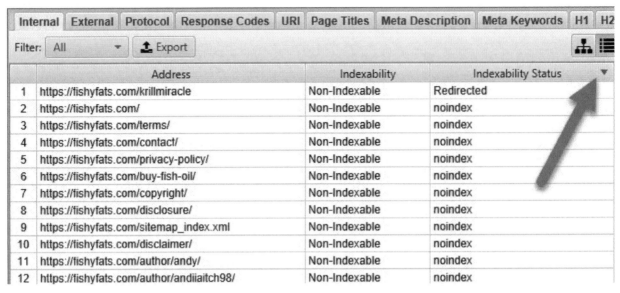

This gives me all of my pages marked with "noindex" at the top of the table.

The very first item in that list is my affiliate link redirect. That is absolutely fine. In fact, all of the noindexed pages are fine with one exception. MY HOMEPAGE!

Look at the second item in the table. My homepage has a noindex tag, so search engines won't include the homepage (the most important page on the site) in the SERPs.

This site uses the Yoast SEO plugin to set the indexability of posts and pages on this WordPress site. In the settings for that plugin, I have chosen to noindex all of the WordPress "Pages" on the site by default. For me, pages on a WordPress site are for legal documents, contact forms, etc. However, I do often use a page for the homepage (and About Us) too, and I need to override that default. I clearly screwed up here.

To fix this, I simply need to login to my WordPress dashboard and edit the homepage so that it doesn't obey the default rules for pages. The Yoast SEO plugin lets me easily override these default settings on a post-by-post or page-by-page basis:

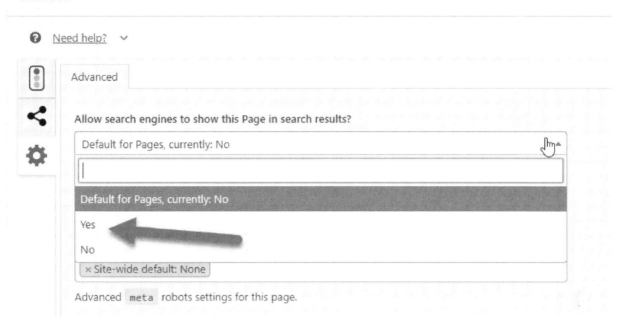

OK, that's done.

If I clear the cache on my site, I can now recheck that page. In the spider, right-click the URL you want to re-spider and select **Re-Spider** from the menu. It will disappear while it is rechecked and will be added to the end of the table:

OK, now click across on the **Directives** tab. You can also select it from the **Overview** box on the right if you prefer:

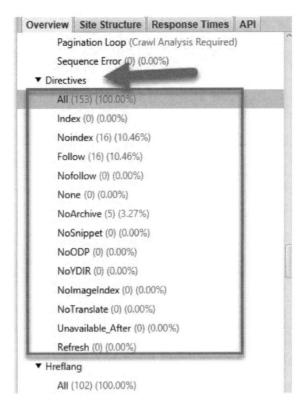

The **Directives** tab gives you a lot more information, and with the directives tab selected, you can now filter by these tags:

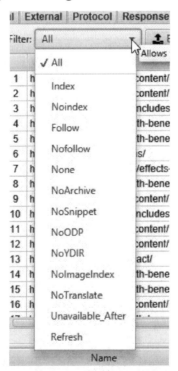

To see all "noindex" pages, select **Noindex** from the **Filter** drop-down box.

	Address	Meta Robots 1
1	https://fishyfats.com/terms/	noindex,follow,noarchive
2	https://fishyfats.com/contact/	noindex,follow,noarchive
3	https://fishyfats.com/privacy-policy/	noindex,follow,noarchive
4	https://fishyfats.com/buy-fish-oil/	noindex,follow
5	https://fishyfats.com/copyright/	noindex,follow,noarchive
6	https://fishyfats.com/disclosure/	noindex,follow
7	https://fishyfats.com/sitemap_index.xml	
8	https://fishyfats.com/disclaimer/	noindex,follow,noarchive
9	https://fishyfats.com/author/andy/	noindex,follow
10	https://fishyfats.com/author/andiiaitch98/	noindex,follow
11	https://fishyfats.com/author/andy/page/2/	noindex,follow
12	https://fishyfats.com/author/andiiaitch98/page/2/	noindex,follow
13	https://fishyfats.com/author/andy/page/3/	noindex,follow
14	https://fishyfats.com/author/andiiaitch98/page/3/	noindex,follow
15	https://fishyfats.com/author/andiiaitch98/page/4/	noindex,follow
16	https://fishyfats.com/author/andiiaitch98/page/5/	noindex,follow

You can see the **Meta Robots 1** column has more information.

As you can see, the directives tab may be more useful if you are doing an in-depth audit to check a site for indexing issues.

Server Response Times

The server response time is the length of time it takes a server to acknowledge a request to retrieve a resource. When you click a link in Google, it's the time from the moment of your click, to the moment the web page starts to download. A fast server response time is essential for quick loading of your web pages.

The screaming spider tool will give you the server response time for each page it downloaded during the spidering phase.

On the **Internal** tab, select **HTML** from the **Filter** drop-down box. Now scroll across to the **Response Time** column and click the column header until response times are ordered with the highest at the top of the table.

	Address	Response Time▼	Content
1	https://fishyfats.com/blog/fish-oil-supplements-periodontal-health/	2.17	text/html; charset=UTF-8
2	https://fishyfats.com/	1.28	text/html; charset=UTF-8
3	https://fishyfats.com/krillmiracle	1.07	text/html; charset=UTF-8
4	https://fishyfats.com/blog/fish-oil-intestinal-barrier-function/	0.68	text/html; charset=UTF-8
5	https://fishyfats.com/blog/fish-oil-prevent-aaa-induced-hypoperfusion/	0.64	text/html; charset=UTF-8
6	https://fishyfats.com/health-benefits/differences-between-krill-oil-fish-oil/	0.62	text/html; charset=UTF-8
7	https://fishyfats.com/health-benefits/fish-oil-vitamin-e/	0.62	text/html; charset=UTF-8
8	https://fishyfats.com/blog/krill-oil-fat-soluble-vitamin-d/	0.62	text/html; charset=UTF-8
9	https://fishyfats.com/health-benefits/healthy-omega-3-to-omega-6-ratios/	0.60	text/html; charset=UTF-8
10	https://fishyfats.com/blog/krill-oil-supplementation-shown-lower-triglycerides/	0.59	text/html; charset=UTF-8
11	https://fishyfats.com/blog/oxidative-constancy-fo-water-emulsions/	0.59	text/html; charset=UTF-8
12	https://fishyfats.com/blog/fish-oil-averts-brain-shrinkage-cognitive-decline/	0.59	text/html; charset=UTF-8
13	https://fishyfats.com/author/andiiaitch98/page/4/	0.58	text/html; charset=UTF-8
14	https://fishyfats.com/health-benefits/health-benefits-fish-oil/	0.58	text/html; charset=UTF-8
15	https://fishyfats.com/author/andy/page/3/	0.58	text/html; charset=UTF-8

I can see three URLs at the top which show response times over 1 second. Chances are that there was a blip when these pages were being requested because all other pages on the site showed response times less than 0.68 seconds. This is similar to the response times I found when I analyzed my site using Pingdom:

Response time

Downtime	Outages	Uptime	Max resp. time	Min resp. time	Avg resp. time
0	0	100.00%	677ms	0	427ms

Response time is something I recommend you check on your own server, as slow response times mean slower loading pages. The only way to fix a slow response time is to switch to a different web host.

Outbound Link Issues

One of the first things we did in this technical audit was to check the response codes for the pages on our website. It is also important to do a check on the response codes of pages your site link to. If a page you linked to has moved, or been deleted, it means you have broken links on your site which need to be fixed.

Screaming Frog makes it super easy to check all outbound links on your site.

Click on the **External** tab to show all URLs and resources that you have linked to from your website. If you want, you can play with the **Filter** drop-down box to select just HTML, or just PDF files, etc. I tend to leave the filter set to **All**.

The columns we are interested in are **Status Code** and **Status**. Order your list by **Status Code**.

	Address	Status Code ▼	Status
1	http://www.nutraingredients.com/Research/Superior-bioavailability-Study-backs-krill-oil-ov...	403	Forbidden
2	http://www.nutraingredients-usa.com/Research/Omega-3-deficiency-causes-96-000-US-d...	403	Forbidden
3	http://www.ncbi.nlm.nih.gov/pubmed/12442909	307	HSTS Policy
4	http://www.ncbi.nlm.nih.gov/pubmed/23703724	307	HSTS Policy
5	http://www.ncbi.nlm.nih.gov/pubmed/10632323	307	HSTS Policy
6	http://www.ncbi.nlm.nih.gov/pubmed/23184014	307	HSTS Policy
7	http://www.ncbi.nlm.nih.gov/pubmed/22596014	307	HSTS Policy
8	http://www.ncbi.nlm.nih.gov/entrez/query.fcgi?cmd=Retrieve&db=PubMed&dopt=Citation&...	307	HSTS Policy
9	http://articles.mercola.com/sites/articles/archive/2014/02/10/krill-oil-supplementation.Aspx	307	HSTS Policy
10	http://www.ncbi.nlm.nih.gov/pubmed/18312787	307	HSTS Policy
11	http://www.ncbi.nlm.nih.gov/pubmed/16879829	307	HSTS Policy
12	http://www.ncbi.nlm.nih.gov/entrez/query.fcgi?cmd=Retrieve&db=PubMed&dopt=Citation&...	307	HSTS Policy

Any item in the list that does not have a "200" status code, probably needs to be fixed.

Click the first item in the list, and then click on the **Inlink** tab at the bottom of the spider:

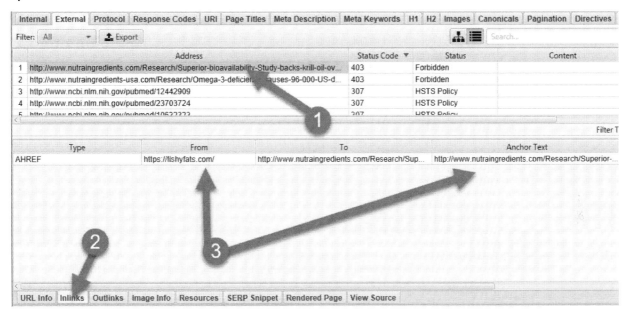

You will be able to see the page that links to this URL, and the anchor text used.

In that lower table, right-click the URL containing the link and select **Open To in Browser:**

This opens the outbound link in a browser so you can check what the issue is. In my case, the URL has changed so I need to update my link.

Work your way through the list of resources with 4xx status codes. If you have time, update any URL where the page has been redirected on the target site.

Pages Titles

On the page title tab, we have a new set of criteria we can filter for, including missing titles, duplicate titles, long or short titles. Let's have a look.

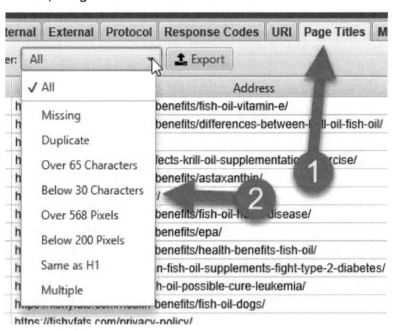

Select **Missing** from the filter box, and make sure all your pages have a title tag. If any don't, then add these.

Now check for **Duplicate** title tags. In my case, I have three:

	Address		Title 1	Indexability	
1	https://fishyfats.com/author/andy/		Krill Oil Articles by Dr. Andy Williams	Non-Indexable	1
2	https://fishyfats.com/author/andy/page/2/		Krill Oil Articles by Dr. Andy Williams	Non-Indexable	1
3	https://fishyfats.com/author/andy/page/3/		Krill Oil Articles by Dr. Andy Williams	Non-Indexable	1

These three URLs represent my author pages on the site. In WordPress, these are archives listing all posts made by an author. This type of duplication of the title is fairly common in WordPress but can be avoided by using the Yoast SEO plugin and variables to make sure all page titles are a little different. However, in this case, the duplication if fine as I have these pages set to noindex. Therefore, Google won't even see the titles.

The next two filters are important because they make sure you use the full "real estate" allowed for your titles. If your title is too long, it will become truncated in the SERPs, and if it is too short, you are losing the opportunity of selling the click to increase your click-through rate.

Google has changed the recommended title length in the past, but fortunately for us, Screaming Spider updates with the latest information regarding titles.

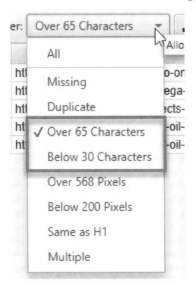

We can see that we are aiming for titles between 30 - 65 characters.

Filter your pages to see if any page has a title tag less than 30 characters. Can you create better titles for these pages?

Repeat the check for titles that are over 65 characters. These titles are in danger of being truncated in the SERPs, so decide whether you need to change the titles on these pages. To help you out, click on the URL you want to investigate at the top, and then in the bottom panel of the screen, select **SERP Snippet**. This will show you what the listing will look like in Google:

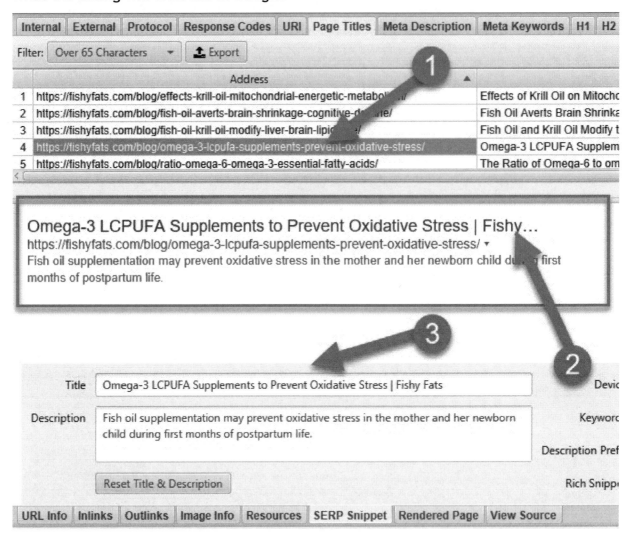

You can see that my title is truncated. I could play with the title at the bottom to see what would fit properly without this truncation. Once happy, I could then update my page with the new title.

The final check I would recommend you carry out on your title is to see if the title is the same as the H1 header on the page. It is good SEO practice to make sure these two tags are not the same. The **Same as H1** filter will identify these for you.

Meta Descriptions

We can use the guidelines from Screaming Frog to also check out Meta Description tags.

Click onto the **Meta Description** tab and check out the **Filter** drop-down box.

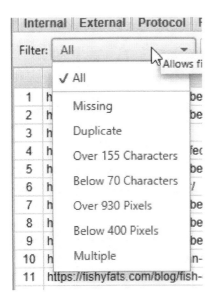

We need to make sure that web pages:

1. Include a Meta Description.
2. No two pages have the same Meta Description.
3. Meta Descriptions are between 70 – 155 characters.

You can once again make use of the **SERP Snippet** tab to see what your SERP listing will look like, and check whether your title, URL, and description, sell your web page to the searcher. Also, note that the SERP Snippet tool gives you the option to check how your listing looks on mobile devices too.

Meta Keywords

As you know, I don't recommend you use Meta Keywords on your page. They won't help you rank better, but if you abuse them, they can help identify you as a spammer. I use the **Meta Keywords** tab for two reasons:

1. To check that if my client's site is using Meta Keywords, they are doing so in a responsible way. That means a limited number of keywords that are also found in the body of the content on the page.
2. To check my competitors to see what keywords they think are important. Run a spider of a competitor site, switch to the **Meta Keyword** tab, and all their keywords will be revealed (if they use the tag).

H1 Headers

The H1 tab allows us to easily check the H1 headers we are using on our website.

Click on it, and look at the **Filter** drop-down box:

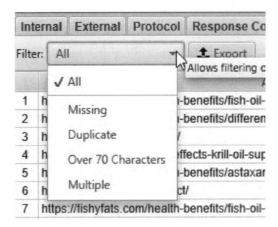

The clues about what we need are all there.

1. Make sure there is an H1 header on all web pages.
2. Make sure the H1 header is unique to each page, so there are no duplicates.
3. Make sure the H1 header is 70 character or less.
4. Make sure pages only have a single H1 header. We use the **Multiple** filter for that.

Any pages that break these rules should be fixed (except for those pages that are noindex).

H2 Headers

The H2 headers should also be checked for the same problems as the H1 headers. The one exception to this is the **Multiple** filter. It is OK to have more than one H2 on a page, so you can ignore that check.

Images

Click on the **Images** tab and look at the **Filter** drop-down box.

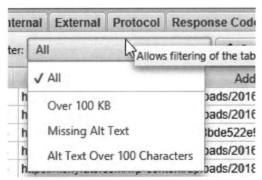

On the images tab, we can check that images have good ALT tags, and aren't too big in size. The **Over 100KB** gives you a good target to aim at (keeping images below 100KB each), but you aren't restricted to the values used by these filters. For example, you might want all images below 50KB, or 25KB.

There are a couple of ways you can do this. The first is simply to order your images by clicking on the **Size** column. You can then select your own cut off point for file size:

https://fishyfats.com/wp-content/uploads/2016/04/fish-oil-during-pregnancy-270x250.jpg	14089	image/jpeg
https://fishyfats.com/wp-content/uploads/2016/03/brain-270x250.jpg	14184	image/jpeg
https://fishyfats.com/wp-content/uploads/2015/11/health-benefits-of-krill-oil-270x250.jpg	14813	image/jpeg
https://fishyfats.com/wp-content/uploads/2016/03/fish-oil-for-kids-270x250.jpg	14815	image/jpeg
https://fishyfats.com/wp-content/uploads/2016/03/fish-oil-for-cats-2...50.jpg	17498	image/jpeg
https://fishyfats.com/wp-content/uploads/2016/03/tuna-omega-3-300x189.jpg	19638	image/jpeg
https://fishyfats.com/wp-content/uploads/2016/03/heart-270x250.jpg	20805	image/jpeg
https://fishyfats.com/wp-content/uploads/2016/03/fish-oil-270x250.jpg	22180	image/jpeg
https://fishyfats.com/wp-content/uploads/2016/03/tuna-omega-3-270x250.jpg	22375	image/jpeg
https://fishyfats.com/wp-content/uploads/2016/04/cured-bacon-stack-xs-270x250.jpg	23597	image/jpeg
https://fishyfats.com/wp-content/uploads/2016/04/cholesterol-270x250.jpg	24693	image/jpeg
https://fishyfats.com/wp-content/uploads/2016/03/sardines-omega-3-270x250.jpg	26757	image/jpeg
https://fishyfats.com/wp-content/uploads/2016/03/krill-miracle-ingredients-1.jpg	27322	image/jpeg
https://fishyfats.com/wp-content/uploads/2018/05/company-stuff-in-privacy-policy.jpg	42346	image/jpeg

The other way you can do this is to **Export** the data to a CSV file and order, sort, and filter in Excel or similar.

To help visually impaired users, use the **Missing ALT Text** filter to show those images that do not have ALT text. All images should use descriptive, non-spammy ALT tags that let visually impaired users know what is in the picture. ALT text should be concise and to the point, so the **ALT Text Over 100 Characters** is a useful filter to use.

Inlinks

Earlier in the book, we looked at the idea of Page Rank where links are "votes" for a page. The more incoming links a page has, the more important that page. Of course, that isn't always true because low-quality links blur the lines.

Incoming links can be from external sources (pages on other websites), or internal sources (pages on the same site). This latter type of link is called an internal link.

If incoming links equal votes for a page, then that holds true for internal links too. The more internal links a page has, the more important that page must be.

Screaming Frog SEO Spider can show us how many internal links a page has pointed at it. We can use that information to check that the most important pages on our website do have the most links pointing at them.

On the **Internal** tab, select HTML from the **Filter** drop-down box.

Now scroll across until you find the **Inlinks** column. Click on the column header to order the results with the highest number of internal links at the top.

	Address	Inlinks ▼
1	https://fishyfats.com/category/blog/	343
2	https://fishyfats.com/	305
3	https://fishyfats.com/health-benefits/differences-between-krill-oil-fish-oil/	255
4	https://fishyfats.com/tag/scientific-literature/	205
5	https://fishyfats.com/privacy-policy/	204
6	https://fishyfats.com/category/health-benefits/	193
7	https://fishyfats.com/health-benefits/omega-3-fatty-acids/	193
8	https://fishyfats.com/author/andiiaitch98/	181
9	https://fishyfats.com/tag/cholesterol/	126
10	https://fishyfats.com/health-benefits/health-benefits-of-krill-oil/	124
11	https://fishyfats.com/blog/need-fish-oil-supplements/	111
12	https://fishyfats.com/blog/can-fish-oil-supplements-fight-type-2-diabetes/	110
13	https://fishyfats.com/health-benefits/health-benefits-fish-oil/	109
14	https://fishyfats.com/blog/fish-oil-possible-cure-leukemia/	109
15	https://fishyfats.com/health-benefits/dha/	108

Do you see your most important pages at the top?

In my screenshot, the Blog homepage is #1, closely followed by the site homepage. These two should be right up there, though I would have expected my homepage to have more links than the blog page.

If you want to see which web pages link to a particular target page, highlight the target page in the **Address** list at the top, and click on the **Inlinks** tab across the bottom. You will now get a list of all URLs that link to that address, including the anchor text used. It can be quite useful to look down the anchor text and see if you really need to diversify it a little, like in my case:

Type	From	To	Anchor Text
AHREF	https://fishyfats.com/blog/fish-oil-possible-cure-leukemia/	https://fishyfats...	The Differences between Krill Oil & Fish Oil
AHREF	https://fishyfats.com/blog/fish-oil-possible-cure-leukemia/	https://fishyfats...	The Differences between Krill Oil & Fish Oil →
AHREF	https://fishyfats.com/blog/fish-oil-possible-cure-leukemia/	https://fishyfats...	The Differences between Krill Oil & Fish Oil
AHREF	https://fishyfats.com/blog/fish-oil-possible-cure-leukemia/	https://fishyfats...	The Differences between Krill Oil & Fish Oil
AHREF	https://fishyfats.com/health-benefits/fish-oil-dogs/	https://fishyfats...	The Differences between Krill Oil & Fish Oil
AHREF	https://fishyfats.com/health-benefits/fish-oil-dogs/	https://fishyfats...	The Differences between Krill Oil & Fish Oil
AHREF	https://fishyfats.com/privacy-policy/	https://fishyfats...	The Differences between Krill Oil & Fish Oil
AHREF	https://fishyfats.com/health-benefits/fish-oil-cats/	https://fishyfats...	The Differences between Krill Oil & Fish Oil
AHREF	https://fishyfats.com/health-benefits/fish-oil-cats/	https://fishyfats...	The Differences between Krill Oil & Fish Oil
AHREF	https://fishyfats.com/buy-fish-oil/	https://fishyfats...	The Differences between Krill Oil & Fish Oil
AHREF	https://fishyfats.com/copyright/	https://fishyfats...	The Differences between Krill Oil & Fish Oil
AHREF	https://fishyfats.com/health-benefits/fish-oil-pregnancy/	https://fishyfats...	The Differences between Krill Oil & Fish Oil
AHREF	https://fishyfats.com/health-benefits/fish-oil-pregnancy/	https://fishyfats...	The Differences between Krill Oil & Fish Oil
AHREF	https://fishyfats.com/health-benefits/fish-oil-kids/	https://fishyfats...	The Differences between Krill Oil & Fish Oil
AHREF	https://fishyfats.com/health-benefits/fish-oil-kids/	https://fishyfats...	The Differences between Krill Oil & Fish Oil
AHREF	https://fishyfats.com/health-benefits/krill-biomass-sustainability/	https://fishyfats...	The Differences between Krill Oil & Fish Oil
AHREF	https://fishyfats.com/health-benefits/krill-biomass-sustainability/	https://fishyfats...	The Differences between Krill Oil & Fish Oil
AHREF	https://fishyfats.com/health-benefits/fish-oil-helps-lower-cholesterol/	https://fishyfats...	The Differences between Krill Oil & Fish Oil
AHREF	https://fishyfats.com/health-benefits/fish-oil-helps-lower-cholesterol/	https://fishyfats...	The Differences between Krill Oil & Fish Oil
AHREF	https://fishyfats.com/health-benefits/fish-oil-healthy-brain/	https://fishyfats...	The Differences between Krill Oil & Fish Oil

The reason the anchor text is identical in all of those cases is that the link to the page is in the sidebar menu on all of these pages. Look back to what we said earlier in the book about Site Wide link. To make my site better, I would remove the sitewide navigation menu in the sidebar and build dynamic menus that changed depending on where in the site the visitor was. For WordPress users, there is a plugin called Dynamic Sidebars, and another called Dynamic Widgets. Both can help achieve this.

Word Count

It's well-known that Google hates thin pages. Thin pages can be defined as pages that have little useful content on them. The Screaming Frog spider will let you check word count on your pages, but be aware that low word count is not necessarily the same as thin content. A page could have a lot of words on it, yet still be thin. For this, and other reasons, Word count is not usually something I will look at on a website.

If you want to use it, you can.

The **Word Count** column can be found on the **Internal** tab.

When you are on the internal tab, select HTML from the **Filter** box, so you are only looking at web pages.

Now scroll across to the **Word Count** column and click on the column title to order your web pages by word count.

	Internal	External	Protocol	Response Codes	URI	Page Titles

Filter: HTML ▾ ⬆ Export

	Address	Word Count▲
1	https://fishyfats.com/krillmiracle	0
2	https://fishyfats.com/contact/	113
3	https://fishyfats.com/category/health-benefits/page/3/	181
4	https://fishyfats.com/copyright/	220
5	https://fishyfats.com/disclosure/	277
6	https://fishyfats.com/author/andy/page/3/	284
7	https://fishyfats.com/category/blog/page/6/	300
8	https://fishyfats.com/disclaimer/	345
9	https://fishyfats.com/buy-fish-oil/	416
10	https://fishyfats.com/category/health-benefits/page/2/	498
11	https://fishyfats.com/category/health-benefits/	524
12	https://fishyfats.com/tag/scientific-literature/page/3	533
13	https://fishyfats.com/author/andy/page/2/	541
14	https://fishyfats.com/blog/effects-krill-oil-supplement...	555
15	https://fishyfats.com/blog/molecular-impact-n3-fatty-...	568

In the screenshot above, you can see that I have ordered my pages with lowest word count at the top.

The very top URL is not a web page. It is a 307 redirect through an affiliate link. Therefore, that one is fine.

Different pieces of content may be different lengths depending on the purpose of that content. It is therefore difficult to generalize on the length of "articles". The only advice I ever give on word count is that the content has to be as long or as short as necessary to cover the topic.

What next?

We have only scratched the surface of how the Screaming Frog SEO Spider can help us in our technical audit. I hope we have covered enough to get you excited about using this tool. There are a number of great resources to help you get the most out of the spider, but the one you should definitely check out is the documentation that comes with the tool. You can find that here:

https://www.screamingfrog.co.uk/seo-spider/user-guide/

Where to go from here

Make sure that your site adds value. Provide unique and relevant content that gives users a reason to visit, bookmark and share your site.

In 2012, SEO changed forever. The last few years have continued that evolution.

Google has become far less tolerant of activities it sees as rank manipulation. It wants to serve web pages that offer its visitors the best possible experience. That means your primary focus should be on your visitor, not Google, not a keyword research tool, and certainly not automated tools that claim to do your SEO for you.

As webmasters, we have been given a choice. Stick to Google's rules, or lose out on free traffic from the world's biggest search engine.

Sure, there will always be someone advertising the next greatest "loophole" to beat the system, and they'll even have examples to prove their loophole works. These examples may even go against everything that Google wants and break all the rules, which will make them tempting to some. However, these loopholes are short-lived. My advice to you is to ignore anyone that tries to sell you a loophole, a trick, or anything ending with the word "quick". If you want long-lasting results, stick to the rules - Google's rules.

The SEO in this book is the SEO I use daily. It's the SEO I teach my students, and it's the SEO that I know works. For those that embrace the recent changes, SEO has actually become easier as we no longer have to battle against other sites whose SEO was done 24/7 by an automated tool or army of cheap labor. Those sites have largely been removed, and that levels the playing field nicely.

Finally, I want to wish you good luck, and I hope that you enjoyed this book.

BONUS Chapter – YouTube SEO

YouTube is owned by the search engine giant Google. YouTube videos that rank in the top 10 probably get quite good click-through rates (CTR), simply because they have a thumbnail image of the video displayed in the SERPs.

Searching for **CurrencyFair review** in Google returns some YouTube videos:

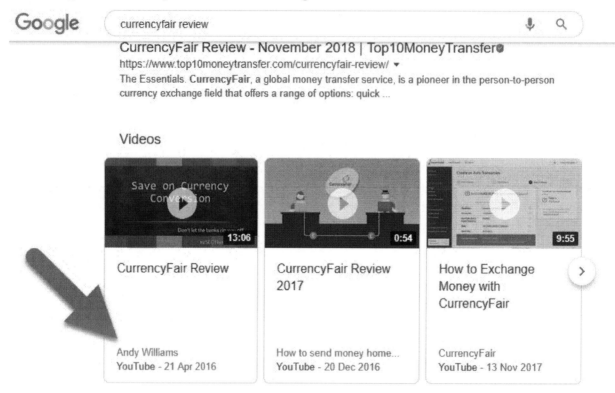

But YouTube is also a major search engine. Ranking high on YouTube can get a lot of eyeballs on your marketing message. However, just because Google owns YouTube does not mean both ranking algorithms are the same. Do a search on Youtube, and repeat it on Google. If Google shows you a video in the SERPs, chances are it is not the same video that ranks #1 on Youtube.

Here is the **CurrencyFair review** search on YouTube:

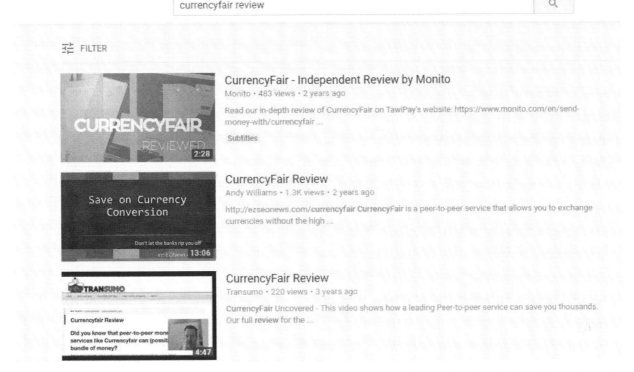

The videos in position 1 and 3 are different to the ones shown in the rich snippet top 3 on Google.

The video in second place on YouTube is mine, and that was shown in position 1 in the rich snippet on Google.

We've already seen that the ranking algorithm for Google is very complex, involving hundreds of different signals, both on the page, and off.

YouTube's ranking is not as complex as Google Search, or at least it does not appear to be.

On YouTube, it is possible to rank a video using just on-page factors in less competitive niches. The ease of ranking on YouTube in low competition niches has gotten some marketers excited. By finding low competition phrases with good search volume, marketers can rank high on YouTube and get easy traffic to their sites.

It sounds great, but let me burst that bubble. Ranking on YouTube is fine, but it's not the best. You really want your video ranking in the Google SERPs. That is where the majority of traffic will come from, not from the YouTube search results.

Let me give you an example.

Here is a search phrase that I found in Google Keyword Planner:

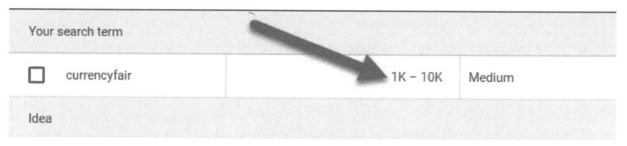

Your search term			
☐ currencyfair		1K – 10K	Medium
Idea			

That screenshot tells me that this phrase is searched for 1,000 – 10,000 times a month.

OK, the first thing to do is see how many videos are actually optimized for that exact phrase.

A search on Google, tells me 420 videos on YouTube use that exact phrase on the page.

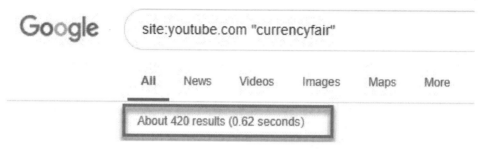

Google   site:youtube.com "currencyfair"

All   News   Videos   Images   Maps   More

About 420 results (0.62 seconds)

An intitle: search tells me that only 60 videos use that exact phrase in the title.

site:youtube.com intitle:"currencyfair"

All   News   Videos   Images   Maps   More

About 60 results (3.81 seconds)

It's probably going to be easy to rank high for this phrase on YouTube using on-page factors.

If you could rank #1 on YouTube for that phrase, how much traffic would it bring?

Well, Google Keyword Planner tells us that the phrase is searched for 1k – 10k per month.

Let's now go over to YouTube and see how many times the top videos ranking for that phrase have been watched:

How to Exchange Money with CurrencyFair

1,099 views

CurrencyFair
Published on 13 Nov 2017

CurrencyFair is the fast, easy, low-cost way to transfer money, with exchange rates up to 8x cheaper than the banks. Find out how to set up a transfer in this video.

SHOW MORE

The number #1 ranked video has been watched 1099 times in the last 385 days (check actual video views count and publish date by clicking on the link in the YouTube results).

This means the video has averaged around 85 views per month. That's around three per day.

The video in position #2 on YouTube is this one:

How to transfer money internationally from Australia with CurrencyFair

2,668 views

Irish Around Oz
Published on 19 Dec 2015

That's 2,668 views in around 36 months, or 74 views per month.

And don't forget that both of these videos probably rank for other search terms as well, so views are not based solely on the search term "CurrencyFair".

What happened to the 1k – 10k searches a month for the phrase **Currencyfair**?

Well, there are two problems with using search volume reported by Google Keyword Planner.

1. The search volume is for Google, not YouTube.
2. The search volume is not very accurate. As you can see, it is a range, and a big range at that.

For a video on YouTube to get decent traffic, it needs either a lot of search traffic ON YouTube, or the video needs to rank for the keyword phrase in Google Search, in the top 10, and preferably near the top.

For any search phrase, if there are videos in the top 10 search results on Google, that's a good sign. However, to make sure people are really using those search phrases, check how many times those videos are watched on a monthly basis.

Before you spend time creating a video for YouTube with the sole purpose of bringing in more traffic, ask yourself whether or not there are YouTube videos in the top 10 for your phrase, and how many views per month those videos get.

YouTube Video Optimization

This really is a two-part process.

1. Get the on-page factors right. This can be enough to get the video ranking high on YouTube (though does depend on competition).
2. Build backlinks to the video from the best sources you can find if you want the video to rank high in Google as well.

These two steps will allow your video to rank near or at the top of YouTube but also have a chance of ranking in Google's top 10 (assuming Google usually shows at least one video in the SERPs for that phrase).

Let's consider the on-page factors for YouTube videos.

The on-page SEO is much more like the Google SEO of old. Keywords are still King here, and spamming does work. I would, however, caution against creating spammy video titles or descriptions. It is only a matter of time before Google cracks the YouTube whip and starts to change things.

OK, here is a checklist of on-page optimization that you can use to optimize your video for a specific phrase.

1. Add the keyword phrase in the video title. Put the phrase at the start and try to make the title as short as possible.
2. Use your main keyword phrase in the video's filename.
3. Think of the description in the same way as you would think of an article for your site. This will give it more chance of ranking in Google. Create a well-themed description that uses the main keyword phrase in the first sentence, plus all important niche vocabulary further down. Include a link back to your website as a bare URL. Make the description as long as it needs to be. Longer descriptions can really work wonders for helping it to rank in Google.
4. You need to add some tags to your submission. Make sure your main keyword is the first one. Include variations on that main keyword in the tags, and any other important niche vocabulary.
5. If you get comments on your videos, moderate them. Remove any spammy comments and reply to any questions you get. Engage with the people who leave comments.
6. Embed the video in a page on your own website and provide a written

commentary (as text) to accompany the video (a video on its own is scraped content even if you created it yourself). I often write longer articles and create a video to cover one aspect. The video then becomes a small unique part of the web page content rather than the dominant feature.

7. If your videos have a lot of speech, you might consider looking into the closed caption features provided by YouTube. YouTube will try to transcribe your video automatically for you, but it's not always good. You can download the file and correct it. If you do this, you can then use the corrected transcription on your own site to accompany the video.

That's all there is to on-page optimization for YouTube videos.

After uploading your video, I recommend you use the social sharing buttons and share it on your social media channels. This will give your video a chance to spread through social channels if your tribe actively share your content.

Things Not to Do with YouTube

There are a lot of services out there that promise to help you with your YouTube promotions. The popular ones offer:

1. To send visitors to your video, boosting the number of views.
2. To provide your video with a gazillion "Likes".
3. To give you subscribers to your channel.

My advice is DO NOT use any services that artificially inflate the metrics of your video or channel, even if they say they are "real" people. They won't be, by the way.

YouTube is a great way to drive traffic to your site through links in the description.

Useful Resources

There are a few places that I would recommend you visit for more information.

My Other Webmaster Books

All my books are available as Kindle books and paperbacks. You can view them all here:

http://amazon.com/author/drandyjwilliams

I'll leave you to explore those if you are interested. You'll find books on various aspects of being a webmaster, such as WordPress, creating high-quality content, SEO, CSS etc.

My Video Courses

I have a growing number of video courses hosted on Udemy. You can view a complete list of these at my site:

https://ezseonews.com/udemy

I have courses that cover the same topics as my books, for those that prefer video to reading books. With the courses, you also get access to me as the instructor to answer your questions.

Google Webmaster Guidelines

https://ezseonews.com/wmg – this is the webmaster's bible of what is acceptable and what is not in the eyes of the world's biggest search engine.

Google Analytics

https://marketingplatform.google.com/about/analytics/– the best free analytics program out there.

Please Leave a Review/Thought on Amazon

If you enjoyed this book, or even if you didn't, I'd love to hear your comments about it. You can leave your thoughts on the Amazon website in the review section for this book.

Printed in Great Britain
by Amazon